The Thistle
and the
Crescent

Bashir Maan

ARGYLL ✠ PUBLISHING

© Bashir Maan 2008

First Published by
Argyll Publishing
Glendaruel
Argyll PA22 3AE
Scotland
www.argyllpublishing.com

The rights of the author have been asserted in
accordance with the Copyright, Designs and Patents
Act 1988.

**British Library Cataloguing-in-Publication Data.
A catalogue record for this book is available from the
British Library.**

ISBN 978 1 906134 14 3 hardback
ISBN 978 1 906134 24 2 paperback

Printing & Binding Bell & Bain Ltd, Glasgow

Contents

Foreword

For the first time, Scotland's historic links with the Muslim world have been explored in *The Thistle and the Crescent*. While the contribution made to Scottish society by our Muslim communities in recent times is better known, I'm sure it would come as a surprise to most people that there may have been contact between Scotland and Islam dating back to the seventh century.

The Thistle and the Crescent provides a fascinating new perspective on a part of Scotland's history which is not documented in its earliest years. Returning from their travels, or even the warfare of the Crusades, Scots will undoubtedly have spoken about what they had seen, and the tales were then told and re-told becoming part of the oral history of our nation.

Later, the writings of Scottish scholars and travellers bring to life their experiences in Muslim countries and remind us that Scots have gone around the globe throughout history, in search of knowledge, trade or just to make a better life. But this book is not just about the far distant past. It brings us right up to date in a section which describes how Muslim communities settled in Scotland in more recent times and also helpfully includes a chapter which outlines the principles of Islam, counteracting many common misconceptions.

Scotland's Muslim communities are now very much part of our nation, part of the great thread which make up the vibrant, colourful tartan of our society. Bashir Maan deserves credit for this first ever attempt to follow the story of Scotland and Islam right back to its earliest beginnings. How inspiring for us now to think that Scots so long ago may have sought out other cultures and learned and changed as a result of that contact. If Bashir is right, from very early in our history we were aspiring to be One Scotland; Many Cultures.

Finally, a word about Bashir's own distinctive contribution to Scottish society. In 1970 he became the first Pakistan-born Scot to be elected to public office as Councillor for Kingston. He therefore was the trailblazer for Mohammed Sarwar MP and Bashir Ahmad MSP and now the group of young Scots Asians who promise so much in their future contribution to Scottish public life – that is a substantial legacy.

Rt Hon Alex Salmond MSP, MP
First Minister of Scotland

Acknowledgments

I wish to express my gratitude to the Senate of the Glasgow Caledonian University, and particularly Dr. Ian Johnston, the ex-Principal of the University, for conferring upon me an Honorary Fellowship and thus making easy my task of writing this book. The staff at the Library of the University were ever ready to provide or borrow for me all the books and material I needed during my research and I thank them all for their help. Prof. Elaine McFarlane deserves my grateful thanks for supervising my work, making useful suggestion and helping me in difficult situations.

I thank the staff of the University of Glasgow Library and the University Archives, the Mitchell Library Glasgow, the National Library of Scotland, Edinburgh and the National Museum of Scotland, Edinburgh, for helping me in accessing the books, documents or other material required by me during four years of my research. My daughters and grand daughters taught me how to use the computer efficiently for word processing and kept my computer in good working order. They all deserve my appreciation for their help and loving support.

Many friends and acquaintances have helped me in various ways during my research and the writing of *The Thistle and the Crescent* and without naming names, I am very much obliged to all of them. However, there are some friends such as Rev John Harvey, Alistair McIntosh, Jean McFadden and Jamil Sharif who have sacrificed a lot of their precious time in order to assist and advise me. Dr Rosemary Harley was kind enough to look at my drafts, make required corrections and suggest useful amendments and alterations. Dr Peter Meadows went through the

7

manuscript and gave valuable advice. Professor Tom Devine read the manuscript, made very welcome suggestions and gave his blessing to this book. I owe them all a debt of gratitude.

Having acknowledged the valuable support and suggestions of all these kind friends I would like to emphasise that I alone am responsible for the text as it stands and any errors it may contain.

Bashir Maan
November 2007

The discovery in 1912 of silver coins from a hoard at Talnotrie, Glen of the Bar, Kirkcudbrightshire, bearing the name of the Abbasid Caliph *al-Mutawakkal ala Allah* (r. 847-862), confirm the connections between Scotland and the Muslim world in the ninth century. Also, over two dozen coins from the eastern Islamic world were found in hoards discovered at Storr Rock in Skye and Skail, Orkney. The discovery, some years ago, of this good quality gold coin bearing the inscription *Offa Rex* in Latin on one side and *La ilaha ill Allah* in Arabic on the other is a conundrum. (see p.28)

Introduction

ISLAM is now the second largest religion in Scotland. Muslims, the people professing the Islamic faith, are living in almost every city and town and participating in every walk of Scottish life. Muslim women wearing the *hijab* (headscarf) and men wearing baggy trousers and skullcaps are common scenes in the streets of Scotland. New, beautiful, purpose-built Mosques, with domes and minarets are changing the Scottish skyline and making the presence of Islam felt in this predominantly Christian country.

Muslims began to settle in Scotland in the third decade of the twentieth century and to date their numbers have grown to nearly fifty thousand. However, there have been contacts between Islam and Scotland since the seventh century. It was a strange coincidence that Islam reached the Holy Land and Christianity became the religion of Scotland at about the same time in the mid-seventh century. By the beginning of the eight century, Islam had spread to Egypt, the north African countries and the Iberian peninsula with which Scotland had minor trading links. These developments led to contacts between Islam and Scotland at first through the Scottish pilgrims to the Holy Land and trade, and later through the Crusades, scholars, embassies, travellers, the Empire and so on. However, there is no collective and comprehensive record in Scottish history, linking these centuries-old varied connections.

This together with the present diversity of Scottish society, with such a large number of Muslims as an integral part of it, prompted me to explore this far-reaching area and fill this gap in the history of Scotland. The subject has been made particularly topical by the anti-Islamic ambience in Britain in the wake of the destruction of the twin towers in New York on 11th September 2001 and the London underground bombing of 7th July 2005.

At this time when Muslims are experiencing a growing alienation from society there can be no better antidote than information and knowledge about the historical relationship between Scots and Muslims. If people can be helped to see the nature of this relationship over many centuries, the likelihood of being influenced by a rhetoric that casts all Muslims as potential terrorists will be lessoned considerably.

It is hoped that this effort would bring about a better understanding of Islam and Islamic culture, help stem the rising tide of Islamophobia and lead to harmonious relations between Muslims and other communities in Scotland.

This task required thorough research in order to locate and gather all available authoritative material, which is spread over the last fourteen centuries. It soon became apparent that information, especially relating to the Middle Ages, was very scarce. Moreover, whatever little is available is fragmented and scattered in many books, chronicles, diaries, letters and government records. This lack of information was caused by most of the Scottish State and Church records, from which material would have been sought, being destroyed in the Middle Ages. The State records up to the thirteenth century were destroyed by the English during the reign of Edward I, the Hammer of the Scots. Some of the Church records including any accounts of the early pilgrims to the Holy Land were lost during the prolonged raids, during the seventh to ninth centuries, of the Vikings who robbed and burned the important monasteries and churches of Scotland. As far as the later State records are concerned, Oliver Cromwell is alleged to have destroyed most of those up to the Restoration of Charles I. Hence, not much information from the medieval period was available to allow building a comprehensive picture of the relationship between Scotland and Islam during that period. This scarcity of the recorded material, especially pertaining to the early Middle Ages, demanded dependence on secondary sources and some historical imagination and hypothesising on certain affairs and events. This has been done with utmost care and consideration.

The Thistle and the Crescent is divided into six chapters and begins with a Prologue that briefly examines the advent of Christianity in Scotland and the rise of Islam and its spread to the Levant. The first chapter, Early Contacts between Islam and Scotland, deals with contacts through pilgrims and traders. Scotland had trading links with Egypt, North Africa and the Iberian Peninsula even before medieval times and before the arrival of Islam to those countries. According to the well-known legend of *Scota*, the very origin of the Scots is linked to Egypt. The profound influence of the Eastern and especially the Coptic Church in the early Scottish (Celtic) Church, confirms these early connections. Islam reached Egypt and North Africa in the seventh century and the Iberian Peninsula in the eighth century. The existing trade and cultural relations between Scotland and these now Muslim countries, continued unhindered. From the late seventh or early eighth centuries, Scottish pilgrims began to visit the Holy Land and this resulted in wider contacts between Islam and Scotland.

During their raids on Scotland, the Vikings captured many young women and girls, who they sold in European slave markets to Muslim traders. These women then ended up in the Islamic world as slaves, concubines and wives in Muslim royal palaces and households. The probability of an Embassy from *Amir Abd al Rahman II*, the Muslim ruler of Spain, coming to Scotland, in the wake of the Viking raids on his territories in about the middle of the ninth century, is investigated to conclude the first chapter.

Chapter 2, The Crusades and Scotland, discusses the impact and influence of Islam on Scotland during the Crusades, spread over four centuries. The numbers of pilgrims from Scotland grew considerably during the Crusade era and especially during the Kingdom of Jerusalem (1099-1187). Scots took part in the first and all other Crusades and performed pilgrimages during that period. In the fifteenth century, Scottish crusaders helped the Spaniards in their wars against the Muslims (Moors) of Spain and took part in many battles against the Turks in Europe. Relics, traditions and stories concerning those old connections through Crusades, are still current in Scotland, some of which are related in this chapter.

Chapter 3, Diplomats, Scholars and Travellers, explores connections developed during the Middle Ages, between Scotland and Islam, through diplomatic relations with the Muslim nations, Scottish scholars seeking knowledge in Spain and other Muslim countries and also travellers journeying through Muslim lands. By the tenth century, the learning institutions and academies of the Muslim world had become famous and quite popular among many of the secular and spiritual elite in medieval Europe. Many students from European countries, including Scotland, went to these universities, especially in Spain, to learn from famous Muslim intellectuals. The fact that this part of northern Britain is mentioned as a separate entity in the ninth century works of Muslim geographers and academics shows that the Muslim world of that period knew of Scotland. Diplomatic relations between what we now know as Britain and Islam began in the eighth century, during the reign of King Offa of Mercia, and became extensive during the fifteenth to the seventeenth centuries.

William Lithgow from Lanark was a seventeenth century adventurer who was one of the Scottish travellers who ventured to the Islamic lands and came back with vast knowledge and experience of the fascinating Islamic world of those times. During the late Middle Ages, Scots went to affluent Muslim lands especially of North Africa to seek employment. Some found respect and riches there and most of them converted to Islam and never returned home.

Chapter 4, The British Empire, seeks to investigate the relationships between Islam and Scotland during the eighteenth to the twentieth centuries. Many Muslim countries came under British rule during this period and remained part of the British Empire until the middle of the twentieth century. Scots soldiers and administrators were deeply involved in the conquest and the running of the British Empire. Many Scots made fortunes in India, Malaya and other Muslim countries that helped boost the economy of Scotland. During their involvement in Muslim lands, British soldiers, administrators and traders became enchanted with Muslim culture especially in Mughal India and many of them became immersed in it. They developed friendships with the Muslim elite, adopted their customs and culture, some even converted to Islam and married Muslim women. However, most of them sent their children to Scotland to be educated and brought up as Christians. From the early nineteenth century, when the British found themselves firmly established as rulers of Muslim countries, they began to distance themselves from the Muslim people and their culture. Nonetheless, the Empire had a very significant effect on Scottish and Muslim cultures.

Chapter 5, Islam in Scotland, relates a brief history of the settlement of the Muslim community in Scotland. It explores the reasons why they came to Scotland, where they originated from, their early experiences in Scotland, their progress and their growth up to the beginning of the twenty first century.

The last chapter, What is Islam?, briefly explains the essence of Islam, the Islamic way of life and the close relationship between Islam and the other two Abrahamic faiths, Christianity and Judaism. Many Scots know little about Islam, and what they do know mostly is based on myths and misconceptions that abound in the West. Hence, there is a need to define the fundamental beliefs of Islam in order to bring about a better understanding of this faith and its adherents.

Detail from the Edinburgh Central Mosque and Islamic Centre

Prologue

A S the first contacts between Muslims and the Scots were in the Holy Land, where the former were the rulers and the latter came as pilgrims, I feel it appropriate to give in this prologue a brief account of the advent of Christianity in Scotland, and the rise of Islam and its spread to the Holy Land. This, I believe, would prepare the reader with a clear understanding.

It has been impossible for historians to establish with any certainty how and when Christianity came to Scotland. Most are of the opinion that it came through the Romans. If it did, then it would have come to Scotland around the middle of the fourth century. The Roman Emperor Constantine (288-337 CE) converted in 312 CE, but it took about two to three more decades for Christianity to be accepted as the official religion of the Roman Empire. Consequently, it was not until about the middle of the fourth century that the Roman policy changed and they began promoting instead of persecuting Christianity in their vast Empire. However, there is also the possibility that in the third century, some missionaries came from England or Ireland, where Christianity had reached much earlier, indeed long before the conversion of the Romans, and introduced this new faith in southern Scotland. In any case, in the last decade of the fourth century, St Ninian was appointed Bishop of south-western Scotland. According to tradition, the Pope would have appointed a Bishop only if there were a sizeable existing Christian community and it had made such a request. That means that by the end of the fourth century, Christianity had firmly planted its roots in Scotland and had a large following in Dumfries and Galloway to justify the appointment of a Bishop.

In 398, St Ninian established the first church and a monastery, north of Hadrian's Wall, at Whithorn, that was known as *Candida Casa* (White House). By the early fifth century, *Candida Casa* had become a strong and effective centre for the preaching and promotion of Christianity in Scotland. St Ninian used this base to successfully preach and spread Christianity to nearly the whole of Galloway, parts of Strathclyde and some areas of Eastern Scotland up to Aberdeen. St Ninian died around 432 but his missionary work continued through his legacy of *Candida Casa*, which produced numerous monks, priests, preachers and saints during the centuries following his death. It was these dedicated and committed men who one after the other kept spreading the faith not only in Scotland but also throughout Northern Britain and Ireland.

One of *Candida Casa's* bright students, St Serf, began his work from south west Scotland. Founding many churches and Christian settlements on his way, he came north to Strathclyde, where he worked for some time and built a church at Dumbarton. From Dumbarton he moved to Culross, on the north bank of the Firth of Forth, in Fife, to spread the Gospel in North East Scotland. He established a church and a monastery at Culross, which also became a well-known seminary that taught and trained a number of successful and well-known missionaries, one of whom was St Kentigern. St Kentigern is reputed to be of royal blood. His unmarried mother became pregnant and as a punishment for her impropriety, her father flung her from the summit of a very steep and high hill. Miraculously she survived the fall and somehow escaped to the east coast of Scotland, where she found refuge with St Serf at his monastery at Culross. At Culross, she became involved in missionary work and in due course became famous as St Thenew. Kentigern was born to her soon after her arrival at Culross in 525 or according to some records in 518.

When Kentigern finished his education and training, he moved to Strathclyde, where he became known as St Mungo, and in about 550 settled on the banks of the Molendinar burn. The original name of this place was Cathures; St Kentigern established his Episcopal See there and renamed it Glasgu or Glaschu, which became the future city of Glasgow. He spent the rest of his life successfully preaching, teaching and spreading Christianity in and around Strathclyde and north east Scotland.

In 563, St Columba, accompanied by twelve monks, came from Ireland to spread the Gospel of Jesus among the pagan Picts and Druids of Scotland. Columba was born in 521, in Donegal. Like St

Kentigern, he also was of the royal blood and closely related to the King of Ireland. By the age of 42, he had already established many churches and monasteries in Ireland. Abbot Adamnan, his biographer, states that he left his home 'desiring to be pilgrim for Christ'. He settled on the barren island of Iona, where with the help of his disciples and his fellow Scots in Dalriada, he established his small monastic community.

Columba attracted many more monks and disciples and soon Iona became the hub of missionary activity and the monastery a source of learning, inspiration and a centre for arts and culture. He travelled extensively in the Pict areas of Northern Scotland and around Dalriada successfully preaching, converting and building churches and monasteries. Columba introduced prayers and services in the Gaelic language. He and his companions also adopted many of the customs and ways of the people they were trying to win over to Christianity. All these innovations in their missionary work helped them to gain converts where others had failed. St Columba died in 597 and St Mungo died in 600. After the deaths of these two champions of Christianity, their disciples and successors continued their work and by the beginning of the eighth century, most of the Scottish people had embraced Christianity.

While Scotland was going through this transformation, far away in another part of the world, in 570, a child was born in the city of *Makkah* (Mecca) who was destined to change the history and the religious and cultural make-up of the whole world. The name of that child was Muhammad. His father had died six months before his birth; hence, first his grandfather and after his death his uncle took over the responsibility of bringing him up. Muhammad spent his childhood tending the goats and camels of his uncle in the barren hills surrounding *Makkah*.

Makkah is situated in the heart of the Arabian Desert. It was founded by Patriarch Abraham about 4500 years ago, who also built in it a Holy House, the *Kaabah*, for the worship of One God, that ever since has been a centre of pilgrimage. Muhammad grew up as a righteous, hard working, and honest young man in a society in which promiscuity, idolatry, drinking, gambling and tribal warfare were the order of the day. Considering his integrity and his concern for others, his fellow citizens bestowed upon him the honorific appellations of *Al Amin* (the trustworthy) and *As Sadiq* (the truthful). He married a rich widow when he was 25 years old and took over as a very successful manager of his wife's flourishing import and export business. In his mid thirties, he grew fond of solitude and began withdrawing to a secluded cave, atop a high hill, a couple of miles outside *Makkah*. As the years passed, his visits to the cave became more regular and longer. He grew very meditative and aware of a pleasant light around him, which he could see and feel but not comprehend. In 610, when he was 40, one night in the cave something appeared to him in the form of a man that said that he was the Angel Gabriel and he had come to inform Muhammad that God had chosen him as His messenger to mankind. After a few more words the Angel disappeared and Muhammad, who by then was shaking with fear, hurried home in a state of panic, went straight to his bed and asked his wife to cover him. When, after some time, he had gained his composure, he told his wife what had happened and not yet realising the full significance of the event, added that he was concerned for his life.

The Angel began regularly appearing to him and giving him further instructions and revelations to prepare him to convey the Divine message to the people around him and beyond. Slowly Muhammad gained his confidence and began his mission from his family and close friends. He told them that he was the messenger of God and they should submit to the Guidance of God through him. He exhorted them to reject idols and other man-made deities and worship the One and Only God, the Creator and Sustainer of the Universe; to live righteously, be charitable and compassionate, believe in the day of Judgment and to believe in the missions and Books of all prophets of God – Abraham, Moses, Jesus and all others who had gone before him.

His close family members and a few others believed in him and the rest especially the rich and influential rejected him and his call and indeed, began to vehemently oppose him. The opposition hardened and turned into harassment and oppression of the Prophet and the small band of his followers. Muhammad, who a few months earlier was adored as a trustworthy, truthful and a respectable member of the community, was now publicly insulted, ridiculed and called a liar and a madman. The poor and the weak and especially slaves who had accepted his call were being tortured by their masters and forced to renounce their new faith that they called Islam. Parents were disowning their sons and daughters who had become Muslims.

Eventually Muhammad and his family were forced to leave the city and take refuge in hills outside *Makkah*. For three years, they lived there, under siege and deprivation, as the city elders had enforced a total boycott of the family and a ban on any communications or dealings with them. Other Muslims in the city were confined to their houses. In spite of all the persecution and hostility towards Islam and Muslims, some people from neighbouring towns and territories were still being influenced by Muhammad and joining him. Word was spreading throughout Arabia that a Prophet had risen in *Makkah* and many of the pilgrims to the sanctuary, *Kaabah,* when there, made a point of meeting the Prophet to find out more about him and his religion.

One night a group of pilgrims from *Yathrab,* a city about two hundred miles north of *Makkah* had a meeting with him, declared their allegiance and invited him to their city. Muhammad, knowing that the *Makkan* leaders were contemplating his murder, accepted their invitation and during one night, accompanied by a friend, quietly left for *Yathrab*. The Prophet arrived in *Yathrab* on 16th July 622. (The Islamic Calendar After *Hegira* (flight) – AH was introduced in 639, from this date.) The Prophet was then 52 years old. Many of his persecuted followers from *Makkah* had already sought refuge in *Yathrab*. They had done some groundwork for the introduction of Islam to the dwellers of that city. The people of *Yathrab* received the Prophet with shouts of joy and songs of welcome.

It was a huge change for the Prophet. Within twelve days, that took him to travel to this city, from a reviled and much disliked person in *Makkah,* he had become the most loved and respected man in *Yathrab*. The people of *Yathrab* accepted him as their spiritual as well as temporal leader. Here, as the head of the tiny city-state of *Yathrab,* he had the authority to preach to whoever he desired whenever and wherever he desired and guide the people to Islam. Consequently, Islam began to spread throughout Arabia. Oppressed Muslims from *Makkah* kept migrating in increasing numbers to *Yathrab*, which became known as *Madinah-tu-Nabi* (the city of the prophet) and then simply *Madinah*.

The rising strength of Muhammad with ever-increasing numbers of followers alarmed the *Makkans*. Their wealth and indeed their livelihood depended on the safety and success of their trading caravans. Their caravans followed the routes that lay near to *Madinah* and were open to attacks from the Muslims whom they had forced to flee penniless from their homes in *Makkah*. To deal with this danger and ensure the safety of their caravans, two years after the flight of the Prophet to *Madinah*, the *Makkans* came out with a force of about one thousand well-armed fighting men. The Prophet could only muster about three hundred ill-equipped volunteers. The two armies met at a place called *Badr*. The weaker small Muslim force vanquished the stronger enemy. The *Makkans* retired in ignominy but came back next year with a force of three thousand to attack *Madinah*. The Muslims, numbering only about 700, faced them a few miles outside the city, but lost the battle. However, they stopped the enemy from entering their city.

While the hostilities were continuing with the unbelievers of *Makkah* and other pagans the Prophet continued preaching and sending delegations to various towns and tribes all over Arabia inviting them to Islam. In response, many delegations of Christians and unbelievers arrived in *Madinah* to meet the Prophet and find out more about Islam. The Prophet also sent letters to Heracles (c. 575-641) the Byzantine Emperor, *Chosroes Pervez* (r. 591-628) the Persian emperor, the Kings of Abyssinia, Egypt, and many other neighbouring rulers inviting them to accept Islam.

Makkah surrendered in 630. The Prophet forgave all the people of *Makkah,* even the chiefs who had conspired to kill him, who mocked and insulted him and who tortured, dispossessed and banished the Muslims. On entering the *Kaabah*, he broke all the idols, cleared it of all the false gods and symbols the pagans had installed in it and brought it back to its original form and purpose, the worship of One Omnipotent, Omnipresent and Eternal God, for which the Patriarch Abraham had built it. After the conquest of *Makkah*, the remaining infidel tribes in Arabia, one by one, sent their delegations to *Madinah*, to pledge allegiance to the Prophet and accept Islam as their religion. Within a year of the surrender of *Makkah*, the whole of Arabia had embraced Islam and instead of being a discordant and seditious people, the Arabs had become a disciplined, devout, compact and caring nation. Then in 632, after a short illness, Muhammad died.

Abu Bakr, (632-634) the closest friend of the prophet who accompanied him on his flight from *Makkah*, was elected as his successor (*Khalifa* in Arabic or Caliph in English). In early 634, the Arabs of the border districts of Syria appealed to *Abu Bakr* for help against the oppression of their Byzantine rulers. *Abu Bakr* responded immediately and dispatched a small force of fighting men to Syria. Emperor Heraclius sent a large army under his brother to repel them. In July 634, the two armies met at *Ajnadain*, a place northwest of Jerusalem, where the Muslim army defeated the Romans.

Soon after this important victory, *Abu Bakr,* died in August 634, and *Umar* (636-644), another close companion of Muhammad, succeeded him as *Caliph*. Following his success at *Ajnadain*, the Muslim Commander, captured Damascus at the urging of and with the active support and co-operation of its Maronite Christian residents who were opposed to Byzantine rule. By the end of 635, the Muslim forces had occupied *Hams*, the second important city of Syria and with it a large area of the country.

The Byzantine Emperor became very concerned at this serious development and gathered a large army of well over one hundred thousand to expel the Muslims from Syria. Knowing the numerical strength of their opponents the Muslim forces abandoned Damascus and waited for the right time and place to face the far superior Byzantine army. At last, on 20 August 636, the two armies met in the valley of *Yarmuk*. The Muslims routed the huge Byzantine army and killed their commander. Beaten again and frustrated, Heraclius returned to Constantinople.

Christians not belonging to the Greek Orthodox Church of the Roman Empire, the Jews and people of other faiths resented the Byzantine rule for their religious intolerance and persecution and exorbitant taxes. When they became aware that Islam respected the Christians and the Jews as People of the Book and forbade its followers to force or coerce anyone to convert to Islam they preferred the Muslim rule to the Byzantine. Thus within a very short time after the battle of *Yarmuk* large areas of Syria and Palestine submitted to Muslim rule and indeed 'welcomed them as deliverers'. Many of the Maronite and other smaller eastern Christian sects, realising the simplicity and closeness of Christianity to Islam, converted to the new faith.

In late 637, Muslim forces besieged Jerusalem. The commander of Jerusalem, Greek Patriarch *Sophronius*, waited in vain for help from Constantinople. After six months, he offered to surrender the city on condition that *Caliph Umar* came in person to sign the treaty and accept the surrender. The Muslim Commander wrote to the *Caliph Umar* informing him of the situation and adding that his presence at Jerusalem could successfully end the siege of the city without any bloodshed. The *Caliph* accompanied by only one servant and a camel came to Jerusalem. The long journey had taken its toll, he was bare footed and his clothes were worn out bearing many patches. He was holding the halter of the camel and leading it while his servant was riding on it. The richly dressed officials and the people of Jerusalem were astonished at the modesty and humility of such a powerful ruler of the nascent Arab Empire. The Patriarch submitted his surrender terms to the *Caliph*. The *Caliph* accepted the terms in full and showing respect and compassion for Christians as People of the Book even added further concessions. This was the first bloodless and most peaceful conquest of the Holy city in its long and tragic history. After the surrender ceremonies were over, *Umar* accompanied by the Patriarch entered the city and asked to be taken to the Holy Sepulchre that he visited with due reverence.

By 640, most of the Levant, that was part of the Byzantine Empire, had fallen to the Muslim Arabs. The couple of coastal towns in Palestine that had not yet submitted to the Muslims were causing them much distress as the Byzantines were supporting and supplying these cities by sea from Alexandria in Egypt. To deal with the source of this menace, in 640 the *Caliph Umar* sent an army to attack Egypt and capture Alexandria. In Egypt, the Coptic Christians welcomed the Muslims as deliverers from the Byzantine rule under which Coptic Christianity was banned and heavy taxes were imposed upon the Coptic people. Within two years, Egypt with all its cities and ports had come under Muslim rule.

Before the end of the seventh century, Libya, Tunis, Algeria and Morocco had submitted to Islam and in the second decade of the eight century, Spain was taken over by the Muslims. In the East Muslims had reached Sind and Punjab in India and in the north they had subdued all the countries up to the Aral Sea and the borders of China. Thus by the second decade of the eighth century, the Muslim Empire had spread to the three continents of Asia, Africa and Europe, covered far more than the combined areas under the Byzantine and Persian Empires at their height and stretched nearly 5000 miles from East to West.

This was then the state of affairs when Scotland first encountered Islam in the Holy Land through its pilgrims and in the North African countries and the Iberian Peninsula through trade.

Muslim map of the known world in the tenth century which shows that the world was considered to be round, and that islands on the north west edge of Europe (Ireland, England, Scotland) were known about – as early as the ninth century, Scotland is mentioned in the works of Muslim geographers

CHAPTER I
Early Contacts
between Islam and Scotland

BEING a country with limited resources and a small population, often in armed conflict with England in the Middle Ages, Scotland 'had to depend to a large extent on the outside world for its trade, education and culture'.[1] Thus, it had to develop trading links with countries beyond England. The primary source of the import of desired goods in that period was the countries of the Eastern Mediterranean. Therefore, trading and cultural connections between Scotland and some countries beyond Europe, such as the Levant, North Africa and especially Egypt, appear to have existed long before medieval times.

The popular legend of *Scota*, as mentioned in the *Scotichronicon*, links the origin of the Scots with Egypt. According to this legend, the Scots are the descendents of *Gaythelos* and *Scota*. *Scota* was the daughter of the Pharaoh *Chencres* of Egypt and *Gaythelos* has various tales attached to his origin. According to one he was the son of a king of one of the kingdoms of Greece, while another makes him the grandson of *Nimrod* the powerful ruler of the kingdom of Babylon. Yet another says that he was the son of a Greater Scythian chief and this appears to be a more credible account. Nonetheless, all various accounts agree that *Gaythelos* came to Egypt, again differing on the circumstances under which he came there. However, from his arrival in Egypt and his and *Scota*'s descendants' entry into Scotland, there are no major differences in the details of the diverse versions of the story.

At the court of the Pharaoh in Egypt, *Gaythelos* soon achieved a high status and the Pharaoh gave him his daughter, the princess

---

[1] McRoberts, Rev David *Scottish Pilgrims to the Holy Land* p.80

Scota, in marriage. After the death of the Pharaoh, by drowning in the Red Sea while pursuing Moses and the Israelites, *Gaythelos* with his wife *Scota*, his family and followers left Egypt and settled in Spain. *Gaythelos* is also reported to have been multilingual and while in Spain, he took out words from each of the languages he knew and constructed a new language that became known as Gaelic after its inventor. From Spain, after many hundreds of years, *Gaythelos*'s descendents, under their leader Simon Brecc, moved on to Ireland.[2]

From Ireland, bringing the Stone of Destiny, some came to Scotland that was then known as Albany, Albyn or Albion. Legend has it that they settled in and around the Isle of Bute. The name of the leader of these newcomers was Eochaid Rothey, the great grandson of the above-mentioned Simon Brecc, who gave his name to Rothesay.[3] As these people were the descendants of *Gaythelos* and *Scota*, some of them called themselves Gaels after *Gaythelos* and others Scots after *Scota*. Later on and still at the present time both peoples are proud to use this last name alone. Hence someone has written:

> The Scots derive their name from Scota
> And all Scotia is derived from Scots,
> While increased use of the name
> of their leader Gaythelos is forbidden.[4]

With the passage of time this land, where the Scots had made their new home, became known as Scotland – the land of the sons of *Scota*.

The Stone of Destiny also has differing accounts about its origin in the legend of *Scota*. One version states that *Gaythelos* brought it with him from Egypt to Spain and the other says that Simon Brecc found it in the sea. As it was of fine marble and shaped like a chair, Simon Brecc took it as a gift from the gods and as an omen that he would be king. However, another version narrates that king Milo the father of Simon Brecc gave it to him. In any case, the Stone has a legendary history and it also carries a prophecy with it, which predicts that if ever the stone was removed by force to any other

---

[2] Bower, Walter *The Scotichronicon* (Vol. I, Book I, pp 27-45)
[3] *ibid* p.69
[4] *ibid* p.67

country the Scots would eventually occupy and reign over that very country:

> If destiny deceives not, the Scots will reign 'tis said
> in that same place where the stone has been laid. [5]

Hence, since time immemorial the Stone has remained a cherished national object of the Scots and until its expropriation by the English in 1296, it was used as throne for the coronation of the Kings of Scotland. It has been known by many names but the Stone of Scone is its most authentic, historical and popular name.

According to the above legend, therefore, the Scottish nation as well as their original language Gaelic has global roots and the Scots were a cosmopolitan people. As regards this legend, it should not be considered just a myth, because unlike other legends it is based not only on myths but also on some historical facts. Firstly, even today, there is a place in Ireland called Glen Scota, a clear reference to *Scota*, the mother of Scots. Secondly, most of the Irish people also claim their origin from *Gaythelos* and *Scota* as Gaels, or Hibernians. Thirdly, Bronze Age archaeological finds in Ireland. . .

> show an evident connection with Spain . . . Of the tombs, the passage graves, while not the most numerous, comprise some of the most impressive antiquities in the country, and there can be little doubt that they are the result of direct influence from Brittany and the Iberian peninsula.[6]

Fourthly, the Declaration of Arbroath also records the origin of Scots from Greater Scythia. Lastly, and more importantly, the Stone of Destiny, which is an integral part of the legend, is a factual reality; it is here with us lying in Edinburgh Castle for everyone to see. Thus, indeed the Scottish connections with Spain and Egypt go back a very long time. Whether it is another legend or fact, the old Scots chronicles also record that during the second century BC certain 'Egyptian philosophers' (probably from the Egyptian mystery temples) came to Scotland to advise the Scots King of the period.

---

[5] *ibid* pp 65-67

[6] *Encyclopaedia Britannica* Vol. 12 p.395

However, the early medieval connections between the Levant, Egypt and North Africa on the one hand and Scotland on the other are not a legend (but may have their origins in the old legendary connections). This is confirmed by the early twentieth century discovery of fragments of fifth century Egyptian and North African pottery in the South West of Scotland.[7] This shows that there were trading and cultural links between Scotland and these countries as early as the fifth century. This pottery must have contained either something like olive oil or wine or some other product from the Mediterranean that was imported by Scottish traders. When Christianity spread to North Western Europe in the fifth and sixth centuries the existing connections between the Levant and Egypt and the British Islands became even stronger. Syria and Egypt where Christianity had reached much earlier had developed asceticism and monasticism by the fourth century AD. Some of the Syrian and Coptic ascetics travelled to western and northern Europe to spread their brand of Christianity. Seven of the Coptic desert fathers are believed to have come to and settled in Ireland. As a result, monasticism and asceticism penetrated the Celtic Church through the influence of the Coptic and the Eastern Churches. William Dalrymple states,

> Even more remarkable, the brethren of dark-age Lindisfarne naturally looked to the fountainhead of Christian monasticism: the desert fathers of Egypt. They consciously looked at St Antony as their ideal and their prototype, and the proudest boast of the Celtic monasticism was that. . . 'This house full of delight/ is built on the rock/ And indeed the true vine/Transported out of Egypt'. The Egyptian ancestry of the Celtic church was acknowledged by contemporaries: in a letter to Charlemagne, the English scholar-monk Alcuin described the Celtic Culdees as *pueri Egyptiaci*. There are an extraordinary number of otherwise inexplicable similarities between the Celtic and Coptic churches, which are shared by no other western churches.[8]

During the fifth and sixth centuries therefore, from Ireland

[7] Ian Bradley *The Celtic Way* p.10
[8] Dalrymple, William *The Guardian* July 12, 2003

and to some extent through its own contacts with the Levant and Egypt, the influence of the Eastern Churches entered Scotland, giving rise to monasticism and asceticism. This influence also affected the Scottish Church rituals and religious arts, as can be witnessed from the similarities between the icons and illustrations in the religious manuscripts of medieval Scotland and the Coptic and Syrian Churches. For example, the Celtic wheel cross. . .

> the most common symbol of Celtic Christianity has recently been found to be of Coptic origin. The Copts were depicting it on their monuments three hundred years before it began to be used in Scotland and Ireland.[9]

In the seventh century, the political topography of the known world completely changed within a short period of fifteen years – from 635 to 650. In this unprecedented short period, the Arab Muslims demolished the Persian Empire and occupied Iraq and Persia (Iran). At the same time, they repeatedly defeated and humiliated the Byzantines, and captured from them the Levant, Egypt, Cyprus and Tripolitania. Soon after, the Arabs also brought under their control Algeria, Morocco and Spain in the West and parts of Central Asia, Afghanistan and Sind in the East. Thus, suddenly the Arabs had become the dominant power of the known world with the largest empire the world had ever seen. The Mediterranean countries, with which the Scots had their cultural and trade relations, had now come under Muslim rule and influence. Scotland therefore had to accept this reality and adapt to the changed world order in order to continue its existing trade relations especially with the Levant, Egypt and North African countries. It appears that in its trading interests, Scotland maintained its existing connections with these countries after their occupation by the Muslims. However, any records or written information about these relations and especially when and how the early contacts developed between Scotland and the Muslim world are almost non-existent.

Written materials for the early history of Scotland are notoriously sparse, and the early Middle Ages, like the so called Dark Ages, are not well recorded.[10]

---

[9] Dalrymple, William *From the Holy Mountain* pp.418-419
[10] Ferguson, William *The Identity of the Scottish Nation* p.19

Nevertheless, there are historical indications that Islamic influence had significantly penetrated Europe and the British Isles by the middle of the eighth century. Muslim traders even from the far-off Baghdad Caliphate were by then visiting the British Isles to sell their exotic merchandise in the British markets and indeed throughout Europe. Communications and some sort of relations existed between Caliph *Harun Al-Rashid* (r. 786-809) and King Offa of Mercia, England. King Offa, who ruled for thirty nine years from 757 to 796, was the paramount ruler and the dominating power in England at that time.

The discovery, some years ago, of this good quality gold coin bearing the inscription *Offa Rex* in Latin on one side and *La ilaha ill Allah* in Arabic on the other is a conundrum. The Arabic inscription means 'there is no God but *Allah*'. This is the creed of Islam. Does this mean that King Offa had accepted this creed and embraced Islam? Or, did Offa do this without realising the significance or the meanings of the Arabic inscription just to conform to the dominant gold currency of the Islamic world that controlled international trade and commerce at that time? Is there more to this unique episode than is known today? These questions beg answers as there were other European rulers who were in closer contacts with the Muslim countries than England, yet there is no evidence that any of them went as far as King Offa and arranged the inscription of the Muslim creed on his coins.

However, it is possible that the Muslim traders engineered the improvement of the quality of Offa's currency in order to make it acceptable to them. In that case, the Muslim traders would have played a direct role in the introduction of new minting techniques in England. It is most improbable though that they would have insisted on Offa's coins being an exact copy of the Muslim gold *dinar* or bearing the creed of Islam. The English minting artisans not knowing the meanings of the inscription and not having any other model to fashion their coins upon may just have thought it convenient to copy the *dinar*. The gold coin of King Offa is an imitation of a dinar struck in Baghdad, during the reign of the Caliph *Al-Mansur* (754-775). On its obverse is inscribed *La illaha illallah* (there is no God but Allah) in Arabic, and on the reverse the legend *Offa Rex*. The English artisan who cut the die for this coin having no knowledge of Arabic language has made many mistakes in the inscription in Arabic. However, in spite of the mistakes made in their execution, the production of these gold coins points to the existence of substantial trading contacts between the Muslim Empire and Britain justifying the minting of coins that would be acceptable to the Muslim traders.[11]

Farhat Hussain in his pioneering work *The Birth of Muslim Coinage* states:

> The coins of this period were shaped in the fashion of the Arabic (gold *dinar*) . . . Stenton speaks of the Abbasids playing a direct role in seeing to the improvement of the coins minted (including in the realm of metallurgy) in Mercia in order to accept subsequent coinage minted as a form of payment for goods and thereby replacing the hitherto low quality coinage in evidence in Mercia which the Abbasids were less than keen to accept. . . As a result of the new minting technique introduced during the reign of King Offa coins minted in England adopted a decimal system of denomination and were minted to a higher standard than had hitherto been the case. The coinage reform of King Offa impacted hugely upon subsequent English coinage whilst the name of King Offa is to be found in history school books across Britain to this day as the father of English coinage.[12]

This Muslim orientated improvement in the English coinage eventually would have had a direct or indirect impact upon future Scottish coinage.

There are also uncorroborated references to a mission sent by Offa to the ruler of Morocco, with whom it appears he had diplomatic or trade relations, seeking military assistance from that Muslim power against his enemies in the British Isles. The outcome of this mission, if there was one, is not known. Precise explanations of such facts or fictions about King Offa may never be found because no contemporary records of his reign have survived and all his available history is merely a collection of fragmentary references. However, the possible despatch of the mission to Morocco and the

---

[11] Stenton, Sir Frank *The Oxford History of England: Anglo-Saxon England* p.223

[12] Farhat Hussein pp.31-32

minting of the coins bearing the Muslim creed tell a very interesting tale and confirm that the influence of Islam was very much present in the British Isles as early as the eighth century.

Whether any Muslim traders visited Scotland or there was any significant fallout of this Muslim influence in Scotland is not certain, but it is very likely that some of that influence must have reached this part of the British Isles. Moreover, when the Muslim traders were frequenting market towns in England and Denmark there was nothing to stop them from coming to Edinburgh, Aberdeen or Dumbarton and the Firth of Clyde. They would bring their beautiful cotton fabrics, embroidered textiles, dates and olive oil and take away wool and woollen cloth, barley and so on.

The most important and lasting contacts between Scotland and Islam however came through religion. More than half of Scotland had embraced Christianity by the middle of the seventh century when Islam reached Palestine. St Ninian's and St Columba's successors and many other saints and preachers were busy promoting the Gospel and spreading Christianity among the rest of the Scottish population. Pilgrimage had been introduced to the Celtic church also from the Syrian and Coptic churches and many monks and missionaries from Ireland were eagerly following the pilgrims' path. They were travelling within the British Isles and to the continent where they paid respects to saints and holy sites and also spent long spells of time preaching to the heathens and spreading Christianity in various parts of Europe. Some went on pilgrimage to Rome and from there to the Holy Land, but only a very few of the Scottish monks, ecclesiastics or laymen, if any, by then joined them on their journeys to Jerusalem. This lack of enthusiasm among Scots to go on pilgrimage at this stage was because Christianity came to Scotland later than to England and Ireland and consequently the urge for pilgrimage to Jerusalem developed later. There were other practical reasons also, such as the remoteness of Scotland from Jerusalem, the scarcity of information about the Holy Land and the holy sites there and of course the occupation of Jerusalem by the Muslims in 638.

The distance to the Holy Land from Scotland certainly would have deterred many a less determined person. It was a very long and arduous journey in those days when Britain was considered to be at the farthest edge of the world. In the seventh and early eighth centuries, not many people in the Levant knew about Britain perhaps even less about Scotland.

The remoteness of Britain is emphasised by an incident concerning St Willibald. When in 720, St Willibald with seven other English pilgrims landed in Syria the Muslim officials, not able to establish where they had come from arrested them on suspicion of being spies. The Governor of the area took them to Damascus to be tried in the court of the Caliph. In the court, the Caliph questioned them about their origin and from where they had come. They answered, 'From the Western shores where the sun sets. . . and we know not any land beyond them, and there is nothing but water.' On hearing this, the Caliph said that they had not committed any offence in his country. They should not have been arrested and brought to the court and gave orders to his officials to 'give them liberty and let them depart'.[13]

Another hurdle the would-be pilgrim had to overcome before he could begin his journey was to acquire certain necessary travel documents. He had to obtain a written permission from his parish priest, entrust his wealth to a church or the king and empower his wife to manage his affairs in his absence. In addition, he needed safe conduct for foreign travel.[14] However, a pilgrim had to accept the necessity of all these formalities and the reality of an arduous journey 'in a spirit of devotion and penitence to expiate some crime, to seek some indulgence or, frequently, in fulfilment of a vow. . .'[15]

Nonetheless, to help and encourage the pilgrims on their way to the Holy Land there were pilgrim-hospices throughout Europe and in the Levant, where the pilgrims could rest, eat and get guidance without charge. Charlemagne (768-814) the Frankish king issued a decree in 802 that pilgrims on the road must not be denied shelter or sustenance. In 813, the Council of Tours instructed the Bishops throughout Europe to offer hospitality to the poor and to pilgrims. Availing upon his good relationship with the Muslim monarch of the Eastern Caliphate *Harun Al-Rashid* (786-809), Charlemagne built a hostel for pilgrims in Jerusalem.[16] The availab-

---

[13] Rev Canon Brownlow, trans. *The Hodeoporicon of Saint Willibald* pp.14-15

[14] Yeoman, Peter *Pilgrimage in Medieval Scotland* p.13

[15] McRoberts, David p.80

[16] Harpur, James *Sacred Tracks* pp.22-24

ility of all these facilities must have encouraged many Scots also, at least from the beginning of the eighth century onward, to take up the challenge of pilgrimage to the Holy Land.

The De Locis Sanctis

The lack of information about the holy sites in the Holy Land was resolved, as by Providence, in the late seventh century. A comprehensive guidebook (*The De Locus Sanctis*) with extensive information about the Holy Land and all its holy places was provided through the narrations of a Frankish bishop named Arculf who returning home from a pilgrimage to the Holy Land was marooned on the island of Iona. Bishop Arculf was a native of Gaul who went on a pilgrimage and spent three years, most probably from 679 to 682, in the Holy Land and the neighbouring countries. For nine months, he stayed in Jerusalem and visited all the holy sites in the Holy City. He also visited Bethlehem, Nazareth, Hebron, the Dead Sea, Galilee and Capharnaum, and travelled to Damascus, Constantinople, Alexandria and many other important places. While returning home to Gaul his ship was caught in a severe storm, was blown off course and ended its journey near the west coast of Scotland. Arculf survived the ordeal and somehow reached St Columba's monastery in Iona, where the monks and particularly the Abbot Adamnan looked after him.

Adamnan, the ninth Abbot of Iona from 679 to 704 AD, was a well-educated Irish monk who wrote the biography of St Columba. When he became aware that Arculf possessed first hand extensive information about the holy sites in the Holy Land, he decided to record it in order to disseminate this much-needed information in Scotland for the benefit of the pilgrims, priests and other interested people. Arculf gave a detailed description of all the holy sites that he had visited within and without the Holy Land and Adamnan wrote down everything in Latin, the language common to both of them. The *De Locis Sanctis* as Adamnan titled this narrative, made the most significant addition to the scant information available about the Holy Land at that time, not only in Scotland but also throughout Britain. It therefore received a wide publication in the British Isles and eventually throughout Europe, and became and remained until the fifteenth century a standard guidebook for the pilgrims to the Holy Land. For the people of Scotland it was perhaps the first window to learning not just about the Holy Land but also about Islam and the Muslims who during Bishop Arculf's pilgrimage were the ruling power in the Holy Land.

Muslims had occupied the Holy Land in 638, just about forty years before the arrival of Arculf in Jerusalem. The memory of the Muslim conquest and related events were therefore still fresh and current in the city. Arculf would have listened with interest and learned much about those events. He also experienced living under the Muslim rule in the Holy Land and in Syria and Egypt when he visited those countries. He lived and travelled extensively in the Levant and Egypt for about three years without experiencing any hindrance or harassment from the Muslim officials or members of the public. His narration does not show any animosity or ill will towards the Muslims though he often refers to them as Saracens, unbelievers or infidels. This was his understanding of the Muslims and his way of distinguishing them from the Christians. In his comments there is no mention of any oppression or harassment of local Christian communities or of the pilgrims. Neither does he express any concern about access to the holy sites or their control that in any case had been given over to the local Christian communities by the Muslim rulers since their occupation of the Holy Land. The itinerary of Arculf was exhaustive as he visited every place of interest in the Holy Land and beyond, where he enjoyed and witnessed the freedom of religion, the freedom of worship, and the freedom of movement for all citizens of the Muslim Empire without any distinction of colour, creed or race.

In a way, he compliments the Muslims when he narrates that Arabs (Muslims) entered Jerusalem after a siege of seven months without causing any damage to the city, whereas the Persians had burnt the city when they occupied it in 614. About his visit to Damascus, he states that the King of Saracens held the principality and his court there, and that there was a great church that had been raised in honour of the holy John the Baptist, which was visited by both the Christians and Muslims and used for their respective prayers. Arculf narrates a story concerning a dispute between the Christians and Jews about the holy shroud that was placed on the head of Jesus when he was laid to rest in the sepulchre. Incidentally, the bishop in this story, quite innocently, reveals the reverence Muslims have for Jesus. This shroud had eventually fallen into the hands of 'infidel Jews'. When the 'Christian Jews' became aware of this, they petitioned the Muslim Monarch Mavias, [*Muawiya Ibne Sufian* 660-680] for the return of the shroud to them as its rightful owners. The Monarch summoned the Jews and said to them:

> Give into my hand the sacred cloth that you have. They obeyed the behest of the monarch, took it forth from its reliquary, and laid it in his lap. The king took it with great reverence, and bade a pyre be prepared in the court before all the people. When it was burning with great intensity, he got up, went right to the pyre, and said in a loud voice to the dissident parties: 'Now let Christ the saviour of the world, who suffered for the human race, who had this shroud (which I now hold in my arms) placed on his head in the sepulchre, judge by the flame of the fire between you who contend for this cloth, that we may know on which of these two contending bands he will deign to bestow such a gift'. And so saying he cast the Lord's sacred shroud into the flames. But the fire was completely unable to touch it. Whole and unimpaired it arose from the pyre, and began to flutter high like a bird with outstretched wings gazing down from above on the two factions of the people thus at variance with one another, two armies set as it were in battle array. For a space of some minutes it fluttered about in the empty air, then gradually coming down it swerved by God's guidance, towards the Christian party, who meantime kept beseeching Christ the judge, and it settled in their midst.[17]

After witnessing this supernatural proof of the authenticity of the shroud and its rightful ownership the Caliph *Mu'awiya* 'respectfully returned it to the Christians'. Arculf says that he saw this shroud and kissed it during his stay in Jerusalem. He further states that Muslims also visit and revere many (Christian) sacred places along with the Christians. It is obvious that Bishop Arculf did not know that Muslims believed in all the Prophets including Jesus, and their scriptures. The *Quran* is very specific on this issue:

---

[17] Meehan, Denis, ed. *De Locis Sanctis* p.55

Say: We believe in Allah (God Almighty) and that which is revealed to us and that which was revealed to Abraham, and Ishmael, and Isaac, and Jacob, and the tribes, and that which Allah gave to Moses and Jesus and the prophets. We make no distinction between any of them, and unto Him we have surrendered. (3: 184)

Hence, the sites and sanctuaries associated with all the Jewish and Christian prophets are sacred to Muslims as well and even now, they do make pilgrimages to them. Indeed, *Al-Hawari*, a Muslim who made a pilgrimage to these sites in 1173, during the Crusader period, compiled an elaborate compendium of all the pilgrimage sites, including Jerusalem that became an important guidebook for Muslim pilgrims to the Holy Land. Mariam Rosen Ayalon, in her essay *Three Perspectives on Jerusalem: Jewish, Christian, and Muslim Pilgrims in the twelfth Century* writes:

The flow of Muslim and Jewish pilgrims was far from attaining the dimensions of the deluge of Christian pilgrims, but must have been more extensive than the surviving evidence attests.[18]

This was the state of Muslim pilgrimage to Jerusalem during the Crusader period, in which the Crusaders harassed and hindered the Muslims from coming to Palestine. It is probable therefore, that during the Muslim rule there were as many, if not more, Muslim pilgrims to the holy places in Palestine as Christians, a fact that testifies that most of the sacred sites in the Holy Land were also revered and respected by Muslims. Jerusalem however has a special place in Islam, as it is its third holiest place after *Makkah* – where the *Kaabah* is, and *Madinah* where the Prophet Muhammad is buried. It has been given several honorific names by Muslims but is popularly called *Bait ul Muqqadas* –The Sacred House or The Sacred Sanctuary:

Looking for an Islamic expression of the spiritual meaning of Jerusalem through history, one inevitably comes across a

---

[18] Levine, Lee. I., ed. *Jerusalem Its Sanctity And Centrality to Judaism, Christianity and Islam* p.301

triple honorary name that the city has borne for at least ten centuries and which is still in use among believers as a mnemotechnical device to remind them of the complex significance of the sanctuary:

Ula al-kiblatayn (First of the two directions of prayer)
Thani al-masjidayn (Scond of the two sanctuaries)
Thalith al-haramayan (Third after the two places of pilgrimage)[19]

Thus many Muslims feel obliged to go on a pilgrimage to Jerusalem. Indeed, before the occupation of Jerusalem by Israel in 1967, many Muslim pilgrims going to *Makkah* from Syria, Egypt and African countries would begin their pilgrimage to *Kaabah* in *Makkah* from Jerusalem and many from the East would end it at Jerusalem. Muslims were well aware of the significance attached to pilgrimage and the feelings and sentiments of pilgrims, especially those who had travelled long distances to perform this cherished rite. That was the most important factor along with their respect for the Jewish and Christian faiths and sanctuaries as ordained in the *Quran* that determined, during their rule in Palestine, the tolerant and accommodating attitude of the Muslims towards the Christian and Jewish people and their pilgrims to the Holy Land.

Early Pilgrims to the Holy Land
The occupation of the Holy Land by the Muslims in 638, naturally became a major deterrent to pilgrims, whether Scots or of other European nations. There was certainly much disappointment and resentment among Christians everywhere that their holy places had fallen under the control of the 'non believing pagans' as they called the Muslims. The prospective pilgrims naturally would have been unsure of the reception they would receive from the 'infidel Saracens' and certainly would have been concerned about their freedom of movement and safety in the Holy Land. Consequently, the number of European Christians going on pilgrimage to Jerusalem dropped drastically after the occupation of the Holy Land by Muslims. Not knowing the true conditions in the Holy Land

---

[19] Levine, Lee I., ed., *Jerusalem, Its Sanctity and Centrality to Judaism, Christianity and Islam* p.315

and uncertain of the new rulers' attitude towards them, most of the European pilgrims, instead of going to Jerusalem began to go to Rome or other holy places within Europe.[20] However, the encouraging reports coming to Europe from the Holy Land, about the tolerant attitude of the Muslim rulers and the freedom to practise their religion accorded to Christians, helped restore the confidence of the European pilgrims within a generation.

In Britain, the favourable reports of the returning pilgrims like Bishop Arculf, St Willibald and others allayed the fears and suspicions of the people and pilgrimage to the Holy Land regained its popularity within a relatively short time. Denis Meehan, in his introduction to the *De Locis Sanctis* confirms this harmonious state of affairs when he states that the *Umayyad* Caliphs (the early rulers of the Muslim Empire) followed a policy of good relations with the Christian world and indeed promoted the Byzantine culture in Palestine and Syria. *Mu'awiya*, the first *Umayyad* Caliph, entered into a treaty of friendship with the Byzantine Emperor *Poganatus* in 678 and it was because of such friendly relations that the journeys of pilgrims to the Holy Land, like Bishop Arculf, became safe.

According to many well-known historians, relations between the *Umayyad* Caliphs of the Muslim empire and the Byzantine Emperors were very cordial. During his construction of the famous Mosque of Damascus and also his rebuilding of the Mosque of the Prophet in *Madinah*, the Caliph *Al-Walid* (r 705-715) asked the Emperor Justinian II (r 685-695 & 704-711 CE) to send him twelve thousand Greek craftsmen, according to some sources and certain materials to help him build and adorn the two Mosques. The Emperor responded with delight and as soon as he could he despatched the best available craftsmen to Damascus and also sent a huge amount of gold and forty loads of mosaic cubes. The beautiful work of these Christian craftsmen, still survives in certain parts of the famous *Umayyad* Mosque at Damascus, which has withstood the vicissitudes of time. Soon after, 'during the reign of Emperor Leo III (r 717-741) a Mosque was constructed in Constantinople'.[21] These were perhaps the first and most practical examples of peaceful co-existence between the neighbouring Muslim and Christian rulers.

The Muslim rulers gave due honour and respect to the local

[20] Harper, James *Sacred Tracks* p.48

[21] Blank, David *Images of the Other* p.119

Christian and Jewish religious leaders and they consulted them concerning the affairs of their respective communities. Many historians have recorded their admiration for the good relations that existed most of the time between Muslims and Christians in the Levant and the prevalence of peace, law and order and religious tolerance in all other areas under Muslim control. The Christian minority sects and Jews were in fact better off under Muslims than under Byzantine Christian rule. Both Christians and Jews enjoyed internal autonomy in their respective religious affairs. Concerning the gracious treatment enjoyed by the Jewish communities living in the Muslim lands, Benjamin of Tudela a Spanish Jew, who travelled in Muslim lands for fifteen years, from 1159 to 1174 states:

> The most elaborate description of Jewish self government is reserved for the Head of the Exile (the Exilarch). He is a descendent of King David, and possesses a complete pedigree of his lineage. The *Emir al-Muminin* [the Caliph) invests him with authority over all the communities under Islamic sovereignty. Mohammed [the name of the Caliph perhaps] himself ordered that every Jew or Moslem should stand up and salute him. A triumphal march through the streets of Baghdad each Thursday precedes his meeting with the Caliph at the royal palace.[22]

The Muslim tolerance of other faiths and creeds was indeed the major factor in the rapid spread of Islam from Portugal to India. S. Runciman, writing about the rule of Muslims in Palestine, states:

> The Patriarch of Jerusalem Theodosius writing (in the ninth century) to the Patriarch of Constantinople, says of the Muslim authorities that 'they are just and do us no wrong nor show us any violence'.[23]

Both the *Umayyad* and *Abbasid* rulers had high-ranking Christian and Jewish officers in their administrations. From the late seventh century until 870 the court physician of the *Abbasid* Caliph was a Christian.[24] In fact, the Christians and Jews as 'People of the Book'

---

[22] (Adler, M. N., ed. The Itinerary of Benjamin of Tudela p.25)

[23] *The History of Crusades The First Crusade* pp.26, 27

enjoyed internal autonomy in their affairs under their own religious leaders in the Muslim empire. Their own clerics and leaders, according to their religious laws, dealt with their internal affairs. The Muslim official had no authority to interfere in their religious matters. The taxes levied on them were not excessive, in fact far less than under the Romans. Muslim rulers were fair and tolerant towards all minorities and no one was oppressed in their dominions.[25] All their holy sites and sanctuaries, religious buildings and institutions were safe under the specific control of the Christians themselves. During their conquest of Palestine, the Muslims had not occupied any inhabited or religious building and had made sure that no damage was done to the holy sites of Christians or Jews. Whereas on their respective occupations of Jerusalem, the Persians and Romans had committed massacres and destroyed all the religious buildings, Muslims behaved humanely. They did not kill or even injure any citizen or damage any building. The Muslim occupiers did not take over even a single building in the Holy City; they set up their camp on a site used as a rubbish dump after cleaning it of all the rubbish. The Muslim conquest therefore had caused no damage to the City and done no harm to any citizen of Jerusalem. Hence, any doubts or fears about the attitude of the Muslims towards the Christian citizens or the pilgrims to the Holy Land began to disappear soon and the pilgrims, who to begin with had hesitated to come, resumed their pilgrimages within a relatively short period.[26]

As regards the good treatment of the Christian pilgrims by the Muslim citizens of the Levant, the compassion shown to St Willibald and his companions by a Muslim merchant speaks volumes. St Willibald narrates that when they were imprisoned in Hams, a local influential merchant wanted to redeem them to set them free (in Islam redeeming and freeing prisoners and slaves is a highly meritorious act), but the governor of the city refused his request. On this, the merchant began sending them food in the prison every day and took them out for a bath twice a week. On Sundays, he conducted the prisoners to a church and on their way passing through a market bought them anything they needed.[27]

[24] Watt, W. M. *Muslim Christian Encounters* p.52

[25] *ibid* p 61

[26] Wilkinson, John *Jerusalem Pilgrims before the Crusades* p.9

It is therefore reasonable to assume that St Willibald and Bishop Arculf's accounts and satisfactory reports coming from other English, Irish or Scottish pilgrims would soon have changed for better the perceptions of Scottish people concerning the conditions in the Holy Land under Muslim rule. These favourable reports, the availability of the comprehensive guidebook – the *De Locus Sanctis* – for the Holy Land and the ever-growing provision of hospices and other support en route should have influenced and motivated Scots to embark upon the pilgrimage.

However, the very few researchers, who have worked in this field, unfortunately have been unable to find any records of Scottish pilgrims to the Holy Land even in the later part of the first millennium by which time most of Scotland had been Christian for more than two to three centuries. The most significant research done on this topic is by Rev. David McRoberts. The first prominent pilgrim to the Holy Land from Scotland that he could trace in the surviving records was John, the Bishop of Glasgow, who in 1122 went to Rome and from there he headed for Jerusalem.[28]

All of this means that either the earlier pilgrims did not record their observations and experiences of their pilgrimages, or their records were lost or somehow destroyed. It certainly does not mean that there were no pilgrims to Jerusalem and the Holy Land from Scotland until the twelfth century. That would be unlikely especially as Christianity had been flourishing since the last quarter of the fourth century and where it had produced very many dedicated priests, preachers and renowned saints. There is significant evidence of pilgrims to the Holy Land during the same period from the neighbouring parts of Northern England with whom the Scottish people on this side of the border had close links. As a memorial of his pilgrimage to Jerusalem, King Arthur is reported to have brought back a wooden statue of Our Lady and a consecrated cross. According to a thirteenth century monk of Durham, in his day the partial remains of that statue existed in the ancient church of Stow in Weedale.[29]

There is also ample evidence that Irish pilgrims were visiting

---

[27] Rev Canon Brownlow, trans. *The Hodeoporican of Saint Willibald* p.14

[28] *Scottish Pilgrims to the Holy Land* (Innes Review xx 1969) p.84

[29] McRoberts, Rev David, p.84

the Holy Land in the eighth century and even earlier:

> Fidelis who visited the Holy Land in 760 mentions . . . some Irish clergy and monks who were in Jerusalem for the purpose of prayer.[30]

The Irish and Scottish were both Celtic Churches and the people of the two countries, being of the same culture and of Celtic stock, having Gaelic as a common language, had very close links in those days and there was a lot of traffic between Ireland and Scotland. The sea between the two countries was not a barrier but a highway for cultural exchanges and continuous communications.[31] Hence it was highly unlikely that nobody went to the Holy Land from Scotland. There is evidence of Scottish pilgrims going to Rome as early as the late fourth century, e.g. St Ninian, and it was normally Rome from where the pilgrims to the Holy Land began their journey. Also, it was the pilgrimage to the Holy Land that offered far more reward than any other place, 'with pilgrims being cleansed of all sins as they entered the Holy Sepulchre, built over Christ's tomb'.[32] Therefore, it is certain that there were pilgrims from Scotland to the Holy Land at least during the ninth and tenth centuries.

As mentioned above Bishop Adamnan wrote *De Locis Sanctis* in the seventh century as an authoritative book of information about the holy places but more importantly as a very useful guidebook for the pilgrims to the Holy Land. It is therefore certain that there was need, at that time, for such a guidebook for the pilgrims going to the Holy Land from Scotland. Medieval Scotland had wide foreign contacts through trade, diplomatic and cultural relations. However, the most extensive contacts were through the constant flow of pilgrims from Scotland to the famous shrines in various European countries and the Holy Land. To protect the interests of the pilgrim, during his absence, certain legal procedures had been introduced since the early times. The earliest collection of Scottish law dealt with many aspects of pilgrimage and during the absence

---

[30] Wikinson, John *Jerusalem Pilgrims before the Crusades* p.139
[31] McIntosh, Alistair 'Saint Andrew: Non-violence and National Identity' published in *Theology in Scotland* Vol. VII. No.I p.59
[32] Peter Yeoman p.117

of the pilgrim on his spiritual journey, his property and his household goods was under the protection of the king.[32] Thus, every need of the pilgrim was attended to in order to help and encourage him on his sacred venture.

Another point that must be considered is that in medieval times the rate of literacy was very low. Most of the early pilgrims would have been illiterate, unable to write and leave any records of their journeys and most of them were not important enough to be noticed and their experiences and observations recorded by others. Some, especially the ecclesiastics, certainly were literate and learned but it is obvious that most either did not bother to record their itineraries or how their perceptions about Islam and the Muslims developed during their pilgrimages. If we consider the case of Arculf, a learned bishop, it was just chance or perhaps destiny that brought him to Iona and Adamnan. It was Adamnan who wrote down his account in *De Locis Sanctus* because he felt the need for publicising in Scotland the information he possessed about the Holy City and the Holy Land. Bishop Arculf himself may never have recorded his journey and his experiences in the Holy Land, in which case we may never have even known that a certain Bishop Arculf from Gaul existed or made a pilgrimage to the Holy Land in the seventh century.

Another case is of St Willibald, an English pilgrim who, as mentioned above, went to the Holy Land in the early eighth century. There are legends and also various records confirming that before him there were many British pilgrims who journeyed to the Holy Land, but St Willibald is the first ever English pilgrim who recorded his observations. Indeed, 'He is the only English pilgrim of our period (before the Crusades) to describe his travel. . .'[33] Even now in this age of enlightenment when nearly every person is literate or learned and every facility is available, very rarely does anyone bother to record his/her experiences whether on a pilgrimage or on any other important or interesting journey. Therefore, the fact that there are no records of or by those who made the pilgrimage should not give credence to the idea that there were no Scottish pilgrims to the Holy Land. As John Wilkinson observes:

---

[32] McRoberts, David pp.80-81

[33] Wilkinson, John *Jerusalem Pilgrims before the Crusades* p.11

Thousands of pilgrims had already come to the Holy Land before the arrival of the Crusaders, but very few wrote about their experiences.'[34]

The most probable reality therefore is that Scottish people like their neighbours and co-religionists the English and the Irish were also making pilgrimages to the Holy Land and coming into contact there with Islam and Muslims during the early medieval times but unfortunately, somehow all their records were destroyed.

Most of the material admittedly, has perished, but sufficient fragmentary scraps remain to allow us to visualise the movement in outline.[35]

How and when those records were destroyed is not known for certain. Some early Scottish historians assert that the destruction of the Scottish State records was deliberately planned and executed by the English. There was a movement in the beginning of the second millennium to establish English claims of suzerainty over Scotland. The English believed that they had a right to rule the whole of the British Isles. Joseph Bain, the editor of the *Calendar of Documents Related to Scotland* (Vol. 1, 1108-1272) states:

The majority of writers on Scottish history who have gone below the surface, have touched with more or less perspicacity on two questions – the nature and extent of the superiority claimed by the English over the Scottish kings and the all but total loss or destruction of the national muniments of Scotland existing at the death of King Alexander III (r.1107-1124), generally attributed to Edward I (r.1272-1307), who was accused by Hector Boece and Buchanan of having burned them. (page. v)

It is alleged that in his efforts to deprive Scots of their national heritage and to strengthen his claim of suzerainty over Scotland, Edward I of England transferred all the existing Scottish State records to England, where some time later they were destroyed. As

---

[34] *ibid* p.1

[35] David McRoberts p.80

referred to above the English took away even the Stone of Destiny in 1296 that had been used for the coronation ceremonies of the Scottish kings for the previous four hundred years. The Stone was not returned to Scotland until Scottish Nationalists stole it from Westminster Abbey in 1950 and now it sits well protected in Edinburgh Castle.

As far as the later records are concerned, Oliver Cromwell is blamed for the destruction of most of the Scottish State records from the time of the death of Alexander III to the Restoration of Charles II. After the flight of Charles II to France in 1651, Cromwell ordered the removal of the records of the Scottish Parliaments and Courts of Justice to the Tower of London. However, it soon became clear that that this unwise move was obstructing the administration of Justice in Scotland. Hence, six year later, some of the records were returned, but the bulk remained in London. Neglect, lack of care and bad storage methods at the Tower of London caused the disappearance or destruction of many of the surviving old and later records of Scotland. After the Restoration when the remainder were being sent back, 'eighty five hogsheads' were lost in the sea during a storm. Consequently, a very small part of the records came back to Scotland.[36]

Most of the Church records and any accounts of the early pilgrims included in them unfortunately were also lost or destroyed by the Vikings during their widespread raids in Scotland in the period between the seventh and tenth centuries. From about the early part of the seventh century the Vikings had begun making desultory raids on the Scottish Islands. Their first raid was on the Island of Eigg in 618, where St Donnan had founded a church. It was the Easter Day and the Saint was celebrating 'the offering'. Many of his monks and the islanders were also present. Suddenly a horde of Norsemen broke into the church. He requested them to wait until he had finished the celebration. Surprisingly they agreed. Nonetheless, as soon as he had finished they murdered him, fifty of his monks and many islanders.[37]

During the eighth century, these raids became more frequent and coordinated. Some of the Vikings by then had settled in the Hebrides and other Scottish coastal islands and were using them as

---

[36] Bain, Joseph ed. *Calendar of Documents Related to Scotland* (Vol 1 pp.ix-xi

[37] Leatham, Diana *Celtic Sunrise* p.95

platforms to launch plundering raids and to capture parts of the Scottish mainland. Consequently, for over one hundred years from the late eighth century to the beginning of the tenth, much of the Scottish mainland suffered havoc and terror at the hands of these savage Norsemen. The people and their property and the monks and their monasteries were subjected to indiscriminate massacres, destruction and plunder.

Candida Casa was attacked and plundered in 776. The monks who survived the massacre deserted the monastery and dispersed to safer places. Raids on Iona began at the beginning of the ninth century. By 831, the situation had become so serious that the surviving few monks felt obliged to send the coffin of St Columba for safety to Ireland. Similarly, many other monasteries and churches all over Scotland were destroyed, with all their relics and records, by the Vikings before they settled down in Scotland and eventually embraced Christianity in the eleventh century. William Ferguson laments the destruction of the Church records by the Vikings:

> As far as Scottish identity is concerned the ravaging of Iona by the Norse dealt a severe blow to the understanding of early Scottish history. The records destroyed at Iona and elsewhere would have cast light on many vexed problems and enabled modern scholars to speak with more certainty about 'Dark Age' Scotland.[38]

The loss, especially of the precious religious manuscripts, records, sacred artefacts and the memorabilia of the saints and founding fathers of the monasteries and churches, was irreplaceable. It is therefore obvious that the Scottish Church as well as State records were lost and destroyed and this is the most probable reason behind the lack of records or any evidence of early Scottish pilgrims to the Holy Land or any contacts between Islam and Scotland.

The Vikings

As far as the plunder and devastation by the Vikings was concerned the situation began to change for the better after the middle of the tenth century. By then, the invading Norsemen had adopted a settled way of life in the islands and the northern and eastern

---

[38] Ferguson, William *The Identity of the Scottish Nation* p.5

mainland of Scotland and had begun their assimilation into the indigenous people. In time they began to be influenced by Christian preachers and teachers and by the end of the eleventh century, almost all of them had embraced the faith. Thus seven hundred years after the beginning made by St Ninian and five hundred years after the death of St Columba, almost the whole of Scotland was brought into the fold of Christianity by the missionaries and preachers trained and imbued with faith by the institutions founded by those two venerable men.

The Vikings had been interacting with Islam and Muslims by trading with them since the eighth century. Among other things, they sold slaves captured from Scotland and other countries to the Muslims in various European markets. Most of these slaves ended up in Muslim palaces and Muslim households in the Middle East, North Africa and Spain. In the Middle Ages slave markets flourished both in Christian and Muslim countries. There is considerable recorded evidence confirming that during that period regular contacts existed between the Viking and the Muslim merchants who traded with each other in the markets of southern Russia in the East and Denmark, France and the Mediterranean in the West. Arab merchants from Cordoba, Spain are reported to have been in Hedeby-Slesvig, a Danish city in the tenth century.[39] In the mid tenth century, an Arab merchant of Spain *Al Turtushi* was in Hedeby, a medieval market town of Denmark, to buy slaves.[40] On the eastern side the Scandinavian traders, who were known as Rus to the Muslims and the Byzantines, travelled down the Russian rivers to various market towns of southern Russia, and traded slaves, furs, fish teeth, amber and honey etc., for luxury goods with the Muslim merchants from the Middle East.

In 922, *Ibn Fadlan*, a member of the embassy from the *Caliph* of Baghdad to the ruler of Khaganate of Bulgars, visited one of these markets at Bulgar on the River Volga. He has left a vivid account of the Vikings, their well-built bodies, fierce appearances, dirty habits and the wares they sold and bought. He admires their physique and states: 'I have never seen people with a more developed bodily stature than they. They are as tall as date palms, blond and ruddy.' However, he abhors their habits especially their engaging in

---

[39] *The Arabian Journey* p.3

[40] Brondsted, Johanne *The Vikings* pp.40 & 42

shameless sexual intercourse with the slave girls, they brought down to sell, in the presence of their companions and even strangers and their total lack of hygiene. He says: 'They are the dirtiest creatures of God.'[41] *Ibn Rustah*, an Arab astronomer and geographer was also in that part of the world in the second quarter of the tenth century. He confirms that many white slaves were brought there by the Norsemen to sell to the Arab and Byzantine traders.[42] Some of these slaves certainly would have been from Scotland:

> In view of the well-organised trade between Swedish Vikings and the Arabic and Byzantine territories of the eastern Mediterranean, it is likely that a large proportion of the captives from the British Isles ended up on the Russian slave route to eastern Islam.[43]

Eastern Islam included roughly the Levant, Syria, Iraq, Iran, parts of Central Asia, Afghanistan, North Western India and the Arabian Peninsula, a huge area where some of the slaves from Scotland would have arrived. The Vikings were traders as well as pirates and raiders. On the Western side, they traded with and also raided the Muslim countries of North Africa and Spain. They traded with the coastal market towns and when they found the seas and the towns undefended, they raided and pillaged the same towns.[44]

Many hordes of coins from various Muslim countries have been found in Denmark and the other Scandinavian countries confirming that in the ninth and tenth centuries, many Arab merchants from Spain and North African Muslim countries visited markets in Denmark to buy their desired goods and especially slaves. On their way up or down to Denmark, they would have also traded in the British markets as their predecessors did in the eighth century during the reign of King Offa. The discovery in 1912 of silver coins from a hoard at Talnotrie, Glen of the Bar, Kirkcudbrightshire, bearing the name of the Abbasid Caliph *al-Mutawakkal ala Allah* (r. 847-862), confirm the connections between Scotland and the Muslim world in the ninth century. These coins would have been

---

[41] Frye, Richard, trans. *Ibn Fadlan's Journey to Russia* pp.63-64

[42] Brondsted, Johanne *The Vikings* p.69

[43] Smyth, A. P. *Scandinavian Kings in the British Isles* p.164

[44] Jones, Gwyn *A History of the Vikings* p.199-200

brought over by the Viking raiders or traders returning to Scotland after their exploits in the Mediterranean. Also, over two dozen coins from the eastern Islamic world were found in hoards discovered at Storr Rock in Skye and Skail, Orkney. These coins are silver *dirhams,* minted at Tashkent and Samarqand between 899 and 943 AD. Some of the *dirhams* bear the name of *Ismail b. Ahmad Al-Shash,* only one of *Ahmad b. Ismail al-Shash,* and the rest of *Nasr II b. Ahmed al-Shash.* These three successive rulers were members of the Samanid family that ruled the whole of Transoxiana from 819 to 1005 under the suzerainty of the Abbasid Caliph of Baghdad. The Vikings frequented the markets in this area especially those near the Caspian Sea. Further, a tenth century Arab *dirham* (not otherwise identified) has been found at Ardeer in Ayrshire.[45] There is no evidence of the presence of Muslim traders in Scotland during this period. Nonetheless, the discovery of these coins of Muslim rulers of the eastern and the western Islamic worlds confirm the continuous wide trading links, through the Viking or Scottish traders, between Scotland and the Muslim world.

The Nordic traders and the Vikings of the British Isles brought North European and British slaves for sale to the various markets in Denmark. The Muslim and Jewish traders visited these markets to buy these slaves, as they were much desired by the royalty and affluent families in Muslim Spain and North Africa. *Ibn Hawkal* an Arab geographer of the tenth century, travelling in North Africa and Spain in the middle of the tenth century, found considerable numbers of white female European slaves in the Muslim palaces and houses and the males in the Muslim armies and as labourers. He also noticed in many places some of the freed male slaves, who had converted to Islam, occupying high government offices or engaged in successful and prosperous businesses. During his travels in the Khazar and Bulgar region, in southern Russia, he came across some Vikings, whom like all Arab historians he calls *Rous* or *Rus.* He gives details of the merchandise they brought down to trade and some of their customs and way of life. His description of their way of life however is not as bad as recorded by *Ibn Fadlan.*[46] *Al-*

---

[45] Stevenson, R.B.K. Sylloge of Coins of the British Isles 6, National Museum of Antiquities of Scotland Part I

[46] Ouseley, Sir William, trans. *Kitab Masalik wa-mamalik tasnif Ibn Hawqal, The Oriental Geography of Ebn Haukal, an Arabian Traveller of the tenth century* pp.190-191

Masudi (d. 956) and *Muqqadsi* (946-991) the two famous Arab geographers of the Middle Ages also record these contacts between the Arab and Viking traders in the East and the West.[47] Many Jewish traders of the time were also engaged in the slave trade. They bought slaves from Scandinavia, the British Isles and other European countries and sold them to Muslims in both the East and the West. Vikings had been raiding the British Isles for slaves and offering them for sale in various European markets since the seventh century. During the ninth and tenth centuries, their raids became extensive and their focus to sell their slaves shifted to the Iberian Peninsula where under Muslim rule there was a greater demand for blond and white skinned European slaves.[48]

The slaves from the British Isles must have included a fair share from Scotland. Thus, many of the Scottish captives, enslaved by the Vikings during their numerous raids in Scotland would have gone to Muslim households and Muslim militias in the Islamic world spread from Western Europe and North Africa to the borders of China and Sind in India. It is certain, therefore, that Scottish blood is running in the veins of some Muslims in the wide Islamic world and especially in the Middle East and the South Mediterranean countries.

It would be appropriate at this point to explain the position of Islam as a religion in regard to slavery. When Islam appeared in the early seventh century slavery was part of life, a part of socio/economic culture of the world. Considering that, Islam overlooked the undesirable practice of slavery, but in order to prevent the abuse and oppression of slaves and to discourage and eventually rid Muslim society of this evil, it introduced a comprehensive code of conduct concerning slaves and slavery. To ensure their humane treatment Islam laid down that a slave must be treated with the same degree of care and compassion as a member of one's family. He/she should be given the same food; similar clothes as worn by the members of the family, equal periods of rest and all other facilities. A slave must not be denied his/her choice to buy his/her freedom at a reasonable price. A slave must not be coerced to change his or her religion and must not be overworked. The children of a slave must not be sold or separated from her or him. A slave should

---

[47] A.P. Smyth, A.P. *Scandinavian Kings in the British Isles* p.160
[48] *ibid* p.161

not be prevented from learning and seeking skills if he/she so desires. Consequently, numerous slaves, male and female, achieved very prominent and influential positions in Muslim society. Indeed, there were many well-known theologians, prime ministers, governors of provinces, commander in chiefs of the Muslim armies and even kings, throughout the history of Islam, who rose to these enviable positions from being slaves in Muslim society. History bears witness to the fact that many of the queens and highly influential queen mothers in the palaces of the Muslim monarchs, especially the Turkish Sultans, came there as slave girls. In the *harems*, they learned the language, acquired knowledge, adopted the Islamic culture, won the admiration of their masters and rose to be their much-loved queens.

More importantly though, Islam encouraged the emancipation of slaves by declaring the freeing of slaves as a highly meritorious act especially for the remission of one's sins, immensely pleasing God Almighty and enormously rewarding in the hereafter. There are numerous exhortations in the *Quran* addressed to Muslims to ransom and free slaves in order to earn the pleasure of God and the remission of their sins. The Prophet of Islam, though not a rich man, himself set an example by freeing sixty seven slaves in his life and indeed adopted one as a son after freeing him. His wife Aysha, who outlived the Prophet by 46 years, is reported to have ransomed about six thousand slaves in her life. Hence, Muslims, right from the time of the Prophet, had been often buying slaves only to set them free in order to earn this virtue. On this topic Riccoldo da Monte Croce, a Florentine monk, crusader and traveller who visited the Muslim lands of the Levant, Iran and Iraq in the late thirteenth century, makes very interesting observations in his *Itinerarius*:

> Yet beyond these things they make great legacies, and put them in a treasury, and at an established time they open them, and give them to a trustworthy Muslim, who goes off to the different provinces and redeems prisoners, and Muslim slaves who are held prisoners among Christians and other nations. Often they even buy Christian slaves who are held prisoners among the Muslims themselves and take them to the cemetery and say I redeem so much for the soul of my

father, and so much for the soul of my mother, and give them letters of freedom and send them away.[49]

Furthermore, Islam did not allow the enslavement of innocent people. It did not permit raiding any towns or territories to capture people to enslave them or sell them into slavery. Hence the widely reported but exaggerated accounts of the sixteenth to eighteenth century slave raiders and traders of Arab or North African origin supplying the transatlantic slave trade of European nations cannot be considered consistent with Islamic principles. Those raiders and traders were flagrantly defying Islamic law and its rules and regulations concerning slavery. Hence, they cannot be considered as true Muslims. The notion of slavery in Islam therefore, was totally different from and indeed opposite to the general concept of slavery in Western and all other cultures.

That aside, the Vikings traded especially in slaves with both Christians and Muslims in Europe and North Africa and when it suited them they also raided Muslim as well as Christian territories. By the mid ninth century, Viking chiefs settled in Scotland were also involved in trading and raiding, along with their kinsfolk from the Scandinavian countries. The first major raid by the Vikings on a Muslim country was in Spain in 844. In August of that year, over three thousand Vikings in their longships attacked Lisbon. The Muslim defenders of the city put up a tough resistance and repulsed the invaders. Having failed to plunder Lisbon the Viking fleet headed south:

> After a fortnight's skirmishing and piracy there they pressed on the Guadalquivir, and with a daring verging on folly went up the river and attacked the city of Seville. Except for the citadel it fell into their hands for a week; its men were put to the sword, its women and children carried off as spoils of war to the Viking base on the island of *Qubtil*.[50]

Seville was attacked in late September or early October 844. Then from their base on the island of *Qubtil*, they raided the neighbouring country for the next six weeks, inflicting havoc, killing

[49] Laurent, J.C.M. ed. *Peregrinatores Medii Aevi Quatour* p.132-133
[50] Jones, Gwyn *History of the Vikings* p.214

and capturing many more people. After recovering from the initial shock, the Muslim forces struck back in late November and by the end of the year they had destroyed most of the Viking ships. 'Their leader and over a thousand men were killed and four hundred taken prisoners.'[51] The Muslim militia surrounded the remainder in their island base with no chance of escape. The Vikings in a desperate situation pleaded for peace. An embassy or a delegation from the Vikings came to Cordoba, the capital of Muslim Spain in order to negotiate the terms for peace and get their trapped men released. It is not known when exactly those negotiations began and when were concluded, but considering all the circumstances, it could not have been before March 845 or even later. Anyhow, to obtain the release of their womenfolk and children, who had been captured by the Vikings and kept in the island of *Qubtil,* and avoid any further harm to them, the Muslims agreed to let the raiders go in safety and to provide them with food and clothes, of which they were in dire need.

During the negotiations between the Spanish government and the Vikings, the possibility of long-term peace, friendly relations and trade would also have been discussed, as in late 845 or early 846, an embassy from the Muslim ruler of Spain went to the king of the Vikings who was based in a 'northern country'. Where or which this northern country was is not known, but it may have been Scotland. *Amir Abd al-Rahman II* (822-852), the ruler of Spain sent as his Ambassador, *Yahya bin Hakam Al-Ghazal,* an academic, a seasoned diplomat, 'a poet of quality, a man of fashion and a celebrated wit', with precious gifts for the king and the queen of the Vikings in their northern country.[52]

Arab historians of the time must have recorded in some detail the progress of this embassy to the land of *Majus* – the Viking pagans, as the North African and Spanish Muslims called them. However, what is available today are only some fragments of those records, copied, recopied and quoted by later Arab historians, giving some vague factual details. They tell us that it was a long journey, how the Muslim embassy was received and especially the very frank and intimate meetings and relations that developed between *Al-Ghazal,* the ambassador, and the Viking queen Nod. There is no mention

---

[51] Allan, W. E. D. *The Poet and the Spae-Wife* p.9

[52] *ibid* p.12

of the name of the king or his country, the embassy went to, except that it was a northern country, nor of any political or economic objectives achieved by the mission. Most of the European writers have based their accounts of this embassy on the narrative of the twelfth century Arab historian *Ibn Dihya,* who had based his narrative on the lost work of a ninth century Arab scholar *Ibn Alcama*. However,

> The historicity of *Al-Ghazal*'s mission to the Scandinavians of the West can no longer be doubted, but since *Ibn Dihya's* narrative was written as a piece of literature rather than a strictly historical narrative, many questions remain unanswered.[53]

Nonetheless, the available information provides some important clues and a few details of the topography of the host country and the time taken by the embassy to complete its assignment. We are told it took a long time for the embassy to reach its destination and indeed, it took them twenty months to complete their mission and return safely home to Cordoba. The king of the 'northern country' lived on an island that had abundance of greenery and many rivers flowing through it. The king's wife was named Nod, or Noud. There were other islands nearby that were inhabited also by his people. The mainland was at a distance of three days journey from the King's island and there also he held power.[54]

Some historians argue that the embassy was to either Ireland or Denmark. They maintain that, 'If the Vikings who attacked Seville were Danes, the embassy was to Horik in Denmark and if Norwegians then to Turgeis in Ireland.'[55] However, there is also an opinion that it was Scotland or a Scottish island that received this Muslim embassy. The description of the land of the 'northern king' fits Scotland better than any other northern country. On considering the available information carefully it appears that Scotland certainly stood a better chance than Ireland. Vikings had flourishing colonies in Scottish islands and parts of the mainland by the middle of the ninth century where there were flowing waters and plenty of foliage and greenery as described by the Arab writers. A long voyage to

---

[53] Smyth, A.P. *Scandinavian Kings in the British Isles* p.162

[54] Jones, Gwyn *A History of the Vikings* p.214

[55] Jones, Gwyn *ibid* p.214

the destination could not have been to Dublin or any other place in Ireland as Ireland is not at such a long distance from Iberian Peninsula. The embassy may have, though it is most improbable, sailed from Cordoba or Seville, travelled through the River Guadalquivir to the open sea and turned north into the Atlantic Ocean. Even then, such a journey from Cordoba to Ireland would not have been very long.

It appears though that *Al-Ghazal* departed from one of the northern or north-western Spanish ports from where the distance to Dublin is between 700 and 750 miles. With that distance, it would have taken him only about twelve to fifteen days to get to Ireland and even less with favourable winds or with favourable ocean currents from the Bay of Biscay. It would have taken longer though, maybe around twenty or twenty five days, if they were travelling at a leisurely pace and stopping during the nights. To their sea journey should be added another about 25 to 30 days, the time it would have taken the Embassy to travel in style by land the distance of around 450 miles from Cordoba, through Leon, to the northern port of their embarkation. That makes a total of six to seven weeks journey time from Cordoba to Ireland. A long journey in those days was not of weeks but of months, at least of three to four months.

Further, we are told that the Viking king who received *Al-Ghazal* gave him a letter to be delivered, on his way back, to the Christian King of Leon, which the Arab ambassador did deliver at Santiago de Compostela on his way home to Cordoba.[56] This means that the Viking king knew or was told by *Al-Ghazal* that he had come through Leon and would be going back by the same route and it would be no problem for him to deliver his letter at Santiago de Compostela. If one looks at the map of the Iberian Peninsula it becomes obvious that *Al-Ghazal* would have travelled through Leon only if he had left from and was returning through a northern Spanish port. Hence, it seems certain that he left and came back through a northern port from where his journey to Ireland could not have been very long.

Other factors to be considered are firstly, the mention of 'other islands' around the abode of 'that king' inhabited by his people. Ireland did not have 'other islands' around it inhabited by the Vikings. However, Scotland or Orkney did have many islands around

---

[56] Smyth, A.P. *The Scandinavian Kings in the British Isles* p.163

them that were definitely inhabited by *Majus*, the Vikings. Secondly, from that king's abode on a 'three days' journey away 'was the mainland that was also under the rule of that king'. The continent or mainland near to Ireland is Europe and it is far more than at three days journey. Furthermore, in the Iberian Peninsula, which at that time was mostly under the control of the rulers of Cordova, or in France 'the northern king' had no territory under his control. If we assume that the mainland or continent was meant to be England, then even in those days it took far less time than three days to get to England from Ireland through the Irish Sea and England was not under the rule of that king supposedly based in Ireland. On the other hand, the Scandinavian mainland was at a distance of about three to five days journey, in the narrow long ships of the Vikings, from Scotland, especially from Orkney, and it is probable that the Viking chief in Scotland had some Scandinavian territories under his control. Thirdly, there is the time factor. It took the embassy twenty months to complete its mission. It certainly would not have taken twenty months if the embassy's destination were Ireland. The journey from Cordoba to and from Ireland would not have taken more than three to four months and considering that this was a peace or a trade mission and not a resident embassy, the stay of the embassy with their hosts, under no circumstances, would have been more than six months but perhaps much less. This makes at the most nine to ten months, far less than twenty months, the time stated to have been taken by the embassy to accomplish its assignment and return home.

Finally and most importantly, W.E.D. Allan states:

> There was, however a serious crisis in the affairs of the Norwegian Vikings in Ireland. Turgeis, had been killed, sometimes in 845, or as I shall suggest later, in 846. Something comparable to 'Sicilian Vespers' flared up against the Norwegian conquerors in Ireland, and in 846-847 they suffered a series of defeats at the hands of the Irish.[57]

The 'crisis' in Ireland makes it not only most improbable but also entirely impossible for Ireland to have received the Muslim embassy in 846. If *Al-Ghazal* were in Ireland in 846, he would have

---

[57] *The Poet and the Spae-Wife* p.10

been caught up in that 'serious crisis' in which Turgeis, his supposed host, was killed. In that case, *Al-Ghazal* and his staff would have been very lucky to return home safely and there would have been no letter from the King of Vikings to the King of Leon, as there would have been no Viking King in Ireland. Moreover, the mission would have been an utter failure and the account of this mission tragic and sanguinary rather than full of flowery pleasantries as we find it now. Considering this and all the other factors mentioned above it is highly unlikely that *Al-Ghazal*'s embassy went to Ireland or it was Turgeis who was the host of the embassy. However, it is possible that on its way to Scotland, the Embassy stopped in Ireland, for a few weeks or so, to take water and replenish provisions or to get some repairs done to their ships. In that case, considering the 'serious crisis' in Ireland during that time, they would have gone to a safe port in an area not affected by the crisis.

Thus, with Ireland an unlikely destinatiou, there is no argument strong enough that conclusively favours Denmark to have received the embassy. To go to Denmark from a north Spanish port would have taken approximately about the same time as to Scotland but this voyage would have been through the English channel, the Straits of Dover and then along the German and Dutch coasts to Denmark. For *Al-Ghazal*, a poet and a highly cultured man and other members of his mission it would have been an interesting if not fascinating journey with considerable traffic in the English Channel and beyond to Denmark, and with many countries visible from the ship carrying the embassy. On this voyage they would have experienced a few notable incidents or episodes that would have found mention in their records. But we find nothing of that sort from the available accounts of their voyage except that it was a 'long journey' meaning perhaps an uninteresting and boring long journey. Such a journey more aptly fits a long uneventful voyage to Scotland from a northern Spanish port. From the Spanish port the ship of the embassy would have taken the Scandinavian route heading north via the Atlantic Ocean, sailing round Ireland by the west coast and then turning northeast towards Scotland. The journey to Scotland would have involved a distance of over 1500 miles by sea plus approximately 450 miles of land journey from Cordoba to the northern Spanish port, making a total of nearly 2000 miles. Such a journey in those days would have taken about three months to complete, a long time indeed. In Scotland by that time, most of the islands and parts of the mainland had been colonised by the Vikings. After plundering Scotland during their frequent raids for about one hundred years, some of the Vikings had begun to settle in the Scottish islands as early as the late eighth century.[58]

By the mid-ninth century, the Vikings had settled in Shetland, Orkney and all the other Hebridean Islands and from there they were slowly penetrating into and settling on the Scottish mainland. Their connections with their homeland were intact and they still owed their allegiance to their Scandinavian kings. That is why in the ninth century, Ragnarr the eldest son of King Halfdan of the Scandinavians came to Orkney when his younger brothers forced him out of the country to prevent him from succeeding their father. The available records of the Vikings are very vague and no precise date or year of his arrival is recorded but it is presumed that he arrived in Orkney around the middle of the ninth century. The middle of the ninth century could mean any time between 840 and 860. It is therefore possible that Ragnarr came to Scotland in the early 840s and the Vikings who raided Spain in 844 were Ragnarr's men or his sons. We are told that his two sons left him either during his flight from Scandinavia or soon after his arrival in Orkney and sailed away with their men on a raiding expedition.[59]

It is therefore probable that Ragnarr's sons were with the Vikings who raided Spain. We know that during the counterattack by the Muslim forces the Viking leader and over a thousand of his men were killed. After the death of the leader, one of the two Ragnarr's sons, being of royal blood, would have taken over the leadership of the remaining Vikings and the peace negotiations with the Muslims in Cordoba would have been conducted by one of them or their emissaries. In that case, Ragnarr's sons would have arranged for the Muslim embassy to go to his father in Scotland. It is also possible that on hearing that his sons were trapped in Spain, it would have been Ragnarr who sent his emissaries to the ruler of Spain, to negotiate peace and the release of his sons and the Muslim embassy was in response to Ragnarr's peace mission. Moreover, as the elder son of the King of Scandinavia, Ragnarr did have a genuine claim to the Scandinavian mainland and this is in perfect accord with an

---

[58] Jones, Gwyn *A History of the Vikings* p.198

[59] Smyth, A. P. p.64

important part of the description by the Arab writers that 'three-day's journey away was the mainland, and here, too the king [who received the embassy] held power.' Thus, Scotland was far more likely than Denmark to have received the embassy of *Amir Abd al Rahman* of Cordoba. Admittedly, there is no contemporary evidence to prove that the embassy actually came to Scotland, but there is enough circumstantial evidence to suggest that it most probably did.

About fifteen years after the episode mentioned above there were more raids by the Vikings on Muslim Spain and the North African coast. These raids had definite connections with Scotland as they were carried out by Ragnarr's sons:

> . . . a Mediterranean expedition was undertaken by a Viking fleet c 860. . . and later Frankish traditions support the Scandinavian claim that the expedition was led by the sons of Ragnarr. . . The expedition of Ragnarr's sons to the Mediterranean has a historical basis, and may be dated to AD 860. [60]

They attacked some Spanish towns and the coast of Morocco from where they captured many slaves – the Blue Men – and acquired much booty. On their return journey through the straits of Gibraltar a great number of the Vikings were slain and their ships destroyed or captured by the Muslims. *Amir Muhammad,* the ruler of Muslim Spain, ransomed some of the captives still in the hands of the Vikings and the rest according to some Irish chroniclers 'were taken back to Ireland, where they survived for a long time.' Now here again one wonders why the slaves were taken back to Ireland when the raiders were Ragnarr's sons and had come from Orkney, Scotland. It is possible that on their way back they stayed a few weeks in Ireland to rest and then continued their journey back to Scotland. However, if they returned to their father or to Orkney as some records suggest, they must have brought with them some of the Moroccan or Spanish slaves to Scotland. Ivarr, one of Ragnarr's sons, who most probably led the raid on Spain and Morocco in 860, according to many accounts did return to avenge the death of his father who had been killed by the Northumbrian king during his raid on Northumbria in early 860s.[61]

---

[60] Smyth, A.P. *The Scandinavian Kings in the British Isles* p.66

[61] *History of the Vikings* p.219

After the ninth century, there are no more accounts of any significant raids on North African or Iberian Muslim territories by the Vikings either from Scotland or anywhere else. By that time, the Vikings had realised that they could not plunder with impunity those countries, that had strong and efficient governments. Once they had settled in Scotland, like the indigenous people, they also established good relations and carried on trading with rather than raiding those rich countries where there was a great demand for goods they had to offer and abundance of commodities they required. But again unfortunately, there are no available records in Scotland of any such dealings or any traders who during that period traded with the Muslim countries. However, Benjamin of Tudela, a Jewish Rabbi from Muslim Spain, who travelled in the Middle East from 1159 to 1174, in his itinerary, mentions Scots among the merchants of many western nations who came to trade at Alexandria in Egypt and who had set up their own hostel there.[62] The existence of a hostel means that during the Middle Ages there was a steady flow of Scots to Alexandria who traded with Egypt and other North African countries. This shows that even during the Crusades period when the Muslims and Christians were engaged in a bloody conflict, trade between the two sides continued unhindered.

By the beginning of the second millennium, the pilgrimage to the Holy Land had become reasonably popular in Scotland. The Crusades and particularly the capture of the Holy Land by Christians boosted the number of pilgrims from Scotland, and from this time onwards it is difficult to distinguish between a pilgrim and a crusader. According to the notes left by a German pilgrim who was in Jerusalem in the mid-twelfth century the Scots were 'among the nations who maintained a pilgrim's chapel for the members of their nation who visited Jerusalem'.[63] Thus, the number of Scots going to Jerusalem would have been quite large to justify the maintenance of a chapel there. The conversion of Vikings to Christianity in the tenth and eleventh centuries further increased the contacts between Scotland and Islam, as there are records of Scottish Vikings also joining the Crusaders and going on pilgrimages. The Crusades and their impact on Scotland shall be discussed in the following chapter.

---

[62] Adler, M.N. ed, *The Itinerary of Benjamin of Tudela* p.76

[63] MacQuarrie, Allan *Scotland and the Crusades 1095-1560*

(Opposite above) *Abbas ibn Firnas* a Muslim adventurous scientist of Cordoba first introduced the concept of flying by a flying machine in mid-ninth century. After many successful experiments of short flights over the desert regions, and improving the design of his machine, in about 855, he attempted his most famous flight from a hill on the outskirts of Cordoba. In the presence of thousands of people, he took off from the top of the hill in his machine with large wings made of silk and eagle feathers. He rose to a considerable height and stayed in the air for over ten minutes before falling down, breaking the machine and injuring himself, but not seriously. (©Ali Amro / MuslimHeritageImages.com

(Above) An illustration showing Al-Idrisi in the court of Roger II of Sicily with a silver globe that he created to show that the Earth was spherical. ©Ali Amro / MuslimHeritageImages.com

(Opposite below) The camera obscura or 'pinhole camera' was invented by *al-Hasan ibn al-Haitham* (*Alhazen* in Latin), in the early eleventh century. Thus, the word camera comes from *kamara* an Arabic word. Ibn al-Haitham was born in Basra and then moved to Cairo, where he remained for the rest of his life and died in 1058. He is known in the West as the greatest Muslim physicist of all times. He was also one of the greatest and most influential discoverers in the science of optics. ©Ali Amro / MuslimHeritageImages.com

The Bishop of Salisbury before Saladin

CHAPTER 2

The Crusaders and Islam

AS a Christian nation, Scotland, according to its resources, played its part in the Crusades and Scots crusaders fought in nearly all of them. In the chronicles of medieval English, French, Latin and Arab writers, there are numerous fragmentary references to the participation of the Scots in the Crusades, but until very recently there was no collective and comprehensive account of their specific involvement in the Crusades Movement. It is to the credit of Dr. Allan Denis MacQuarrie that he researched and put together all these widely scattered bits of information first in his exhaustive and well researched thesis *The Impact of the Crusades Movement in Scotland, 1095 c.1560*, (1982), and then in his book *Scotland and the Crusades 1095-1560* published in 1985. These two publications appear to be the only extensive record of the part played by the Scottish nation in the Crusades. Hence, much of the material in this chapter is derived from these two sources.

Since the capture of Jerusalem by Muslims in 636, the Christian world had resented that reality. However, during the first four and a half centuries of Muslim rule their military might deterred the Byzantines and other European Christian powers from planning or taking any serious action to recover the Holy Land. In addition, the prevalence of peace and order in the Holy Land, the just treatment of the Christians and the tolerance and respect manifested towards the Christian religion and religious institutions by the Muslim rulers, even during trying times, contributed to the maintenance of the *status quo*. For example, during the prolonged warfare between the Muslims and the Byzantines in the tenth century, the Muslims were the losers. As a reaction to their reverses, the Muslim mobs sometimes attacked the Christians for their sympathies with their co-religionist Byzantines. After such attacks, the Muslim ruler, the *Caliph*, always made restitution for the damage done to his Christian subjects and/or their properties. [1] Such was the attitude of the Muslim rulers towards their Christian citizens, when on the other side, during their reconquest of some territories in Armenia, Syria and Anatolia the Byzantines in their intolerance and bigotry were destroying mosques and had their soldiers 'under orders to gather up copies of the Koran and burn them'.[2]

So far, the Muslims had seldom indulged in such sacrilegious acts, even in retaliation, as burning Bibles or demolishing churches. However, the situation of tolerance and co-existence in the Muslim Empire changed during the eleventh century. The political fragmentation of the Abbasid Empire based at Baghdad led to disorder and chaos in the Levant. The central governments had become so weak and ineffective, that the local petty chiefs and in some places, even brigands had taken control of many of the outlying areas of the Empire. In the tenth century the Fatimid Caliphs of Egypt, who were of the minority Shiite sect, had occupied Palestine and parts of Syria. Early in the eleventh century the sixth Fatimid Caliph *Al-Hakim* (r. 996-1021), who was a bigot and an eccentric ruler, became very intolerant towards Christians and Jews as well as Sunni Muslims. He introduced excessive taxes and oppressive policies that made life very difficult for the local inhabitants and the pilgrims to the Holy Land. Even some churches and religious buildings, against specific commandments of the *Quran*, were destroyed on his orders. The returning European Christian pilgrims carried back to their countries all these disturbing reports, which exacerbated the concern and anger in the Christian world against Muslim rule in the Holy Land.

Soon after the death of *Al-Hakim* in AD1021, the situation concerning pilgrims and the safety and security of life and property of the Christians in the Holy Land began to improve and by the middle of the eleventh century, the conditions had again become satisfactory. But the excesses committed by *Al-Hakim* had transformed the desire of Christian Europe to recover Jerusalem from Muslims into an intense passion. The crunch, however, came in the last quarter of the eleventh century when the Byzantine Emperor came under greater pressure from the Seljuk Turks, after they had conquered Armenia in 1064. The Seljuks, who had recently converted

---

[1] Runciman, S. *The History of Crusades* Vol. I, p.27

[2] Fletcher, Richard *The Cross and the Crescent* p.67

to Islam, being a warlike tribal society, were constantly attacking and encroaching upon the Byzantine territories. After suffering many reverses at the hands of the Seljuks and especially the humiliating defeat at the battle of Manzikert in 1071, the Byzantine Emperor appealed for military assistance from the Pope and the European rulers. The situation became more serious when the Seljuks took control of Jerusalem in 1075, and law and order broke down in the Holy Land. By this time, the Normans had taken Sicily from the Muslims and Alfonso IV of Castile had recovered Toledo from the Moors in Spain. These two very important Christian victories against the Muslims enhanced the confidence of the European Christians nations and convinced them of the weakening of Muslim power. Consequently, it strengthened their resolve to reclaim the Holy Land. Realising this favourable situation Pope Urban II declared a crusade to recover Jerusalem from the Muslims.

On 27 November 1095, at Clermont, he delivered an emotional sermon exhorting the Christians to march to the Holy Land and wrest Jerusalem from the Muslim oppressors. Within a few months of the Pope's sermon, a huge Christian army led by various European princes and prelates was marching towards Constantinople to cross over to Anatolia, from where to travel to Jerusalem. This was the first campaign of a series launched by Western European powers against the Muslims of the Near East, during the Middle Ages, which became known as the Crusades.[3] These Crusades continued off and on, from the end of the eleventh century to the middle of the sixteenth, first against the Muslim rulers of the Levant and then against the Muslim Moors of Spain and the Muslim Ottoman Turks.

In spite of the fact that there was no Scottish representative at the Council of Clermont, in November 1095, the echoes of the Pope's sermon clearly reached Scotland. The Pope's call 'to set out to liberate the holy city of Jerusalem' was received fervently and answered enthusiastically by a number of Scots. 'His summons was eagerly obeyed. From as far as Scotland. . . men hastened to make their vows.'[4] Nearly every chronicler of the time has acknowledged the presence of the Scots among the 100,000 men who joined the first Crusade. The one nobleman from Scotland known to have

---

[3] Hillenbrand, Carole *The Crusades; Islamic Perspective* p.20

[4] Runciman, R. *The History of Crusades* Vol.I p.112

joined the first Crusade with his followers was Logmann, the king of the Isle of Man and the Hebrides. To expiate his heinous crime of blinding and mutilating his estranged brother, Logmann renounced his kingdom and 'took the cross in remorse for the cruelty he had shown towards his rebellious brother'.[5] Logmann did not return to his native land as he died somewhere in the Holy Land. There were others, unknown ordinary people, from Scotland who left their hearths and homesteads to go to France and join the Crusaders. They were seen arriving in France 'with bare legs, shaggy cloaks, a purse hanging from their shoulders, offering the help of their faith and devotion to the Franks'.[6]

These ordinary Scots joined the army of Robert Duke of Normandy, who earlier had been in Scotland and who some of them knew or had heard of, and probably stayed with, throughout the first Crusade. Scotland's scarce resources and lack of interaction with mainland Europe was reflected in the comparative backwardness of the contingent of the Scottish Crusaders. They were noted for their faith, but their armaments and armour were inferior, their dress shabby, their language totally unintelligible to their comrades in arms and they did not know the language of the Franks. For everyday contact and for crusading purposes, therefore, communication was possible only through hand gestures and body language. Hence, Scottish Crusaders were considered primitive, undisciplined and not rated as effective fighting men. Nonetheless, the Scots with the other multitude of Crusaders reached Syria in 1097, and laid siege to the city of Antioch in October of the same year. The besieged city after negotiating acceptable terms, surrendered to the Crusaders on 3 June 1098. However, on their entry into the city the Crusaders, in total disregard to the terms of surrender, killed every Muslim and Jew they found there before the sunset:

> . . . you could not walk on the streets without treading on corpses, all of them rotting rapidly in the summer heat. But Antioch was Christian once more.[7]

---

[5] MacQuarrie, Allan *Scotland and the Crusades* p.122

[6] *ibid* p.122

[7] Runciman, S. *The History of Crusades* Vol.I p.235

From Antioch the Crusaders moved on south towards Jerusalem capturing many other towns on their way and in most cases, in spite of giving solemn indemnities of safety to their residents, slaughtering them all – young, old and infirm. After receiving the surrender of the town of *Ma'arra*, they not only butchered the citizens as usual, but here they also ate their flesh. They cut out pieces of flesh of dead people, cooked them and ate with relish.[8]

The Crusaders captured Jerusalem on 15 July 1099. Their treatment of the residents of the Holy City was far worse than any other place conquered by them on their way to Jerusalem. They had committed massacres of the people of nearly every town and every habitation that surrendered to them with or without a fight, but their indiscriminate massacre within the sacred precincts of Jerusalem was more barbaric than all their previous atrocities:

> The Crusaders, maddened by so great a victory. . . rushed through the streets and into the houses and mosques killing all that they met, men, women and children alike. All that afternoon and all through the night the massacre continued . . . When Raymond of Aguilers later that morning went to visit the Temple area he had to pick his way through corpses and blood that reached up to his knees. The Jews of Jerusalem fled in a body to their chief synagogue. . . The building was set on fire and they were all burnt within. . . No one can say how many victims it involved; but it emptied Jerusalem of its Muslim and Jewish inhabitants. . . It was this bloodthirsty proof of Christian fanaticism that recreated the fanaticism of Islam. When later, wiser Latins in the East sought to find some basis on which Christians and Moslems could work together, the memory of the massacre stood always in their way.[9]

About the fate of those Muslims of Jerusalem who took refuge in the *Al-Aqsa* Mosque and who had been given a pledge of safety, Fulcher of Charters, a participant in the first Crusade, in his *Historia Hierosolymitana*, has this to say:

---

[8] Wheatcroft, Andrew *The Infidels* p.182

[9] Runciman, S. *The History of Crusades* Vol.I p.286/7

Many of the Saracens who had climbed to the top of the temple of Solomon in their flight were shot to death with arrows and fell headlong from the roof. Nearly ten thousand were beheaded in the temple. If you had been there your feet would have been stained to the ankles in the blood of the slain. What shall I say? None of them was left alive. Neither women nor children were spared.[10]

The day after their capture of Jerusalem, the streets of the Holy City ran with blood. The Crusaders rode thorough blood coming up to their knees and bridle reins. Heaps of severed human heads, hands and feet were everywhere. Mounds of rotting bodies were choking the streets. Piles of bodies had to be burnt to make way for the Crusaders to visit the holy sites. The number of people massacred was so great that in spite of burning pile after pile for many days, bodies were still lying around and inside the city five months later and the stench of rotting human bodies was unbearable. The once intensely populated and flourishing Holy City had been turned into a stinking and silent city of the dead by the Crusaders.[11] Having massacred and cleared the Holy City of all the Muslims and Jews the Crusaders banned the future residence and even the entry of Muslims and Jews into Jerusalem.

Not much is known about the progress of the Scottish contingent in their journey from France to the Holy Land or their part in the atrocities committed by the Crusaders in the cities and towns captured by them. In the middle of 1097, they are reported to be with the Crusading armies on their advance from Nicaea to Antioch. Nothing is known about their participation in the capture of Jerusalem or their interaction with the Muslims they came across during their marches in the Levant or their battles with them. There is no available information about the number of Scots who participated in the first Crusade or the number of those who died in action except King Logmann. Neither are there any records of those who survived the brutalities of the battles and the rigours of the return journey and came back to Scotland. However there are signs and some tangible evidence that point to the fact that some did come back.

---

[10] Ryan, Frances Rita, Trans. pp.121-122

[11] Armstrong, Karen *History of Jerusalem* p.274-75

Soon after the first Crusade King Edgar of Scotland is reported to have owned a camel, 'an animal of remarkable size', which only a returning crusader could have brought with him from the East. Some years ago a gold coin bearing the Islamic date AH 491 corresponding to AD 1097, belonging to a *Murabit* ruler of North Africa was discovered buried in Monymusk churchyard, which again could only have arrived in Scotland in the purse or the pocket of a survived Crusader or a trader. These returning Crusaders must also have brought back many tales of their adventures and their contacts with Muslims of the Levant that would have disseminated some information among the Scots about the culture and customs of the Muslims.

The news of those momentous successes of the Crusaders had spread like wildfire in Europe and many more volunteers, to share the spoils of a successful war perhaps, or to expiate their sins, were rushing to join them in the Holy Land. From Scotland another nobleman, Edgar Etheling is known to have left with his retinue to join the Crusaders. In May 1102, he reached *Ramleh* and took part in the capture of that town which at his arrival was under siege by the Crusaders. He stayed in the Holy Land for about four years and took part in many battles and expeditions before he returned to Scotland. King Alexander I (r. 1107-1124) of Scotland is reputed to have owned an Arab horse and Turkish armour 'which he had proudly displayed during a visit to the church of St Andrews'.[12] It is not known who brought over this horse and the armour King Alexander was so proud of or how he got them. It may have been Edgar Ethleling, who was a relative of the King and who returned from taking part in the Crusades at about the time when Alexander succeeded his brother Edgar to the throne of Scotland. On the other hand, it could also have been some other nobleman or an unknown Scottish Crusader who knew about the King's passion and deep interest in the Crusades Movement and wanted to oblige his Sovereign by bringing back something for him as a memento from the Holy Land. The horse and the armour may have been the spoils of war of whoever brought them over for the king. In any case, this again shows the contacts that were being established between Scotland and the East and the influence of the Muslim culture that was slowly reaching Scotland.

---

[12] MacQuarrie, Allan *Scotland and the Crusades*

The establishment of the Latin kingdoms in the Levant in the beginning of the twelfth century and their continued conflicts with the neighbouring Muslim rulers resulted in the unprecedented growth of traffic in Crusaders and pilgrims between Europe and the Holy Land. The trend now for most of the European Christians was to go as both Crusaders and pilgrims. John, Bishop of Glasgow went on a pilgrimage in 1122 and there must have been many more of whom we have no knowledge. There is evidence to the fact that by that time, pilgrimage to the Holy Land from Scotland was a common phenomenon. The *Melrose Chronicle*, a record of that period, relates the pilgrimage of Bishop John as if it was nothing of much importance. With the Holy Land under Christian control, pilgrimage to the Holy City had become very popular and like other European Christians Scots were also taking advantage of this favourable situation.[13]

In 1124 King David I succeeded his brother Alexander. David was deeply interested and indeed remained very much involved in the Crusading movement all through his life. Hugh de Paiens, First Master of the Knights Templars, visited Scotland early in David's reign to recruit more Crusaders and to collect funds for the Crusading movement. David entertained him with great respect and actively helped him in his mission. As a result, a significant number of volunteers, mostly common Scottish folk, joined thousands of others from England and Europe and followed Hugh to the Holy Land. From there Hugh led them to the disastrous campaign against Damascus where many, the Scots among them, were killed. But that did not dampen the crusading zeal of King David. To promote the Crusading movement more effectively he actively supported the establishment in Scotland of the two famous Crusader Military Orders, The Order of The Knights of The Temple, the Templars and The Order of The Knights of St James, the Hospitallers and to both he made liberal grants of land.

In the Muslim world, ever since the capture of Jerusalem by the Crusaders followed by their indiscriminate massacres of Muslims and the desecration of the Muslim holy places, there had been extreme anger against them and an earnest desire to eject them from the Levant. In December 1144, *Imad ad Din Zangi,* the ruler of Mosil and Mesopotamia, captured the Crusader stronghold of

---

[13] McRoberts, Rev. David *Scottish Pilgrims to the Holy Land* p.18

Eddesa and started the process, which, forty-three years later, culminated in the victory of Saladin (*Salah-ed-din Yusaf ibn Ayyub*) at the battle of *Hittin* and the surrender of Jerusalem. The loss of *Eddesa* was the first serious reverse suffered by the Crusaders since their capture of Jerusalem in 1099. It came as a terrible shock to them and they issued earnest calls for help to the Pope and the European kings. The response as always was tremendous. King Louis of France and Conrad III of Germany took the crusading vows and announced their readiness to go to the assistance of the Latin kings. King David I of Scotland also expressed his earnest desire to join them. However, his nobles, the clergy and the common people thought it against the interests of the nation for their sovereign to leave the country for such a considerable time and successfully pleaded with him to change his mind. The King, then, to play his part from here in the Crusade, helped and motivated many of his nobles and ordinary people to go and in early 1147, a strong Scottish contingent travelled south, to join the English, in order to take part in the second Crusade.

The fleet taking the Scottish, English and Flemish crusaders left for the Holy Land in June 1147. When they were near Lisbon, they came to know that King Alfonso Henrigues of Portugal was besieging that city which then was under Muslim (Moors) control. The commanders of the Crusaders decided to help the Christian King against the Muslims and achieve the credit of crusading nearer home before going to Jerusalem. Four months later the city surrendered to the besiegers. The Scottish contingent displayed great courage during the siege of Lisbon though their image still was the same – rough and rugged barbarians.

After the victory celebrations, the Crusader fleet went on its way to the Holy Land. The French and German kings had reached the Holy Land early in 1148 where Baldwin III of Jerusalem joined them. Before trying to recover Edessa the three kings resolved to capture Damascus. However, Damascus proved to be so well defended that after suffering huge losses, within four days of the siege in July 1148, the Crusaders were forced to an ignominious retreat. Thus, the second Crusade ended in utter disaster. Soon after their defeat the German and French kings returned to their respective countries with whoever of their soldiers had survived.

Encouraged by the defeat of Crusaders at Damascus, *Nur-ed*

din Zangi, the successor to *Imad-ed-din,* consolidated his position in the county of Edessa, and in 1149 defeated, and killed Raymond of Antioch. Again, there is no information about the fate of the Scots who joined the second Crusade, except one nobleman William de Warenne, who was connected to the Scottish royal family. He was captured by the pursuing Muslim forces during the flight of the Crusaders from Damascus, but nothing appears to be known about him or his fate after his capture.

In 1151 Earl Rognvald of Orkney, a Viking lord, with his entourage, sailed to the Holy Land on a Crusade and a pilgrimage. On his way he attacked and plundered Moorish Spanish coastal towns. In the Mediterranean he captured a Muslim merchant ship (according to some sources two ships) laden with rich merchandise and killed most of the crew – 'Saracens, whom we call Mahote's infidels.' In the Holy Land the earl visited all the holy places and bathed in the River Jordan. He did not engage in any crusading during his pilgrimage and his stay in the Holy Land. What he had already done round the coast of Spain and in the Mediterranean on his way to the Holy Land was his only contribution to the Crusade against Muslims. From Jerusalem the earl went to Constantinople from where he returned to Orkney in late 1153.[14] By this time, according to the observations of a German pilgrim John of Wurzburgh, a Scottish pilgrim's chapel had been founded in Jerusalem.[15] The foundation of this chapel means that there must have been a considerable flow of Scottish pilgrims to the Holy Land to justify its existence and maintenance.

On the other side, the Muslims had increased pressure on the Crusaders and were slowly but steadily pushing farther and farther into the territories held by them. With the arrival of *Salah Al-Din* (Saladin), the Sultan of Egypt and Syria, on the scene in the last quarter of the twelfth century, the situation began to change rapidly. He was a leader who had the courage, the foresight and the power to wrest Jerusalem from the Crusaders. He had united Syria and Egypt under his rule thus surrounding Christian territories from three sides. Realising the danger, in late 1184 Hercalius, Patriarch of Jerusalem, hurried to Europe to apprise the European rulers of the seriousness of the situation and seek their aid in defending the

---

[14] Taylor, A.B. *The Orkneyinga Saga* London 1938
[15] Allan MacQuarrie p.22

kingdom of Jerusalem. At the beginning of 1185, he arrived in England to enlist the help of Henry II King of England. Henry called a meeting of his knights and nobles and also invited King Malcolm IV of Scotland to discuss the matter and decide how to respond to the appeal of the Patriarch of Jerusalem. On his return, King Malcolm urged the Scots to join the Crusade and again, many knights and ordinary Scots vowed to and went to defend the Holy Land. It is rumoured that David the brother of King Malcolm also was in the Scottish contingent. However, the chivalry and sacrifices of the Scots and other Crusaders could not prevent *Salah Al-Din* from capturing Jerusalem on 2 October 1187.

Salah Al-Din was one of the most chivalrous, just and compassionate leaders and army generals in history. Having defeated the Christians at the battle of *Hittin*, he wanted to negotiate the surrender of Jerusalem, in order to avoid laying siege and shedding blood on the sacred soil of *Bait-ul-Muqqadus* – the Holy City. The terms he offered the residents of Jerusalem were to feel free to strengthen the fortifications of the city, cultivate the surrounding land without any fear and live in peace until the following Pentecost, on the condition that if no help came to them from outside by that time they would surrender the Holy City. He promised that on the surrender of the Holy City those who wanted to leave would be escorted in safety to wherever they wanted to go with all their possessions. The Sultan in his benevolence also offered them as much money and food as they required during that period. However, the Crusaders defending the city spurned the generous terms of *Salah Al-Din*, for a peaceful surrender:

> The Sultan was anxious to spare the Holy City the misery of siege. 'I believe,' he told them, 'that Jerusalem is the House of God, as you also believe, and I will not willingly lay siege to the House of God or put it to the assault.' . . . The offer was chivalrous, even quixotic, when the notorious bad faith of the crusaders is remembered, and the lack of any security for their keeping a promise. But the delegates from Jerusalem refused it without hesitation.[16]

Thus, *Salah Al-Din* was left with no choice but to mount an attack

---

[16] Lane-Poole, Stanley *Saladin and the fall of Jerusalem* p.164

on the Holy City. The city surrendered within a week, on 27th September 1187 and after a forced absence of 88 years the Muslims were back in Jerusalem. As previously mentioned, when the Crusaders captured Jerusalem in 1099, they massacred all the Muslim and Jewish residents of the city including women, children, old and infirm. However when the Muslims had occupied the Holy City in 638, they harmed none of the citizens on its sacred soil and granted amnesty even to the Christian combatants. *Salah Al-Din* also, on his capture of Jerusalem, according to nearly every Christian chronicler of the time, some of whom were present there, showed great reverence and respect for the Holy City and unprecedented kindness and forbearance towards its Christian citizens. S. Runciman states:

> The victors were correct and humane. Where the Franks, eighty-eight years before, had waded through the blood of their victims, not a building now was looted, not a person injured. By Saladin's orders, guards patrolled the streets and the gates, preventing any outrage on the Christians.[17]

The victors followed the humane principle of forgiveness, compassion and respect towards the citizens and did not tarnish the precincts of the Holy City with any wanton and merciless massacres. The Sultan posted guards in every street of the city to protect the citizens from any harm from his soldiers. No one was forced to leave the city. Those who wanted to leave of their own volition were given forty days within which to go in peace with all their goods and movables on the payment of a fixed small sum of ransom. After the period of grace expired there still remained thousands of the poor in the city who wanted to leave but could not pay the ransom. To them *Salah Al-Din* treated with exceptional favour:

> Then *el-Adil* came to his brother and said: 'Sire I have helped you by God's grace to conquer the land and this city, I therefore pray you give me a thousand slaves from the poor people within'. To Saladin's question, what he would do with them, he answered he would do as he pleased himself. Then

---

[17] Runciman, S. *A History of the Crusades* Vol.II p.466

the Sultan gave him the thousand slaves, and *el-Adil* set them all free as an offering to God. Then came the Patriarch [of Jerusalem] and Balian [a Christian knight who had negotiated the surrender of Jerusalem], and begged likewise, and Saladin gave them another thousand slaves, and they were set free. Then said Saladin to his officers: 'My brother has made his alms, and Patriarch and Balian have made theirs; now I would fain make mine.' And he ordered his guards to proclaim throughout the streets of Jerusalem that all the old people who could not pay were free to go forth.[18]

To the daughters, wives and widows of the Christian knights and soldiers, who had been fighting against him and indulging in all kinds of atrocities against the Muslims, he showed unparalleled compassion and unprecedented generosity. After the surrender of the city, these ladies went before *Salah Al-Din* crying and pleading with him to show mercy to them and release their imprisoned husbands. The Sultan was so overcome by their earnest and pitiful pleas that he himself began weeping with them and told them that if they could tell him when and where their husbands were captured or where they were being held he would search for them and release them. When he had obtained that information, he gave orders for all of them to be released as soon as his messengers could reach their holding places. Further, he gave all the widows, wives and daughters of those knights, considerable sums of money according to their status from his own treasure. It is reported that he gave them so much that 'they gave praise to God and published abroad the kindness and honour which Saladin had done to them.'

Thus, did the Saracen show mercy to the fallen city? One recalls the savage conquest by the first Crusaders in 1099, when Godfrey and Tancard rode through streets choked with dead and dying, when defenceless Muslims were tortured burnt down and shot down in cold blood on the towers and rooftop of the Temple, when the blood of wanton massacre defiled the honour of Christendom and stained the scene where once the gospel of love and mercy had been preached. 'Blessed are the merciful, for they shall obtain mercy' was a

---

[18] Lane-Poole, Stanley *Saladin and the fall of Jerusalem* p.169

forgotten beatitude when the Christians made shambles of the Holy City. Fortunate were the merciless, for they obtained mercy at the hands of the Muslim Sultan.[19]

It is not known whether any Scottish Crusader participated in the defence of Jerusalem or any widow, wife or daughter of a Scottish Crusader was among those who experienced the generosity of Sultan *Salah Al-Din* after the fall of Jerusalem. However, not all the Christians left Jerusalem. The Orthodox and other smaller Christian sects remained in the city. They had always preferred Muslim rule to escape from the oppression of their co-religionist Latins and Franks.

The generosity, compassion and indeed the chivalry of *Salah Al-Din* was very well and widely 'published abroad'. Returning knights and other Crusaders told to their countrymen, the tales of the courtesy and generosity of their Muslim enemy. Out of these tales the minstrels, the poets and writers of the West in the Middle Ages and later made up numerous legends and myths about *Salah Al-Din* and his good deeds. He became the hero of so many plays, chansons and romances in which, over and above his other adventures, he is portrayed as having love affairs with many dames of the Christian knights and queens of Christian kings. In one of these legends, Eleanor the queen of the French king falls in love with him. She '. . . sends a dragoman to tell him so; offering to have him for her lord, and to change her religion for his sake'.[20] In another myth, he is made to have accepted the baptism and gone through the ceremony of Christian initiation to knighthood. To deny him his Muslim heritage perhaps, he was even from his mother's side 'endowed with noble French descent, from the counts of Ponthieu'.[21] In short, *Salah Al-Din*, or Saladin as he is called in the West, became the epitome of tolerance, chivalry and generosity in medieval Europe.

Even today, over 800 years later, facts, legends and myths about him, mostly in his praise, abound in the West. Poets and writers like Dante, Voltaire, Shakespeare and Sir Walter Scott have given him literary immortality. Nonetheless, in spite of *Salah Al-Din's*

[19] Lane-Poole, Stanley p.170

[20] Lane-Poole, Stanley pp.255-56

[21] Daniel, Norman *The Arabs and Medieval Europe* p.189

supposed Christian ancestry and baptism, Dante in his Divine Comedy, still places him in Limbo in the company of famous non-Christians, philosophers like Aristotle, Plato and Homer etc. Nonetheless, the legends surrounding Saladin did influence the thinking of the Europeans of the time to the effect that Muslims were not as evil as they were being presented to them by their clerics.

The fall of Jerusalem shook the whole of the Christian world. The Pope issued a desperate call for a new Crusade. Most of the European rulers including the King of England began to make preparation to embark upon their sacred journeys to the Holy Land to recover Jerusalem from Muslims. A tax called the 'Saladin tithe' – a tenth of rent and movables – was levied in most of the Christian countries of Europe to finance the Crusade. The English King Henry sent his messengers to Scotland to collect the Saladin tithe and also to exhort the Scots to participate. The Scottish King William and his court were not very enthusiastic about paying the tithe until the English king restored to the Scots the Scottish royal castles that he held. However, Henry died in 1189, and Richard the Lion Heart succeeded to his father's throne. At a meeting between King Richard and William of Scotland, at Canterbury in December 1189 the two sovereigns amicably resolved their differences. Richard consented to meet all the demands of the Scots and William agreed to pay Richard 10,000 marks as the Scottish contribution toward the Crusade. The Saladin tithe and the wrangling on it, between the two governments, would have raised many questions and caused very many discussions among the people of Scotland. That would have led to much focus on Saladin, his character and his religion, disseminating more information, about Muslim culture and religion.[22]

After settling his differences with the Scottish King, Richard crossed the English Channel on 12 December 1189, to join the Third Crusade. Not much enthusiasm was evinced by the Scots to take part, but from among those who did join Richard, Robert de Quincy was the most important Scottish personage. Robert de Quincy was married to Orabile, a grand daughter of King William. Probably he had accompanied William to Canterbury and had met Richard. Others from Scotland who are considered to have taken part in the Third Crusade include Osbert Olifard of Arbuthnott,

---

[22] MacQuarrie, Allan *Scotland and the Crusades 1095-1560* p.28

and Alan son of Walter the Steward, with their respective followers. Earl David, the brother of King William is also rumoured and indeed mentioned in some legends to have taken the cross and gone on the Third Crusade. Many early historians like Hector Boece have included in their works the exploits of Earl David in the Holy Land. Following them probably, in his novel *The Talisman*, Sir Walter Scott also narrates many feats of David in the Crusades.[23]

After a year and half's vacillation, King Richard, with his forces and the small Scottish contingent, reached Acre on 8 June 1191 and joined the King of France and other Crusaders who were besieging that port city. A few days later Richard sent a request for a meeting with Sultan *Salah Al Din*, who declined to meet him saying that it was not proper 'for kings at war with each other to meet in friendly converse until a treaty of peace was actually afoot.' However, *Salah Al Din* agreed to a meeting between his brother *El Adil* and Richard, to negotiate a peace treaty between the Crusaders and the Sultan. That meeting had to wait because Richard suddenly became very ill. Nonetheless, the exchange of messages and the negotiations for peace continued through envoys during the illness of Richard. When *Salah Al Din* became aware of Richard's illness and high fever he continuously kept sending to him snow and fresh fruit to help lower his fever and facilitate his recovery. As the peace negotiations were dragging on between the Sultan and the English King through their respective ambassadors, the Muslim garrison in Acre became so hard pressed by the Crusaders that they themselves negotiated terms with the besiegers and surrendered the city. However, in spite of giving a solemn pledge, in the peace treaty, to let the garrison and the citizens leave in safety Richard gave orders that they all be beheaded. Even the old, the invalid and women and children were mercilessly massacred. Considering *Salah Al-Din's* grace, courtesy and compassion towards the Christians of Jerusalem and indeed his concern for Richard during the latter's illness, Richard's atrocity, will appear incomprehensible:

> But the students of the Crusades do not need to be told that
> in this struggle the virtues of civility, magnanimity, toleration,

---

[23] *ibid* pp.28-29

real chivalry, and gentle culture, were all on the side of the Saracens.[24]

In spite of Richard's endeavours, the Third Crusade also failed to recover Jerusalem from *Salah Al-Din*. However, the Scottish noble, Robert de Quincy played an important part in this Crusade. Soon after joining the English contingent, he won the confidence of the English King, who entrusted him with some very important missions during his campaign in the Holy Land. For example, Richard sent Robert de Quincy as his emissary to settle a dispute with Conrade of Montferrat, one of the claimants to the throne of Jerusalem, concerning some Muslim prisoners and he was appointed 'constable and leader' of a force of the one hundred and fifty English knights and fifty sergeants sent for the defence of Antioch.[25] As confidant of his King, Robert de Quincy would have also participated in the various negotiations between Richard and *Salah Al-Din* and the many very amicable meetings and dialogues between Richard and *Salah Al-Din's* brother *el-Adil*.

Having failed to win the Holy City with force, King Richard tried diplomacy and even a marriage alliance with the Sultan to achieve, if not full control, at least some kind of hold on Jerusalem. During their protracted negotiations, Richard had developed a warm friendship with *el-Adil*, the brother of *Salah Al-Din*, to whom he proposed that he (*el-Adil*) marry his sister Joan, the widowed Queen of Sicily. Richard was then to give the coast cities of Acre, Ascalon, and Jaffa that were in his possession, in dowry to Joan who would live with *el Adil* at Jerusalem. On the other side, *Salah Al-Din* was to endow *el-Adil* the area under his control and the couple would reign together over the whole of Palestine. *Salah Al-Din* had to also surrender the true Cross and allow the establishments of Templars and Hospitallers in the Holy City. However, when Richard's sister came to know of this proposal she angrily refused to marry a Muslim. Richard then came up with another absurd idea that *el-Adil* should embrace Christianity, that was rejected by *el-Adil*. However, before he and his English and Scottish Crusaders left to return to Britain, Richard through his rapport with *el-Adil* had secured from the sultan an honourable treaty of peace for three

---

[24] Lane-Poole, Stanley p.213

[25] MacQuarrie, Allan, pp.28-29

years. The treaty allowed Christian pilgrims to visit Jerusalem, gave the coast cities he had conquered from Acre to Jaffa to Richard, and Muslims and Christians were to pass freely in each other's territories. Before his departure from the Holy Land, Richard invited *el-Adil* to his camp where he hosted a sumptuous dinner in his own tent in *el-Adil's* honour and they parted in renewed friendship.[26]

Nevertheless, the Christian world was in sombre mood for having failed a third time to recover the Holy City. In 1198, the new Pope Innocent decreed the fourth Crusade to try again. The Pope sent his legates to all countries to stir up interest in the Crusade and arouse the kings, barons and commons to take the cross. In 1201, a papal legate came to Scotland and held a council at Perth. The Council was attended by the bishops of Aberdeen, Moray, Dunkeld, Ross, St Andrews and Glasgow: the abbots of Holyrood, Jedburgh, Arbroath, Melrose, Kelso, Lindores and Kilwinning; the dean of Glasgow and archdeacons of Lothian and many other church leaders. Gilchrist Earl of Strathearn, Duncan Earl of Fife and a number of important laymen were also present. Out of this impressive gathering only David Rufus of Forfar, who was also present, is known to have taken the cross.[27] However, the fourth Crusade ended up capturing Constantinople, a Christian city, instead of Jerusalem and David Rufus, most probably did not get to the Holy Land.

Pope Innocent had been deeply disappointed at the failure of the fourth Crusade. He was however busy with other important affairs until 1212. In early 1213, he proclaimed the fifth Crusade to recover the Holy City. He sent letters to all the spiritual and temporal leaders of the Christian world seeking their financial and military assistance and appointed legates in most countries to 'preach the cross'. In Scotland, the bishops of St Andrews and Glasgow were appointed as preachers and collectors. The preaching of the two Scottish legates and other church leaders produced very encouraging results and a large number of Scots, mostly from the common people, vowed to participate in the new Crusade. However, the journey to the Holy Land did not commence until mid-1218,

---

[26] Lane-Poole, Stanley p.225/26

[27] MacQuarrie, Allan *Scotland and the Crusades 1095-1560* p.32

as it took a few years before everybody and everything could be made ready.

From among the rich and powerful of Scotland Saher de Quincy, son of Robert de Quincy, and only three or four others took the cross. Another notable, Ranulf, Earl of Chester who had connections with Scotland through his relationship with Earl David was also in this Crusade. From the ordinary common people though, nearly 'a multitude from throughout Scotland' joined this crusade. Among them were the two Gaelic poets Gille-Brigde Albanach and Muiredhach Albanach O Dalaig. They survived and came back to Scotland to tell their tales. Their poems that were preserved give much interesting information about the Scottish contingent's progress to and in the Holy Land. These poems most probably are one of the scarce first hand surviving records of the participation of ordinary people of Scotland in the crusades. Saher de Quincy died in August 1218, of an illness at Damietta in Egypt, before he could see or take part in any action in this Crusade. After nearly a year of inconclusive warfare between the Crusaders and Muslims, the Sultan *Al-Kamal* of Egypt offered generous terms to end the conflict.

> If they would evacuate Egypt, he would return them the True Cross, and they could have Jerusalem, all central Palestine and Galilee. The Moslems would only retain the castles of Oultrejourdain, but pay a tribute for them. It was a startling offer. With no more fighting, the Holy City, with Bethlehem, Nazareth and the True Cross, could be restored to Christendom. . . But Pelagius (the papal legate) would have none of it, nor would the Patriarch of Jerusalem. They thought it wrong to come to terms with the infidel.[28]

In vain did King John of France and the Scottish noble, Earl Ranulf show their sagacity and foresight by earnestly advocating the acceptance of the favourable terms offered by the Egyptian Sultan *Al-Kamal*. Earl Ranulf returned home disappointed soon after. Eventually the Crusaders were forced by the Egyptians to leave empty handed. Thus, the fifth Crusade also failed to achieve its

---

[28] Runciman, S. *A History of the Crusades* Vol.3 p.161

objective mainly due to incompetence and bigotry, especially of the papal legates.

However, where others had failed with arms and might, Emperor Frederick II of Sicily succeeded with diplomacy and peaceful negotiations. Frederick, who admired Muslim culture and had many learned Muslim courtiers, was a wise and tolerant ruler. Instead of confronting Sultan *Al-Kamil,* a nephew of *Salah Al-Din,* by this time the ruler of Egypt and Syria (*Salah Al-Din* had died in 1193 at age 56), Frederick entered into negotiations with him seeking a peaceful resolution to the Jerusalem conflict between Christian and Muslims. The negotiations bore fruit and *Al-Kamil* and Frederick signed the treaty of the Peace of Jaffa on 18 February 1229. According to the terms of the treaty, *Al-Kamil* agreed to transfer the control of Jerusalem, Bethlehem, Nazareth, Lydda, Toron and Sidon to Emperor Frederick. The two parties were bound to keep the peace for ten years. The Muslim holy places in Jerusalem were to remain under Muslim jurisdiction and Muslim worship was to continue in them without any hindrance. Lastly, Jerusalem was not to be fortified by Frederick. Thus after 42 years of long and bloody struggle, the crusaders recovered Jerusalem not by force but by friendly and very favourable negotiations.

The success of these delicate negotiations most probably was achieved through the diplomatic skill and the academic excellence of an Arabic scholar Michael Scot, a trusted courtier and physician of the Emperor Frederick. Michael Scot, as we shall discuss in the next chapter, was from Scotland. He took up the service of Frederick in the early 1220s and was with him in the Holy Land in 1229. As he was very proficient in the Arabic language and well aware of the customs and culture of the Muslims, he would have acted as the leading negotiator for his Emperor. Thus, this single Scot contributed perhaps more, towards the recovery of Jerusalem, than all the Scots and hundreds of thousands of other various crusaders in forty to fifty years.

This singular success and the remarkable treaty obtained by Frederick, very surprisingly, was condemned by the European Christian leaders and especially the Pope. Their main objection was the concession to Muslims to retain their religious places and perform their prayers in Jerusalem. Considering that they had failed to recover Jerusalem by force and that Muslims during their occupation of the Holy City had respected the religion and religious places of the Christians and allowed freedom of worship in them, the opposition to this treaty appears to have been based on lack of any semblance of tolerance and sheer zealotry. Thus in spite of the recovery of Jerusalem by the Christians the fervour for the Crusades continued in Europe, but the truce held for ten years.

It appears that in Scotland also there was more enthusiasm for taking part in the Crusades in the thirteenth century than ever before. In the early thirteenth century the 'General Statutes of the Scottish Church' that provided ecclesiastical protection for Scottish Crusaders had been drawn up. This provision motivated and encouraged more Scots to take the cross. In 1235, Earl Richard of England decided to go on a Crusade. From Scotland in 1236, John the Scot, son of Earl David of Scotland, with many other Scots joined Earl Richard in England, but soon after John the Scot died. In 1238, Richard de Toni, nephew of King Alexander II of Scotland took the cross and joined Earl Richard. In 1239, Pope Gregory IX began his campaign to inspire more Christians to take the cross. In the early 1240s, many responded to his call and rushed to the Holy Land but there the Crusaders suffered many reverses and in October 1244 at Gaza, they were annihilated.

Pope Innocent IV declared yet another crusade, the seventh in the series at the Council of Lyons in June 1245 that was attended by the Bishop of St Andrews from Scotland. As usual, Scotland also received the summons to join the crusade and from the barons, Earl Patrick of Dunbar took the cross. King Louis IX of France became a great champion of this crusade and a great number of noblemen from Europe joined him. Earl Patrick with his contingent including some notables left in January 1248 to join King Louis in France but died on the way. King Louis decided to capture Egypt before going to Jerusalem, and attacked *Damietta*, which he captured in June 1249. Next, he headed for Cairo but in April 1250, was defeated at the battle of *Fariskur* near *Mansurah* and captured by the Egyptians with all the surviving crusaders. There is no information about the Scots killed or captured by the Egyptians in this battle, but there must have been some. It is not known either, if any of the Scots were redeemed from the Egyptians when King Louis and other French captives were ransomed.

In spite of all the setbacks, the enthusiasm to take the cross continued unabated in Scotland. The Knights Templars and the Hospitallers had become very well established and very effective in Scotland by the second half of the thirteenth century. These two military Orders played a significant role in generating that enthusiasm and sustaining it.

In the meantime, a new and powerful dynasty the Mamluks had taken control of the Near East. Their sultan *Baybars* (1260-1276) began determinedly encroaching upon the Christian territories in Palestine and Syria, and in 1268 captured Antioch. Realising the new dangerous situation King Louis had declared another crusade in 1267. In Scotland, a large sum of money was collected to support the Crusade and many Scots joined King Louis' Crusade. From among the Scottish nobles the Earls of Atholl and Carrick, Robert de Bruce and Robert de Bruce Younger, Alexander Balliol and three other Balliol noblemen volunteered. John de Vescy, Adam de Gordon, David de Lindsay, Alexander de Seton and many more, all with their knights and squires, also took the cross and joined the French king.

This time Louis began his crusade from Tunis and besieged that city. However, the heat of a dry summer in Tunis badly affected the health of the King and his crusaders and many of them fell ill and died. King Louis died in August 1270 and so did David the Earl of Atholl. At King Louis' death most of the Scots crusaders who had been with him at Tunis and had survived, joined Lord Edward the son of King Henry III of England and with him sailed away to Acre, where the Earl of Carrick also died. While narrating the siege of Tunis the *Chronicle of Melrose* mentions that when the city surrendered the population beseeched Louis to spare them because as Muslims, they believed in One God but not in three persons and that, they were not in any way connected to the Jewish faith. About the eventual fate of the citizens, the *Chronicle* is silent. However, to write and publicise that Muslims believed in One God was something quite unusual and indeed unique in that atmosphere where the common belief in Western world was that Muslims were idol-worshipping pagans who worshipped the idol of Mahout (Muhammad). This also shows that Scotland, though at the periphery of the then known world, through its contacts and Chronicles was quite abreast of what was happening in the world.

Some Scottish barons such as Robert de Bruce the Elder and

others joined Lord Edmund the other son of the English King Henry III, who sailed to the Holy Land and joined his brother Edward there in the summer of 1271. It is obvious therefore that a considerable number of Scots, perhaps more than ever before, both very important and common folk, took part in this Crusade. However, they did not achieve any positive results. This time again the crusaders were unable to expel or even stop the advances of Muslims in the Holy Land. Lord Edmund and most of the Scottish crusaders returned home in 1272; the rest came back with Lord Edward in 1274.

From 1273 to 1291, the Popes and other ecclesiastics in the whole of Christendom, without success continued to attempt to revive the enthusiasm for another Crusade and exhort the faithful to take the cross. But in 1291 came the final blow. The Sultan *al-Ashraf Khalil*, one by one, captured all the cities still held by the Crusaders in Syria and the Holy Land, and put an end to the Kingdom of Jerusalem. With no base or a seaport left in their possession on the Syrian or Palestinian coast at which they could land their forces, it became nearly impossible for the crusaders to recover the Holy Land and Jerusalem.

In the fourteenth century, realising the odds against the recovery of the Holy Land, the focus of the Crusade in Europe began to shift towards the Moorish Kingdom of Granada in Spain and the Ottoman Turks in Eastern Europe. A crusade was a war against the unbelieving heathens – the non-Christians. The Moors and Turks both being Muslims were termed Saracens and considered heathens by the Christians; hence they fitted their criteria for a Crusade. Therefore, to expel the Moors from Christian Spain, or to halt the advance of the Turks into Christian Europe, was considered as good a crusade as to fight for Jerusalem against the Muslims. Confirming the Scots participation in the Spanish wars against the Muslim kingdom of Granada, the following entry is recorded under 3 June 1309 AD in the *Calendar of documents relating to Scotland*:

> Warrant to the Chancellor for letters of special recommend-
> ation to the K. of Spain, for Sir Robert de Tony, who goes by
> the K'.s leave to serve God against the 'Sarazyns' there; also
> protection till All Saints next for him and Sir Wauter de

Kynggeshemede his bachelor, who accompanies him to
Spain.[29] (Vol. III, 1307-1357)

King Alexander III had died childless in 1286 and as a result,
Scotland went through internal dissension and the wars of
independence with England during the following forty years. Thus,
not much attention was paid to the Crusades during this time as
the Scots were engaged in their local 'crusade' against the English.
After the Treaty of Edinburgh in 1328, in which the English King
Edward III recognised Robert the Bruce as the rightful king of
independent Scotland, peace and order returned to Scotland.
Robert the Bruce, like his father and grandfather was very much
devoted to the cause of Jerusalem and had vowed to take the cross.
However, his struggle against the English did not allow him, during
his lifetime, to join a Crusade or effectively help that cause in any
other way. Nonetheless, before he died he directed Sir James
Douglas, one of his trusted knights, to take his heart, after his death,
to Jerusalem and the Holy Sepulchre in order to atone for his failure
to keep his vow. Accordingly, Douglas accompanied by seven knights,
twenty squires and a considerable number of men at arms, left
Scotland on his mission in early 1330.

'This was to be a Scottish Crusade and a pilgrimage to fight for
the cross in reclaiming the holy places.'[30] Passing through Spain on
his way to the Holy Land, he came to know that the King of Spain
was at war with the Moorish king of Granada. Douglas presented
his contingent to the Spanish King and joined him in his crusade
against the Spanish Muslims. In a battle with the Muslim forces
soon after, Douglas and most of his senior comrades in arms from
Scotland were killed. Thus ended the only Crusade declared solely
by anyone from the Scottish nation. The casket containing the heart
of Bruce was found near the body of Douglas and was brought back
to Scotland and buried at Melrose Abbey.

The long conflict between England and France prevented
Europeans from planning any new crusade to recover Jerusalem
until 1362, when King Peter I (1359-1369) of Cyprus took the
initiative. It was his ancestors the de Lusignans who were the kings
of Jerusalem before Muslims captured the Holy Land. He therefore

---

[29] Vol. III, 1307-1357

[30] Peter Yeoman *Pilgrimage in Medieval Scotland* p.119

had a vested interest in recovering 'his dominion'. He toured Europe from 1362 to 1364 to revive the interest in recovering the Holy Land and to promote a new crusade. King David II of Scotland hastily travelled to London to meet with the king of Cyprus when the latter arrived there to visit Edward III of England. The Scottish king decided to support and join that Crusade and on his return to Scotland enthusiastically began recruiting volunteers for his army of Crusaders. The response from some other European countries to King Peter's campaign was also encouraging and a considerable army of Crusaders gathered under his banner. The Scottish king could not go himself but the Scottish recruits who went on this Crusade included at least six magnates and a number of knights, squires and soldiers. King Peter sailed from Rhodes in October 1365, attacked Alexandria in Egypt and captured the city.

> . . . the victors pillaged and massacred throughout the city; and the following day, gathering their booty, they retreated to their ships. . . the Egyptians were able to reoccupy the city almost as the last of the crusaders were boarding their galleys and sailing for Cyprus. Peter's great Crusade was over almost as soon as it began, with nothing achieved but plunder and butchery.[31]

However, the gallantry and the commitment to the cause of Crusades displayed by the Scottish contingent during and after the attack on Alexandria was noticeable. Sir Norman Leslie one of the Scottish nobles, in spite of showers of stones being hurled upon the attackers by the defenders from the wall of the city, succeeded in kindling a fire against one of the gates that facilitated an early entry of the Crusaders into Alexandria. This brave Scottish noble was killed in front of the city gate by a big stone before he could retreat to safety.

The fiasco of this campaign and the many previous unsuccessful attempts to recover the Holy Land began adversely affecting the zeal for the Crusades in Europe and in Scotland. Another factor that lessened the enthusiasm of the Scots towards the Crusades movement was perhaps the decline, in the early fourteenth century, of the influence and the activities of the Templars in Scotland. Since

---

[31] MacQuarrie, Allan *Scotland and the Crusades* 1095-1560 p.82-83

their arrival in Scotland in 1128, during the reign of King David I, the Templars, because of that Order's admirable record, had enjoyed royal patronage and acquired many grants of land and other favours. Later on however, their conduct, their integrity and their commitment to the cause deteriorated very badly. Eventually, in 1309, their misconduct and misappropriation of the funds of the Order led to the arrest of the Master of the Order and in 1312, to the abolition of the Order in Scotland.

The fifteenth century saw the Scots resigned to the reality that the Crusades to recover the Holy City were not being effective or productive. Thus, instead of going to fight, some Scots began to adopt the idea of going on peaceful pilgrimages to the Holy Land. Before his death at Perth in 1437, King James I of Scotland decreed that his heart should be taken on a pilgrimage to Jerusalem. His decree was obeyed and this sacred duty was entrusted to Sir Alexander Seton who, with the king's heart, embarked upon this peaceful pilgrimage to the Holy Land. He reached Jerusalem safely where he found peace and order under Muslim rule and free and easy access to the Christian sanctuaries. In accordance with his mission he presented his king's heart at the Holy Sepulchre. During his return journey Sir Alexander, unfortunately, died at Rhodes. The king's heart, however, was returned safely to Scotland and was buried at the Charterhouse in Perth.[32]

In the early part of the fifteenth century, many adventurers joined the Knights Hospitallers or went on their own to the East to fight against the Turks who were getting dangerously close to Constantinople. There is a strong probability that in the 1450s Scottish mercenaries and volunteers fought against the Muslim Turks, outside and inside the walls of that city, along with the defenders of Constantinople. It is also certain that Scots were in the forces of King Ferdinand of Spain during his siege and conquest of Granada in 1492, ending nearly eight hundred years of Muslim rule on Spanish soil.

The steady advance of the (Muslim) Ottoman Turks in Europe, since the mid fourteenth century, had alarmed the European nations. In the fifteenth century, after capturing Constantinople in 1453, the Turks had become a serious threat to the whole of Europe. The crusading zeal that for so long had been focused on the Holy

---

[32] Yeoman, Peter *Pilgrimage in Medieval Scotland* p.119

Land had now to be diverted towards the Turks. At the same time however, in this age of Renaissance, some Christian intellectuals, like the Spanish John of Segovia (d. 1458), who had studied Islam and found a lot in common between Christianity and Islam, began to think about turning confrontation into conciliation with the Muslims. They intended to win over the Muslims through peace instead of war. They argued that to create an atmosphere of mutual understanding the Christian should first get to know Islam and then have a dialogue with Muslims to dwell on common points that were many, as against the points of difference between the two religions. However, not pleased with such conciliatory notions, Pope Pius II (1458-1464), planning a Crusade against the Turks asked a gifted intellectual and accomplished philosopher, Cardinal Nicholas of Cusa (d. 1464) to write something against Islam and in support of his Crusade.

> . . . he must have been dismayed at what he got. The work, entitled *Cribratio Alcorani* (The Sieving of the Koran), is dedicated to the proposition that if the Koran is intensively studied in the proper spirit ('sieved') it will be found to be compatible with the teaching of Christianity as found in the New Testament. Beneath discrepancies and differences there lay a shared basis of belief.[33]

Such good advice and sensible suggestion unfortunately were not entertained by those in authority who were intolerant and ignorant of the teachings of the *Quran* and the confrontation between Cross and the Crescent continued unabated. The Turks captured Belgrade in 1521 and were soon after knocking at the doors of Vienna. The sixteenth century therefore saw much propaganda and diplomatic activity among European rulers aimed at planning a crusade against the Turks. Early in the sixteenth century, King James IV of Scotland had become very much interested in the idea of a Crusade to check the Turkish advance in Europe and also to perform his pilgrimage to the Holy Land. He became so obsessed with the idea that in late 1509 he wrote to the Pope saying that he had learnt from the King of France that the Pope was thinking of summoning a Crusade against the Turks that

---

[33] Fletcher, Richard *The Cross and the Crescent* pp.147-48

he would lead himself. He told the Pope that he was anxious to join his Crusade and ready 'to shed his blood for Christendom.' He asked the Pope if he should make the necessary preparations to leave for the Holy Land the following year.[34] It is not known what the reply was from the Pope, if there was one.

But as had happened many times before, the dissent and the internal wrangling among the European kings frustrated the sincere, but perhaps naive, aspirations and efforts of the Scottish King, as an agreement could not be arrived at as to when to start the Crusade. James however, was soon to be involved in a war with the English in which he was killed at Flodden, in September 1513. After James death, none of his successors showed any serious interest in the recovery of the Holy Land or the danger of the Turks. The Crusade age was coming to an end not only in Scotland but also in Europe. The pilgrims, nevertheless, kept up the traffic from Scotland to the Holy Land and kept alive peaceful contacts with the Muslims during the sixteenth and seventeenth centuries.

The spirit of the Crusades did not fade away completely. There were some individual Scots whose conscience, religious fervour or chivalry kept prompting them to keep up their crusading zeal and to go and fight against the Turks in Europe. The military Order of the Hospitallers – the Order of the Knights of St John – kept alive in Scotland some interest in the crusades against the Turks. In 1522, a number of Scottish knights fought along with the Hospitallers against the Turks to defend the island of Rhodes. One of these was Thomas Douchty from Musselburgh who returned from his exploits in 1533. After they lost Rhodes to the Turks in 1522, some Scots travelled to Malta, where the new HQ of the Order had been set up, to join the Hospitallers and fight against the Turks. Even in 1612, when during his travels he visited Malta, William Lithgow (about whom there will be more in the following chapter) met there a fellow Scot who was still following a chivalrous career with the Hospitallers.

However, in 1560 the Scottish parliament broke its connections with Rome and in its place instituted the Reformed Church of Scotland. As the Order of the Knights of St John was considered to be a Roman Catholic institution, all its property was taken over by the Scottish Crown after the Reformation and that was the end of

---

[34] MacQuarrie, Allan p.109

the Hospitallers in Scotland. The saints and their marvellous shrines, with many relics from the Holy Land, also suffered badly during and after the Reformation. Indeed most of the shrines were destroyed by the end of 1560.[35]

Some other smaller religious/military Orders had also arrived in Scotland during the Crusades period. Those also disappeared after the Reformation. With all the Orders gone and the cult of saints abandoned by the end of sixteenth century, the tradition of pilgrimage also began to weaken in Scotland. The seventeenth century saw very few, if any, of the Scots embarking upon a pilgrimage even to the Holy Land. And those few who did make a pilgrimage, did not receive from their communities the same degree of reverence or admiration on their return as did the returning pilgrims of the past, which further discouraged the would-be pilgrims.

Nonetheless, the idea of pilgrimage did not disappear altogether; it remained embedded in the memories, folklore and literature of Scotland. Consequently, owing to the arrival in Scotland, during the eighteenth to early twentieth centuries of a considerable number of Catholics from Ireland, complementing the small indigenous Catholic community, the culture of pilgrimage saw a significant revival. Hence, in the past two centuries many Scots have been going on pilgrimages to the shrines in Europe and of course, to the Holy Land.

In the twentieth century the facilities for safe and speedy travel further enhanced the interest in pilgrimage. In 1927, the Archbishop of Glasgow and the Bishop of Galloway led a group of 153 pilgrims to the Holy Land. They travelled by train and steamship and reached the Holy Land in six days.[36] The situation has further improved since then with the introduction of affordable air travel. In spite of the continuous uncertainties in the Holy Land, the latter half of the twentieth century saw the number of pilgrims from Scotland rise considerably.

Scottish Muslims have, to some extant, contributed to this rise in the numbers as they also have begun to go on pilgrimages to Jerusalem. With nearly 50,000 Muslims now living in Scotland and Jerusalem being holy to them also they are joining their Christian

[35] Yeoman, Peter *Pilgrimage in Medieval Scotland* p.15
[36] McRoberts, David. p.105

compatriots on these sacred journeys. One such pilgrimage left Glasgow on 28 March 2005, led by Councillor Alex Mosson, ex Lord Provost of the city. What was unique about this pilgrimage was that it included over 200 Christian and Muslim pilgrims (I was one of the Muslims) from Scotland. This combined pilgrimage shows how relationships have changed in the last century and that there is so much in common in them that unites Christians and Muslims. This trip has further enhanced the cordial relationship between these two major faiths not only in Scotland but also in the Holy Land where Muslims and Christians received this mixed group of pilgrims with delight and the Christian Mayor of Bethlehem gave them a civic reception. This unique pilgrimage will go a long way in further reviving and strengthening the pilgrimage tradition in Scotland and motivate many more Christians and Muslims to embark upon this sacred journey.

The contacts between Islam and Scotland during the Middle Ages through pilgrimage and Crusades introduced considerable Islamic and Middle Eastern influence into Scottish culture. Many legends arose from imaginary as well as actual exploits of Scottish crusaders. The pilgrims and the crusaders also brought many novelties and relics back from the Holy Land. Some of the interesting legends are as under:

> The 'Lee Penny' is a famous lowland example of a Crusader's talisman, said to have been brought back from the Holy Land by Sir Simon Lockhart of Lee in the fourteenth century; he had used it as a medical amulet, for the arrestment of haemorrhage, fever, etc. . . An alternative of the version of the tradition states: 'it is said to have been given, along with ransom money, to Sir Simon Lockhart of Lee by the wife of a Saracen chief whom he had taken prisoner in Palestine.' And 'The Stewarts of Ardvorlich were proud possessors of the clach dearg of Ardvorlich, a small red charm stone, which had properties to cure sick cattle when they drank water in which it had been dipped. . . and the family tradition is that it was brought back from a Crusade.'[37]

---

[37] Allan MacQuarrie *Scotland and the Crusades 1095-1560* p.4

Another well-known legend is about the fairy banner of Dunvegan:

> The legend of its origin is that a Macleod who had gone on a Crusade to the Holy Land when returning home in the garb of a pilgrim was benighted on the border of Palestine in a wild and dangerous mountain pass, where by chance he met a hermit who gave him food and shelter. The hermit told him that an evil spirit guarded the pass and never failed to destroy the true believer; but by the aid of a piece of the true cross and certain other directions given by the hermit this Macleod vanquished and slew the 'She Devil' called Nein a Phaipen, or daughter of thunder, around whose loins the banner had been tied; and that in reward for conveying certain secrets which she wished some earthly friends to know she revealed the future destinies of the Clan to her conqueror, in whose family this knowledge was supposed to be deposited to its final extinction, and desired that her girdle should be converted into this banner which was to be attached to her spear, which became the staff which is now lost.[38]

A belt of thick red morocco leather, brought over by a Crusader of the Clan Cluny, is among many other relics found in Cluny Castle. Local people believe that there is a charm in the belt for the safe delivery of women in childbirth.[39] There are of course many other relics, charm stones and mysterious objects scattered all over Scotland and preserved in the National Museum of Antiquities, with various legends attached to them, reputed to be associated with the Holy Land and Arab/Islamic culture.

Scottish literature also benefited from this interaction as is evident from the extensive and accurate reporting of the events in the Holy Land, Mediterranean and Europe during the Crusades period, found in the *Chronicle of Melrose*, the *Holyrood Chronicle* and other such documents of the Middle Ages. The *Chronicle of Melrose* contains some rare first hand accounts of happenings in the Holy

---

[38] Proceedings of the Society of Antiquaries of Scotland, Vol. XLVII, Relics Preserved in Dunvegan Castle, Skye, Edinburgh, 1912-1913 p.112

[39] MacQuarrie, Allan *The History of Crusades* p.4

Land and in parts of Europe and North Africa. It relates that before the capture of Jerusalem the Crusaders 'suffered so great a famine that they ate Saracens' flesh' (p.30) and on their capture of Jerusalem the Christian Crusaders killed many Greek and Jacobite Christians some even while they were in their Church of St James. (p.93) The Muslims during their occupation respected the lives of all Christians and allowed them to celebrate the 'divine mysteries' with complete freedom. (p.95) As referred to above, for the first time in British history, it also tried to correct the prevalent common conception of the Scots that Muslims were polytheists and idol worshippers, by narrating so clearly and perhaps so boldly, in that anti-Islam milieu that the Muslims worshiped only One God. About this passage in the *Chronicle of Melrose* Rt. Rev. Allan MacQuarrie states:

> What is of interest is the chronicler's description of Islam; as a Scottish attempt to understand Islamic belief, rather than to malign Muslims as idolaters or polytheists (almost a total reversal of the truth), this passage is unique. The writer was impressed to learn that Muslims acknowledge one God, though not in three persons and in a way that was distinct from the Jewish law. This is perhaps a faint reflection of the change in attitudes towards Islam which is perceptible through Europe in the second half of the thirteenth century, less intolerant and more inquisitive than before.[40]

As is obvious from the plays of Shakespeare, medieval English poetry and drama were also greatly influenced by Muslim/Arab legends and culture. The poems of the thirteenth century Scottish bards Muiredhach Albanach and Gille Brigde, who took part in the fifth Crusade, reflect much Arab influence. Their poems contain many references to the 'Saracens', the pilgrims and the Crusades. The writings of Sir Walter Scott are a good example of the influence of the Muslim and Arab culture on later Scottish literature. The Crusades had widened the cultural and trading links between the Muslim world and European countries. That resulted in Europeans embracing Muslim learning and customs such as bathing regularly and keeping one's clothes and body clean. The Turkish bath was

---

[40] MacQuarrie, Allan *The Impact of the Crusades Movement in Scotland, 1095 c.1560* p.385

introduced into Europe by the Crusaders who had enjoyed it in the Levant and realised its benefits in the cold climate. They also learnt from Muslims the arts of soap, sugar and glass production, castle fortification, many branches of textile manufacturing, and above all the spirit of chivalry. The Scottish crusaders and traders would have also learnt these arts and customs and brought back beautifully woven and embroidered cloth, spices, sugar and many other commodities from the Levant and introduced these exotic things to Scotland. Through centuries old trade and other contacts between Muslim countries and Europe, a significant number of Arabic words have entered English and the other European languages. Words such as chiffon, cotton, damask, muslin, tariff, douane, cheque, lute, guitar, tambourine, sugar, sorbet, admiral, arsenal, and hundreds more are all of Arabic origin. Certain important words used in nautical science such as zenith, azimuth and astrolabe are also Arabic, which were borrowed from Arabic technology in the Middle Ages.[41]

Alcohol is an Arabic word and is derived from *kohl* that is the name of a black powder, which is applied to the eyes and used extensively in the East. It was the Arab alchemists who invented the art of distilling alcohol, though according to some Western historians the Arabs learnt it from the Egyptians. In any case, they refined this art and used it for chemical experiments, medicinal purposes and to produce perfumes. The Arabs introduced it to Europe in the eighth century through Muslim Spain. By the eleventh century, the Europeans were using this skill to distil wine. Alcohol was also being used medicinally and in the production of gunpowder. From Europe it would have reached Scotland in the thirteenth or fourteenth century – '. . . by the fifteenth century Scotland was making *acqua vitae* as the alcohol produced was termed.'[42] By the end of the fifteenth century, whisky was being produced under the patronage of King James IV, and now it is considered the most famous product and profitable export of Scotland. The art of distillation therefore, probably is one of the most significant contributions of Arab culture to Scotland. The Arabs, though as Muslims, would hate even to think that they were

[41] Hillenbrand, Carole *The Crusades Islamic Perspective* p.397-98

[42] Hume, John, S. & Moss, Michael, S. *A History of Scotch Whisky Distilling Industry* p.22

in any way responsible for the introduction of the distillation of whisky to Scotland, because under the Islamic Law the manufacture, trade, storage, conveyance and the consumption of alcohol are all major sins and hence prohibited!

As far as Muslims were concerned their image or conception of the Crusaders and their culture was a very negative one. They were amazed at the filthy habits, rude, ignorant and savage attitudes and ways of the Crusaders whom they called *Afranj* or *Franji* – the Franks. To the Muslims, whether they were French or English, Germans or Italians, Spanish or Scots, as Crusaders, they were all *Franji* – the Franks. Before embracing Islam and becoming Muslims in the seventh century the Arabs also were a most savage, rude and backward people with no influence in the world. Within a century, Islam had tamed them and transformed them into the world's most powerful and civilised nation. By the time they came into contact with Crusaders, they had developed a highly literate and sophisticated culture, far ahead of any nation in the world. They followed a thorough code of personal hygiene as purity and cleanliness lies at the very heart of Islam. They took regular daily showers or baths and had to wash their faces, arms and feet five times a day to perform their five daily prayers. The Franks or the Crusaders on the other hand were not used to such sophistication. They were not accustomed to washing or bathing their bodies even once a month.

For example T. B. Simpson in his review of Marjorie Plant's *The Domestic Life of Scotland in the Eighteenth Century*, states:

> Urban life in eighteenth-century Scotland saw people huddled together in great 'lands', divided into flats. Sanitation there was none, and the rule of life was 'the clartier the cosie'. . . The children of the Royal Family used to have a bath once a fortnight, on alternative Mondays, but that was a luxury which nearly all their Scottish subjects lacked.[43]

That was the state of affairs in eighteenth century Scotland. It can reasonably be assumed that perhaps things would have been worse in the twelfth and thirteenth centuries in Scotland and of course in all other European countries from where the 'Franks'

---

[43] *The Scottish Historical Review* Vol. XXXII pp.150-51

arrived in the Holy Land. The Muslims in contrast had humane and dignified standards of personal, social, moral and religious attitudes. Riccoldo da Monte Croce, a thirteenth century Italian crusader and traveller, travelled through Syria, Iraq and Iran, disguised as a Muslim. He recorded his experiences and observations in his *Itinerarius*. Concerning the Muslim way of life he observed, he has this to say:

> We therefore describe certain Muslim works of perfection thus briefly, in order to shame the Christians and not to praise the Muslims. For who will not be amazed if he carefully considers how great among the Muslims is the attention to study, the devotion to prayer, pity for the poor, reverence for the name of God and the prophets and the holy places, their serious ways, their kindness to strangers, and their concord and love towards each other.[44]

Thus, the disgust and disappointment of the Muslims at the savagery and uncivilised ways of the Franks was understandable. Phillip K. Hitti the translator of the *Memoirs of Usamah Ibn-Munqudh an Arab Syrian warrior in the period of Crusades*, (1098-1188) states:

> . . . he (Usamah) sees them as animals possessing the virtue of courage and fighting, but nothing else; just as animals have only the virtues of strength and carrying loads. (p.161)

Usamah was a contemporary and an intimate friend of *Salah Al-Din*. He deplores the absolute faithlessness of the Franks – all the Crusaders, where their solemn promises and their earnest treaties with Muslims were concerned. Many of the Western historians also confirm this and record that during the Crusades the Popes and the Archbishops had lain down the rule that oaths and promises made to the infidel, i.e. Muslims, were invalid. Hence, the Christian kings and army commanders usually broke any pact or promise they made with the Muslims. On the contrary, Muslim clerics always condemned Muslim leaders who broke their solemn promises or pacts made with a friend or foe. History records many incidents where a faltering Muslim ruler or leader was forced by Muslim

---

[44] Laurent, J.C.M. ed. *Peregrinatores Medii Aevi Quatour* p.132-133

ecclesiastics to uphold the oath or treaty made with an enemy or anyone else.

Commenting on the crude skills of the Crusader doctors and surgeons *Usamah* pities the patients who had to go through their rough and dangerous treatment that killed more than it cured. He paints the Crusaders, especially those who had arrived recently, as filthy, lacking in personal hygiene, having no sexual morality and with no sense of marital dignity and honour. He narrates many anecdotes about the customs of the Franks that according to the Muslim norms were strange, disgraceful and shameless. He mentions that on one occasion he witnessed a Frank coming home and finding another Frank in bed with his wife. The husband did not show any feelings of hurt, humiliation or jealousy; the only thing he did was to say to the other man 'if thou shouldst do it again, thou and I would have a quarrel'.[45]

In another case, he relates a story, which he heard from his father's bath keeper, who narrated:

> I once opened a bath in *al-Ma'arrah* in order to earn my living. To this bath there came a Frankish knight. The Franks disapprove of girding a cover around one's waist while in the bath. So this Frank stretched out his arm and pulled off my cover from my waist and threw it away. He looked and saw that I had recently shaved off my pubes. So he shouted 'Salim!' As I drew near him he stretched his hand over my pubes and said, 'Salim good! By the truth of my religion, do the same for me.' Saying this he lay on his back and I found that in that place the hair was like his beard. So I shaved it off. Then he passed his hand over the place and, finding it smooth, he said, 'Salim, by the truth of my religion, do the same to madame. . . referring to his wife.' He then said to a servant of his, 'Tell madame to come here.' Accordingly the servant went and brought her and made her enter the bath. She also lay on her back. The knight repeated, 'Do what you hast done to me.' So I shaved all that hair while her husband was sitting looking at me. At last he thanked me and handed me the pay for my service.[46]

---

[45] Hitti, Phillip, K. trans. *Usamah Ibn-Munqidh* p.165

[46] *ibid* p.166

There is no information in the *Memoirs of Usamah* about the origin or nationality of the couple in the above anecdote. As Muslims called all European Crusaders, pilgrims and traders Franks during the Crusades period that couple could have been French, German, Italian, English or possibly even Scottish. Hitti further states: '*Usamah* draws a distinction between "acclimatised" Franks in Muslim lands and the outlandish, rude "recent comers".'[47] Whereas Usamah kept his distance from the outlandish, rude 'recent comers', he had close friendships with some of the 'acclimatised' Franks. He was a keen sportsman and in his memoirs he mentions many occasions during the times of peace in the Holy Land when his Frank friends accompanied him on hawking and hunting expeditions.

Professor, the Rev. William Montgomery Watt even alludes to Christians being embarrassed living with the Muslims in those days:

> The feeling of inferiority with which Western Europe confronted Islamic civilisation had various facets. . . For any Christian who had come in contact with Muslims, too, their unshakable sense of superiority must have been disturbing. In general the feelings of western Europeans over against Islam were not unlike those of an underprivileged class in a great state.[48]

The Europeans who had lived among the Muslims for some length of time in the Levant, therefore, became very impressed and highly influenced by their superior culture. Most of them while there adopted many of their ways, even the Muslim dress, and became outwardly just like them.[49]

The Scots crusaders and pilgrims who had lived in the Holy Land for some time would also have become influenced by that sophisticated society and brought back new ideas about social conduct, hygiene, food, dress and other aspects of life derived from the exquisite Muslim culture. The introduction in Scotland of an Arab horse, a camel, Turkish armour, other such novelties and various legends were the result of the Scottish Muslim contacts

---

[47] Hitti, Phillip, K., p.16

[48] *Influence of Islam on Medieval Europe* p.82

[49] Watt, W. M. *Muslim Christian Encounters* p.81

through pilgrimages and Crusades. With the passage of time and the scarcity of available records of that period, that specific influence may not now be noticeable or even traceable but in the Middle Ages, it must have made a significant impact on Scottish life. There is no doubt that the experiences of the Crusaders living with Muslims in the Muslim countries must have introduced many elements of Islamic culture not only in Scotland but also in all Western European countries.[50]

Scotland benefited in many other ways from the influences derived through the Crusades. Rev. Allan MacQuarrie states:

> In oral tradition, in factual participation, in propaganda, in diplomacy, in the writing of history, in generosity to institutions, in the survival of these institutions the Crusading Movement can be seen to have had a significant impact in Scotland, which did not begin to decline until the sixteenth century. Indeed, much of medieval thinking cannot be properly understood except in the context of the crusading thought, and this is true no less of Scotland than elsewhere. The Crusades can be said to have had a significant part in bringing remote little Scotland 'beyond which there is no dwelling place at all' into the fold of unified western Christendom, and there after the movement had a long history, some remnants of which are still with us today.[51]

---

[50] Montgomery Watt, Prof. the Rev. William *Influence of Islam on Medieval Europe* p.28

[51] *The Impact of the Crusades Movement in Scotland* 1095 c.1560 pp.133-134

CHAPTER 3

Diplomats, Scholars and Travellers

Diplomatic Contacts

By the early eighth century, the Muslim Empire had extended to all the North African countries and the Iberian Peninsula. The British Isles, including Scotland had trading links with these countries; the development of good relations with their new rulers therefore, was not only a matter of course but also a necessity. As mentioned earlier, King Offa had trading relations with the *Caliph* of Baghdad – the ruler of the vast Muslim Empire. He also appears to have had diplomatic relations with the Muslim ruler of North Africa from whom he is alleged to have sought military assistance against his enemies in Britain. Early medieval Muslim geographers and cartographers were well aware of the British Isles. *Muhammad bin Musa al Khwarizmi* (780-850) in his *Surat ul Ard*, (The Shape of the Earth) written around 817, mentions a number of places in Britain. In his map of the world, the well-known Muslim historian and geographer, *Al Masudi* (871-957) places the British Isles – England and Scotland above France, in roughly the same position and shape as they are in the current maps. The twelfth century famous Muslim cartographer *al-Idrisi* (1199-1180) is known to have visited Britain in about mid twelfth century.[1]

All this shows that in the early Middle Ages, the Muslim world was familiar with Britain and the location of Scotland and the conditions in this country. Indeed, their knowledge and information of the topography of the world by the ninth century was ahead of the time. The Arabs had borrowed and learnt from the Greeks and Romans. After the weakening of the Roman Empire and their neglect of their learning traditions, the Arabs took up and maintained those traditions. In time, they made significant advances on the Greeks and Romans in every field of knowledge and in

---

[1] Watt, W.M. *Influence of Islam on Medieval Europe* p.21

especially geography, they left Ptolemy and Strabo, the famous Greek geographers, far behind.[2]

The geographical knowledge of the Muslim cartographers of those days was so extensive that in his map of the world, *Al-Masudi* shows a large land area he calls *Ard Majhoora* (the Unknown Territory), southwest of the continent of Africa, in the Atlantic Ocean that is identified today as South America. This indicates that in the ninth century, the Muslims new the existence of the Americas. Further:

> . . . *al-Idrisi* (1099-1180) the famous Arab physician and geographer who established himself in the Arabicised court of King Roger II of Sicily, reported in his extensive work *Kitab al Mamalik wa-l-Masalik*, in the twelfth century, on the journey of a group of seamen who reached the isles of the Americas. . . This astonishing historical report not only describes contacts between Muslim seamen and the native people of Americas, but it also describes travel between islands, probably the Bahamas chain of the Lesser Antilles. The islanders had developed the ability to speak Arabic, a language that cannot be mastered by a single contact. They must have been regularly visited by Arabic speaking Muslim merchants or adventurers, or they had lived in Muslim territory.[3]

There are many other accounts by sixteenth century Spanish and Portuguese chroniclers and modern American writers of the presence of North Africans, and especially the West African *Mandinka* Muslims, in the Americas long before the voyage of Columbus. Such achievements of Muslim adventurers and sailors and the vast geographical knowledge of the Muslim academics of that time, suggest that it is highly probable that some North African or Spanish Muslim traders or sailors would have ventured to Scotland and traded with its people. It would have been quite easy for the Muslim traders who visited England, in the eight century, to travel up to Scotland from there either by sea or by land. The

---

[2] Dunlop, D.M. Scotland according to Al-Idrisi, *The Scottish Historical Review* Vol. XXVI p.114

[3] Quick, Dr.A.H. *Deeper Roots* pp.15-16

trade relations between Scotland and North Africa had continued after the advent of Islam and the Scots traders were visiting these countries and trading with them. It would therefore, have been quite natural and indeed expected of the Muslim traders to come to Scotland. In any case, it is evident that trading and diplomatic relations between Islam and the British Isles began soon after the spread of Islam in North Africa and Spain, in the late seventh and early eighth centuries, and have continued to the present time.

By the early twelfth century *studia Arabum*, i.e. studies of the Arabs or Arabic learning, had reached Britain through Latin translations of the writings of Arab philosophers and scientists. Realising the magnitude of the knowledge of the Arabs, the Christian scholars of Italy and Spain had begun these translations in the late tenth century. The English King Henry II (r.1154-89) was so charmed with the knowledge and sciences developed by the Muslims that during his reign he always kept Arabic scholars in his court. Henry was very keen 'to understand the opinions of the Arabs'. He had acquired his interest in Arabic learning from his tutor Adelard of Bath who had spent fifteen years in Syria and Spain learning from the Arab scholars and proudly acknowledged them as 'his masters'. Through trade or his love of Arabic knowledge perhaps, King Henry appears to have developed some sort of relationship with Sultan *Nur ad-Din*, the powerful Muslim ruler of Aleppo and Syria. When in 1168, Henry had a quarrel with the Pope concerning the appointment of Thomas Becket as the Archbishop of Canterbury he threatened to follow the religion of that ruler – in other words to convert to Islam, if the Pope did not depose Thomas Becket.

> Perhaps this threat could have been taken more seriously at the time than modern scholars are inclined to believe. For, if we follow Adelard's words, Henry had been imbued in philosophy and curious about the *studia Arabum* from his very infancy.[4]

King Richard, the Lion Heart (r. 1189-1199), as has been mentioned in the previous chapter, wanted to build matrimonial

---

[4] Burnett, Charles *The Introduction of Arabic Learning into England* p.60

relations with Muslims by marrying his widowed sister Joan to *Al-Adil* the brother of *Salah Al-Din* (Saladin), the ruler of Egypt and Syria. Richard's brother King John (r. 1199-1216), went even further. When he had a quarrel with the Pope and his nobles, he sent a diplomatic mission to *Emir Mohammad Al Nasser*, the powerful Muslim monarch of Morocco and Spain to offer him suzerainty over England. Mathew Paris (1200-1259), a Benedictine monk and the authentic and respected thirteenth century historian, in his *Chronica Majora* reveals that to confound the Pope and his barons, with whom he was in constant conflict, King John offered to hand over his kingdom to the King of Morocco and convert to Islam. He sent a secret embassy consisting of his confidants, the knights Thomas Hardington and Ralph FitzNicholas, and Master Robert, a cleric of London. The message to be conveyed to the *Emir* was that he (King John) would willingly hand over himself and his kingdom to him and if he pleased, would hold it as tributary from him; and that he would also abandon the Christian faith, which he considers false, and would faithfully adhere to the law of Mohammad (Islam).

Mathew Paris paints an impressive picture of their entry into the palace of the *Emir*, as described by Master Robert, how they had to pass through many entrances and how every entrance was guarded by heavily armed and elegantly dressed fierce soldiers with swords drawn. When the ambassadors were brought in the presence of the *Emir*, they greeted him reverently in the name of their king, explained the reason for their arrival and handed him the royal letter. An interpreter who was summoned to be present opened the letter and read it to the *Emir*. After contemplating for a while, the Emir said: 'I say this of your king of England, who, having given up his holy law of the Christians, longs to go over to another – what an unstable man he is.' Then he questioned the ambassadors for some time about their king and country and after listening to their answers the *Emir* remarked: 'Your king is a petty monarch, already losing his senses and growing old. I have no regard for him; he is unworthy of being my ally.' Looking at Thomas and Ralph with stern expression, he added: 'Do not come back again into my presence and do not let your eyes look at my face.' However, he kept hehind the cleric Robert, with whom he had a private conversation and treated him kindly. On the following days, the *Emir* had many more conversations with Master Robert in which the cleric gave the *Emir* some unsavoury details of King John's tyranny upon his people, the adulterous ways of his wife and much more.[5]

We only can wonder what would be the socio/political and especially the religious state of Britain, particularly Scotland today, if King Henry's threat to follow the religion of *Nur-ed Din* had materialised. Or, if King John's hair-brained scheme to 'hand over his kingdom . . . to abandon his faith . . . and faithfully adhere to the law of Mohammad' had been accepted by the *Emir Mohammad Al Nasser*. Perhaps the *Emir*, accompanied with his court and a strong *Berber* army would have sailed through the English channel, entered the Thames estuary and docked near the Tower of London where King John would have paid his obeisance to him and conducted him to his palace. One also wonders what kind of response or reception the people of London and especially the English Church would have given to the *Emir*, once they had seen and known what was happening. Would the *Emir Al Nassar* have been able to subdue the English people and the Church? If so what would be the state of affairs of Britain of today? Over and above other things, what A.R. Gibbon wrote about the after effects of the battle of Tours if the Moors had won, would also perfectly apply in this situation:

> . . . and the Arabian fleet might have sailed without a naval combat into the mouth of the Thames. Perhaps the interpretation of the Koran would now be taught in the schools of Oxford, and her pupils might demonstrate to a circumcised people the sanctity and truth of the revelation of Mahomet.[6]

Nevertheless, if King John's plan had succeeded it is certain that one day the Muslim English forces would have marched into Scotland as the Romans did after their subjugation of the English and as English armies have been doing since the early medieval times. Hence, Scotland also, would be a very different place from what it is today and perhaps St Giles Cathedral and the Glasgow Cathedral would now be the principal mosques of the cities of Edinburgh and Glasgow.

---

[5] *Chronica Majora* ed. Luard, Henry Richards, pp.559-563
[6] *The Decline and Fall of the Roman Empire* vol. vi, p.15

That aside, the first Scottish sovereign to make some sort of official diplomatic contacts with the Islamic world was King James III (r.1460-88). He encouraged his confidant and friend, Anselm Adornes, to travel to the Islamic lands of North Africa, Egypt, Syria and the Holy Land to bring back reliable information about the culture, the customs and the power of those countries. Adornes was an influential member of a rich and well-known Burgundian family of Bruges. He had come to Scotland on a diplomatic mission and had won the admiration and trust of the Scottish King. He left on his mission with his son in February 1470, as a kind of a roving ambassador of King James. First they went to Tunis where he was well received and granted the king's safe conduct. After a week's stay in Tunis they boarded a ship for Alexandria to go to their next destination, Cairo, where they arrived in early August. They stayed for about eight days in Cairo and left for the Holy Land via Mount Sinai reaching Jerusalem on 11 September. After visiting all the holy sites in and around Jerusalem, they left for Damascus. Calling at Nazareth and the Sea of Galilee on their way, they arrived at Damascus on 16 October. From Damascus they left for Beirut arriving there on 29 October. From Beirut, they boarded a ship to return home. They reached Bruges in early April 1471, where Anselm Adornes asked his son, who had accompanied him, to write down the account of his journey. His *Itinerarium* was completed in about six months and Adornes dedicated it to King James III of Scotland. He arrived in Scotland probably in November 1471 and presented his *Itinerarium* to the king. The king was so pleased to receive the *Itinerarium* of Adornes that he honoured him with a knighthood, gave him a barony and appointed him a royal counsellor.

Though his stay in the capital cities of those parts of the Islamic world he visited was exceptionally short, Adornes stresses in the account of his journey that wherever he went he promoted the reputation of the king and the people of Scotland:

> His voyage, says the writer, was undertaken to enhance the glory of the king of Scotland, which, though already considerable, has now been further enhanced; Anselm has missed no opportunity to expound on James' power, virtue and nobility among the barbarous and distant lands he has

visited. As a result, James is now more admired among these nations than any other western prince, and his subjects with him.[7]

It is not known what effect his diplomatic skills really had 'to enhance the glory of the king of Scotland' in the lands he visited. Nonetheless, according to available historical records, King James III appears to be the first Scottish ruler who sent a diplomat to introduce Scotland and its ruler to a part of the Muslim world with which it had had trade and cultural links for centuries.

The fifteenth and sixteenth centuries saw the advance of the Ottoman Turks up to the heart of Europe and the strengthening of their control on the Mediterranean. Until the end of the seventeenth century, their domination and the awe in which they were held influenced and indeed regulated the political, trade and diplomatic affairs in Europe. The power and the fear of the Turks was so great that most European sovereigns desired and tried to establish good relations with them. King Edward VI (r. 1547-1553) of England developed diplomatic relations with the Turkish regencies of North Africa and the king of Morocco and in 1551, received the first Moroccan Ambassador in London. Queen Elizabeth I (r. 1558-1603) of England and James I of Great Britain and Ireland (r.1603-25) and King of Scotland (r. 1567-1603 as James VI) both had trade and diplomatic relations with the Ottoman Sultans, the Shahs of Persia, the Mughal Emperors of India and some Muslim rulers in North Africa. King James also, following Queen Elizabeth perhaps, had begun developing good relations with some Muslim rulers. He had been in correspondence with the Shah of Persia from Edinburgh, before his accession to the English throne and his coming to London in 1603.[8]

The mounting Catholic threat in the 1580s and the 1590s, especially from Spain, forced Queen Elizabeth to establish closer ties with the mighty Ottoman Sultans and with the Muslim rulers of North Africa. Consequently, she received the ambassador of the Ottoman Sultan in 1579 and many other Muslim diplomats during

---

[7] MacQuarie, Allan Ansalem Adornes of Bruges: Traveller in the East and Friend of James III *The Innes Review* XXXIII (1982) p.16

[8] Chew, Samuel, C. *The Crescent and the Rose* p.282

her reign. She is believed to have made requests to the Ottoman Sultan *Murad* III and his son *Muhammad* III, for military assistance against Spain. However, no practical assistance appears to have come from the Turks, but perhaps the alliance with them was a deterrent of some effect to the enemies of Britain. Throughout her reign, Queen Elizabeth 'offered the Turkish and the Moroccan rulers mutually beneficial agreements'.[9] During the 1570s, steps were taken to regularise English trade with the Turks. In 1580, through the diplomatic skills of the English ambassador Sir William Harborne and in spite of the intense opposition of Venice, an agreement was secured for 'the safety of English traders, the right to trade and the permission to establish consulates' in the Turkish Empire.[10] To develop trade with India, Queen Elizabeth wrote a letter to the Mughal Emperor Akbar requesting permission and protection for British traders. John Mildenhall a British trader presented that letter to the Emperor at Agra in 1603.[11] The Emperor did not reply, but the letter did produce the desired result as a few years later, in the early years of the reign of Elizabeth's successor James I of Great Britain and Ireland (James VI of Scotland), the East India Company began trading with Mughal India.

Elizabeth developed a friendship with Queen *Safiye*, the influential wife of Ottoman Sultan *Murad* III and corresponded with her. *Safiye's* son *Muhammad III* became the Ottoman Sultan at the death of his father in 1595 and that enhanced the influence of *Safiye* as the all influential *Walde Sultan* –Mother of the Sultan or Queen Mother. Three of the letters from Queen *Safiye* in Turkish, accompanied with their Italian translations, have survived. The first of these arrived in England in 1593 and is preserved in the British Museum. The other two are in the Public Records Office. The first letter appears to have been written by an official professional court scribe in elaborate oriental style with all the usual Eastern royal trappings. The side of the thick paper that contains the writing is flecked with gold. The scribe has used the ink of five colours, black, blue, crimson, gold and scarlet and changes the ink three times in every line. The other two letters are simpler private personal letters from one woman to the other, probably written by a maid of the

---

[9] Matar, Nabil *Islam in Britain* p.20

[10] Chew, Samuel, C. *The Crescent and the Rose* p.152

[11] Schimmel, Annemarie *The Empire of the Great Mughals* p.43

Royal household in 1599. Many valuable gifts came with these letters. The summary below of the English rendering of the second letter by S.A. Skilliter gives an insight into the relationship that had developed between Queen Elizabeth and the Ottoman Queen Mother, and the gifts that they exchanged:

> After greeting the Queen, the *Walde* (Queen Mother) notifies the receipt of her letter and promises to act as her intermediary with the Sultan in the matter of the English capitulations. She urges the Queen to be firm in friendship. The arrival and acceptance of a coach from the Queen is mentioned and in return the *Walde* sends various items of Turkish ladies costumes and certain jewels all of which are listed; in this respect only do the two letters differ. The first delivered by the *Bostanjibashi*, accompanies a robe, a girdle, sleeves, various handkerchiefs, and a crown of pearls and rubies; the second, by the *Kira*, accompanies a crown of diamonds and rubies.[12]

Elizabeth had developed such good diplomatic and commercial relations with the Turks that they were noticed with concern in Scotland as it is recorded in *The Calendar of Scottish Documents*, that James VI was 'perswaided that no Christian prince (except Queen Elizabeth) ever had in the Turk suche great estimation'.[13] Many European rulers and the Pope became suspicious of her being 'a confederate with the Turk'. She also had become very fond of Turkish clothes and other Islamic paraphernalia and often wore the princely Turkish attire the Ottoman Queen Mother had sent her as a present. Unfortunately, 'the attire for the head' which the Queen had so much desired, was "imbeazelled" on the way'.[14] Her donning Turkish dress encouraged other British women to imitate their Queen and Turkish clothing, the turban especially, became quite popular in Britain.

As a symbol of Ottoman might, the turban was not only desirable but also exquisite. Since the early sixteenth century, many British

---

[12] Stern, S. M. ed. Three Letters from Ottoman 'Sultana' Safiye to Queen Elizabeth I in *Documents from Islamic Chanceries* p.133

[13] *The Calendar of Scottish Documents* (1589- 93, 10: 404)

[14] Blank, David *Images of the Other* p.42

travellers had been returning wearing the turban and Muslim dress. After centuries of crusading wars and enmity, this age was seeing an amicable engagement with Islam and a fascination with Islamic culture. By the early seventeenth century, therefore, the turban and eastern clothes had become part of the fashion scene in Britain and many ladies, gentlemen, including members of royalty, and others were wearing the turban and Turkish dress. Later on in the seventeenth century, King Charles II himself adopted and patronised the turban and Muslim dress:

> The turban was a powerful symbol – of both authority and fashion. No wonder that. . . King Charles II used the turban to challenge the French fashion of his court: in 1667, he adopted a Persian dress with a glowing turban on his head.[15]

This was happening when strict dress code was enforced in England and dress was linked to social status and difference between the nobles and aristocracy on one hand and the rest of the lower class sections of the population on the other. Those who broke the code and wore clothes that were above or below their status were prosecuted. However, Scottish and English travellers who had dressed in Muslim attire and turban in the Muslim lands, on their return home, were considered immune from such prosecution.[16] Following their monarch in London, some Scots in Edinburgh, Glasgow or any other Scottish city would probably also have donned turbans in keeping with the trend in southern Britain. However, no recorded evidence to that effect has been found in Scotland.

After the death of Elizabeth, her successor King James I, though not well disposed towards Islam and Muslims, in the better interests of Britain, followed her policies and maintained diplomatic and trade relations with the Mughals, Persians, Turks and the North African rulers. Like Elizabeth, he also received many Turkish and North African diplomats during his reign.

All this diplomatic activity, during the early Caroline period, resulted in the development of extensive commercial and diplomatic relations and amicable social contacts with the Turks and the North

---

[15] Blank, David *Images of the Other – Europe and the Muslim World before 1700* p.47

[16] *ibid* p.43

African Muslims. In fact, during this period, the Muslims of the Turkish Empire, Eastern Mediterranean and Morocco had better relations with Britain than any other non-Muslim country. They were coming to Britain as traders and visitors and out of the non-Christian people on English soil they were the most obvious.[17]

The first Turkish diplomat who arrived at the court of King James was *Mustapha*, who presented his credentials in July 1607. Thus since the Union of Crowns of Scotland and England in 1603, there have been continuous diplomatic and, later, colonial relations between Scotland and the Muslim world.

James I received two embassies from *Shah Abbas* of Persia, the first in 1611 and the second in 1624. The ambassador in both cases was a Briton, Robert Shirley, who having lived in Persia for many years had won the confidence of the Sophie – the *Safvi* Shah of Persia. As Ambassador of the Persian Emperor, Shirley was in Persian dress and wearing a turban. That created a problem, as King James was not well disposed towards the turban and did not expect one of his subjects and a Christian to approach him dressed as a subject of the Persian king. Shirley a clever diplomat solved the problem by attaching 'a small cross to the turban thereby demonstrating that he had not deserted Christianity'.[18] James accepted the letter from *Shah Abbas* at Hampton Court on 1 October 1611. As there was great animosity between the Persians and the Turks, in his letter naturally, the Persian King urged the English Sovereign that 'the Turke ought to be assaulted by dyvers ways' and to outline a plan of campaign 'to ruyne hym and to blott out his name'.[19] However, James did not show any interest in such a campaign or an alliance with the Persians that could give offence to the Mighty Turk.

To develop trade and diplomatic relations with India, James I sent Sir Thomas Roe as his ambassador to the Mughal Emperor *Jahangir*. Sir Thomas presented his credentials, with many presents from his king for the Emperor and his family, at the court of the great Mughal at Agra, in 1615. Among the presents, along with other precious gifts, were European paintings that were much liked by the Emperor and red wines that were cherished by him. The introduction of European paintings had a profound influence on

---

[17] Matar, Nabil *Turks Moors and Englishmen in the Age of Discovery* p.3

[18] Blank, David *ibid* pp.48-49

[19] Chew, Samuel, C. p.303

the Indian miniature painters and inspired them with new ideas. To the Mughal Queen *Nur Jahan*, Sir Thomas presented an English carriage 'which she greatly enjoyed using'.[20] With his diplomatic skills and of course the presents he gave to the royal family members and the Mughal nobles Sir Thomas obtained permission to set up a British factory at Surat, a very important port on the east coast of India, and protection for the British traders in India. During his four years at the Mughal court, he won many more privileges for British traders.

To maintain good relations with the Muslim rulers, James I, like his predecessor, encouraged the freeing of Muslim seamen captured from the Spanish galleys and sent them to their countries or exchanged them with British sailors in the captivity of Muslims. This appreciative gesture resulted in further enhancing British links with the Muslim world and in increasing the number of Muslim seamen using British ports and vice versa. James' successor King Charles I, soon after his accession to the British throne in 1625, received the new Ambassador, *Naqad Ali Beg*, of *Shah Abbas* of Persia and a messenger from the ruler of Algeria who brought Barbary horses, tigers and lions as presents for the British King. In 1632 and 1637 King Charles I signed two treaties with the Moroccan Kings resulting in wider interaction between Britain and North Africa. Also in 1637, 'King Charles authorised his fleet to assist *Siddy Hamid al-Ayayashi* of Old Sallee, against his rival'.[21] This most probably was the first instance ever that the British naval forces had gone to the assistance of a Muslim ruler.

King Charles was also a keen collector of Arabic and Persian manuscripts.[22] Whether he had learnt to read and understand them is doubtful, nonetheless, a keen interest in the study of Arabic grew in Britain during the Stuart period. The Muslim influence in Britain was so strong in this period, that in dealing with the Muslim rulers, 'Britons followed Muslim rules'. As for Cromwell, 'in his correspondence with the North Africans, he used the Muslim calendar'.[23]

---

[20] Schimmel, Annemarie *The Empire of the Mughals* p.43

[21] Matar, Nabil *Turks Moors and Englishmen in the Age of Discovery* p.54

[22] Matar, Nabil *Islam in Britain 1558-1685* p.30

[23] Matar, Nabil *Turks Moors and Englishmen in the Age of Discovery* pp.104-105

During the Elizabethan and Stuart periods, the good relations between Britain and the Muslim world encouraged many British people to go to the Muslim countries and seek employment, as wages and the conditions of service there were often far better. Also, as Islam allowed diversity of religion and liberty of conscience they had no fears of religious persecution, which was then widespread in Christendom. Thus many Scottish and English soldiers, sailors and freebooters entered the armed and naval forces of the Muslim world, not only around the Mediterranean but also as far as central Asia and India: 'From the Atlantic coast to the valley of the Nile and from Istanbul to Salee, Britons lived and worked among the Muslims'.[24]

Some of them died fighting for their Muslim employers, some converted to Islam and stayed there. Others returned home with their riches. Most of them were common soldiers but there were also some from the British nobility. They sought employment as soldiers, seamen and gunners in the Ottoman, Persian and North African armed forces because there they could get a good and reliable wage. Indeed the attraction for service in the Muslim countries was so great that throughout his reign James I had to issue decrees urging Scottish and English soldiers and sailors serving abroad to return home and join the British armed forces.[25]

Some English and Scottish pirates sought service and often refuge in North African Muslim countries. Many of them settled there and operated from the safe havens of North African ports. English, Scottish, Welsh and Irish pirates flourished under Muslim flags.[26] Morocco was the most accessible and attractive place for the British pirates. On many occasions the Muslim and British pirates combined their forces and together committed foul and flagrant piracies. During the sixteenth and seventeenth centuries the Muslims of North Africa and the Ottomans used Scottish and English ships for transportation, especially during their pilgrimage season. The Scottish and English ships were easily available in the Mediterranean. The good relations and the trust built between the two peoples assured Muslims of a safe journey in the British ships and so they preferred to travel in them to the financial gain of

[24] *Turks Moors and Englishmen in the Age of Discovery* p.66

[25] *ibid* p.44

[26] *ibid* p.63

Britain. This extensive interaction between Muslims and Britons in those days was so effective and the influence of Islamic culture so powerful that, like the Crusaders in the eleventh and twelfth centuries, these British traders, pirates, seamen and soldiers also adopted much of Muslim culture, habits and ways. They learned the language of their hosts, clipped their beards according to the style in Muslim countries, adopted Muslim dress, ate the local food and learned the games played by their Muslim hosts.[27]

The harmonious connections between Muslims and British people during that time were not confined to the Turkish Empire and the North African countries. Indeed, they extended to the whole of the Muslim world including India and Indonesia. British traders had also developed good relationships in the Far East. These extensive and profitable relations changed for the better the attitude of British Christians towards Muslims throughout the world and many close friendships and even marriages resulted from these relationships.

During the seventeenth century Britain, legal sexual liaisons between Christians and Muslims came to be viewed as tolerable if not desirable. For instance, in 1614, the East India Company conducted negotiations for the marriage of the Sultan of Sumatra with the daughter of an honourable English gentleman because it was thought that this marriage would bring benefits to the Company. In this case, some theologians objected to a Christian girl marrying a Muslim but others approved of it as lawful and legitimate according to the scriptures. However, the negotiations failed and this marriage did not take place but others did. In the second half of the seventeenth century, a marriage had taken place between the ruler of Algiers and an English woman and at about the same time, the King of Morocco had married an English girl. In 1682, a companion of the Moroccan ambassador to Britain, a Christian convert to Islam named Hamed Lucas married a Christian girl during his stay in London without any objections from any quarter against this union.[28]

The British people appreciated the tolerance proffered to Christians especially Protestants living in the countries under Turkish rule in Central and Eastern Europe and this led to further

---

[27] *Turks, Moors and Englishmen in the Age of Discovery* p.58
[28] *ibid* pp.40-41

strengthening the atmosphere of harmony between Britons and Turks. The nascent Protestant minority in most parts of Europe in the sixteenth and seventeenth centuries was under severe persecution from the Catholic Church and the Catholic rulers. The Turks in their vast European territories allowed them liberty of conscience and granted them religious freedom. The Protestant minorities living under the Muslim Turks valued this freedom, preferred to live under them, and even supported them against the Catholic Hapsburgs. In fact, in the sixteenth century, the Turks proved to be the allies of the Reformation movement against Catholicism. The spread of Protestantism in the European part of the Turkish Empire, especially Hungary was because of the Turks' tolerance and freedom of religion for all their subjects.[29]

Tolerance of all religions and especially of Christianity and Judaism – the other two Abrahamic faiths – was and is a matter of course in Islam. During the Muslim dominance of the world, normally all religions prospered in their empires and intolerance or persecution of minority religions were very rare. In fact, persecuted Christian minorities, especially Jews living in Christendom, always found safe havens in the Muslim countries that practically demonstrated religious tolerance that was unparalleled in the countries of western Christendom. During the Inquisition in Spain from the fifteenth to seventeenth century, Muslims and Jews were being forced to convert to Christianity or burnt at the stake. However, in the Islamic world there were no repercussions of these barbaric atrocities against the Christians. Christians and Jews living under the Turks in the Levant, Eastern Europe and the North African Muslim countries were going about their daily life freely, practising their religion, and worshipping in their churches and synagogues respectively with full freedom. For example, the following quotation provides a picture of seventeenth century Smyrna, an important city in Turkey, based on the observations of the British Consul working there:

> The skyline of Smyrna reflected the cosmopolitan and tolerant character of the city. There were thirteen (or fifteen) mosques, seven Synagogues, three Roman Catholic churches,

---

[29] Matar, Nabil *Islam in Britain 1558-1685* p.138

two Greek Orthodox and two Armenian. The English, the Dutch and Genoese worshipped in their Consular chapels.[30]

Islam's toleration and empathy for Christianity and especially its closeness to the new reformed Christianity – Protestantism – gave expectations to some seventeenth century European Protestant theologians of the possible conversion of Muslims to their creed. Lacking the power to convert them forcibly, those who had experienced or known the humanity and especially the anti-idolatry fervour of the Turks somehow became hopeful of their 'redemption' through intellectual and rational evangelism. Under pressure from the Catholics, they wished the conversion of the powerful Muslims to have their support and strength. Thus, there were hopes and out of hopes rose 'prophesies' to the effect that the Muslims will convert to Protestant Christianity. However, before their conversion they were to destroy the Pope and other Catholic dominions and 'Conversion to Christianity would be God's reward to the Muslims for helping His cause against . . . the Papist'.[31]

These feelings and hopes were shared among many Protestants in Britain. In the seventeenth century however, some Scottish and English Christian clerics and eschatologists were working on another fanciful intrigue through which they were hoping for the conversion of the Jews and the destruction of Islam. They believed that the Jews were desperate to end their Christian-imposed exile and to live in the Promised Land. The Jews were therefore eager to capture Jerusalem and to turn the Arabs and Turks out of Palestine. However, to achieve that objective the Protestants had to encourage and support the return of Jews to Palestine. Thus began the controversial movement for the 'Restoration' of Jews to Palestine. The capricious idea was that once the Jews were restored to Palestine the Jewish warriors would fight the Arabs and the Turks, vanquish them and convert to Christianity. Then they would establish in Palestine the Protestant kingdom of Christ. 'The reason for this. . . lay in Paul's promise to Romans 11:24, that the Jewish 'branches' would finally be grafted to the Christian tree.'[32]

It would have been highly unlikely that the Jews, who had been

---

[30] Anderson, Sonia, P. *An English Consul in Turkey* p.7

[31] *Islam in Britain 1558-1685* p141

[32] *ibid* p.168

persecuted, forced to convert or burnt alive by the Christians in Europe as well as in Britain would suddenly turn against the Muslims who had given them refuge and saved them from extermination. Secondly Jews had no power, no armies and no government that could pose a possible threat to the Muslims. It was perhaps the desperation of the British eschatologists arising out of the unassailable power of the Turk that made them willing to believe anything in which they saw the imaginary downfall of Islam that had dominated them for nearly one thousand years. In other words they were clutching at straws.

There were very few Jews in Britain at that time, as Cromwell had only recently allowed them back in the country. Nonetheless, some Scottish and English religious leaders became fervent supporters of the scheme for the 'Restoration' of the Jews so that they could conquer the Holy Land and Islam. The fantastic expectation out of this intrigue was that the Jews would defeat the Turks with the support of the *Shiite* Muslim Persia, the perpetual enemy of the *Sunni* Muslim Turks. After capturing Palestine and the rest of the Levant, and killing all the Turks and the Arab inhabitants they would take seven years to purify Jerusalem and its sanctuaries. After completing that sacred task they would accept Jesus as the Promised Messiah, renounce their Jewishness, declare their conversion to Protestant Christianity and their allegiance to the British Crown.

Though nothing practical had been done yet in Britain to restore the Jews to Palestine, in that charged atmosphere of these eschatological intrigues, many rumours and letters were widely circulating in Scotland and England to the effect that the Jews had already started their victorious campaign against Islam. For instance, one of the letters written in August 1665, from 'Saley in Barbary', gave information that the Jews had already captured many cities and massacred all their Muslim residents. Another letter from Antwerp revealed that the Jewish forces were poised to capture Makkah.[33]

However, the most whimsical news came from Scotland in a letter sent to Oxford on 15 November 1665. I take the liberty of quoting this long letter *verbatim* to give the reader the true taste of what was going on:

---

[33] Matar, Nabil *Islam in Britain* pp.177-178

Having received a more full account of the proceeding of the Jews, I shall here present you with such occurrences, in this juncture of time, wherein scarce any thing else is either talkt of, or lookt after, in comparison of them. The whole World we see is out of order, nothing to be expected by Intestine Broils, and whether the Lord will be pleased in the midst of these combustions to call in his Ancient People, and magnify his Name in them, He only knoweth. On the 23 of October, by the foulnesse of the weather and storms, put into Aberdeen a Ship, from whence they came 'tis uncertain; but the Profesour of that City, of the Tongues and Languages, having Notice thereof, went down unto them, and by their Discourse perceived they spoke broken Hebrew, and bound for Amsterdam, as was intimated by a Letter in High-Dutch, to have Correspondence with their Brethren (the Jews) there; Which Letter further relates, That there is Sixteen hundred thousand of them together in Arabia, and that there came into Europe Sixty thousand more; withal, that they had many encounters with the Turks, defeating several Bodies, and killing many thousands, none being able to stand against them. They give Liberty of Conscience to all, except the Turks endeavouring the utter Ruine and Extirpation of them. But for the ship, the Sails thereof are white branched Sattin, and all their Ropes are Silk of the same colour; and in the Sails was this inscription in fair Red characters, **These are of the Ten Tribes Of Israel,** Which was to discover them to be Jews; There Food on board was only Rice and Honey: Their Habit [or Clothing] Black and Blew. It seems they have sent to the most of chief Cities in the world to their Brethren, to give them Notice of their Proceedings, to the end they may come and joyn with them. The Great Turk having had a Dream, that a Jew had taken the Crown from his Head, resolved to put all to death within his Dominions; But his Council disswaded him from that Bloody Design. The Jewish host are said to increase daily, and that many of them believe in the true Messiah, and that it was the Saviour of the World that was crucified at Jerusalem.[34]

---

[34] The Jewes Message to their Brethren in Holland; and a New Letter touching their further proceedings sent from the Kingdom of

Another letter gave even better good news. It said that the Israelites, having besieged *Makkah*, have defeated the King of Arabia and the *Bashaw* of Alexandria who came to relieve the Holy City of Islam with sixty thousand troops. The commander of the City sent four bodies of troops against the besieging Israelites but not a single man returned alive. It goes on to tell about a 'sad and fearful dream' of the 'Great Turk'; the gathering of sixteen hundred thousand Israelites in the dominion of the Turk; the mysterious miracles performed by the 'Captain General of the Israelites'. It ends with a prophesy foretelling the downfall of the Turks in 66 (probably 1666), 'and the year of Reformation for the Gospel to be preached throughout all nations' etc.[35]

One can only wonder who was spreading such imaginary rumours and reports. It could be argued that it might have been the recently re-admitted Jews who perhaps, through such propaganda, were trying to acquire some degree of acceptance and respect in Britain. However, considering the terrible consequences of such a blatant deception no rational Jew would have thought of it. On the other hand, it is most probable that the Scottish and English religious thinkers and writers who, according to the current 'prophesies', in their wishful thinking dreamt up and devised these intrigues. Through them, they imagined inducing the Jews to destroy Islam and advance Protestantism in the Levant and the realm of the Turks or perhaps they just wanted to boost the morale of the pressured European Christians and give them courage and hope. However, it is not known if in reality these machinations had any influence in the Levant and the Turkish Empire. The chances are that the happily living and prospering Jews in the realm of the Turks and the Turkish authorities would never have heard of such fantastic plots being designed in Scotland and England. The British government of the day had no part in this subterfuge either and it was maintaining its good relations with the Turks and other Muslim powers.

In spite of good diplomatic and trade relations between Britain and the Muslim world, with both sides enjoying the benefits of

---

Scotland: printed for George Freeman, Anno Dom. 1665, pp 1-2

[35] Another Letter from Dr. Serarias, to Dr. Homes, Mr. Bruce and others, printed for George Freeman, Anno Dom. 1665, pp.2-6

lucrative and essential trade with each other, there was also a point of conflict, representing a very dark side to this relationship. Over and above those adventurous Britons who went to Muslim countries of their own volition to better their lot, unfortunately there were thousands of unwilling British captives in the Turkish Empire and especially in the North African countries. These captives were there mainly through widespread piracy in the Mediterranean, the English Channel and the Atlantic. In the sixteenth and seventeenth centuries, British ships and some coastal areas of Britain appear to have been easy prey for the technologically superior and powerful Turkish and North African pirates. During the reign of James I of England, scores of English and Scottish ships were captured or sunk and their crews and passengers taken captive. In January 1618, a Scottish ship was captured by Turkish pirates, and between 1620 and 1621, North African pirates captured more than 100 British ships. Thus, by mid 1626 there were about 3,000 British captives in Algiers and nearly 1,500 in Sali.

> The Britons who were captured in these attacks came from all over the British Isles . . . from Dundee to Hull and from Edinburgh to Barnstaple.

Turkish pirates during this period were so powerful and daring that on many occasions, they even attacked and plundered some port towns and coastal villages in the British Isles and took away many captives '. . . in March 1636, it was reported that 36 English, Scottish and Irish ships have been taken, and there are now 400 captives of English, Scots, and Irish.' [36]

In the *Calendar of Documents of Scotland* and the *Register of the Privy Council of Scotland* there are many accounts of Scottish captives in the hands of 'Saracens' and the efforts being made for their release. To mention a few:

> March 1st. 1541, Edinburgh. 21. Queen Margaret to King Henry VIII. Begs a safe conduct for Friar Joachim, Sacristan of the Holy Sepulchre at Jerusalem, who is coming from Scotland to England to solicit alms for the redemption of the Abbot and monks of his convent, taken prisoners by the

---

[36] *Islam in Britain 1558-1685* pp.7-9

Saracens and that the said friar may procure and receive alms of his Majesty's lieges.[37]

December 1582, London. 93. Petition of Robert Oliphant to Queen Elizabeth, praying her assistance towards an expedition undertaken by himself and others for the relief of the Master of Oliphant and Master of Morton, reported to have been made slaves by the Turks, and to be detained in captivity in the town of Algiers on the coast of Barbary.[38]

Edinburgh, 25th Jan. 1620. Circular letter in favour of a collection for the ransom of Robert Cowan, skipper and 6 of his crew, captives with the Moors.[39]

Holyrood house, 29th July 1624. Recommendation and warrant for a collection for the payment of the sum demanded (twenty pounds Sterling) by the Moors for the ransom of William Dawson, a Scottish captive in Algiers.[40]

The relatives of the captives and/or the government usually made efforts to get them freed as soon as possible through exchange of prisoners or the payment of ransom. There was always great concern in Britain for the fate of these captives and the relatives were ever anxious to secure their release before any harm came to them or they followed their compatriots, who had converted to Islam and achieved honour and success in Muslim society. Conversion to Islam of European Christians in those days was a common phenomenon. Europeans who had lived for some time in the materially rich and culturally sophisticated Muslim world, and had witnessed the respect and riches of those who had converted, could not resist the temptation. Therefore, many captives as well as freemen, after experiencing the lure of Islam during their captivity or residence converted to Islam and did not wish to return.

Some well-known Britons who converted during this period were Captain Ward, Captain Sampson and Sir Francis Verney. They settled in Muslim lands and never returned to Britain:

---

[37] *Calendar of Documents of Scotland*, 941.05 CAL [1509-1589] 'Vol.V. 1541

[38] *ibid* 941.05 CAL [1509-1589] Vol. XXX

[39] *ibid* 941 REG Vol. 12, [1619-1622]

[40] *ibid* 941 REG Vol. 13, [1622-1625]

In 1635, two Scotsmen were captured by Spaniards on a Turkish vessel and detained because they were renegadoes (had converted to Islam).[41]

Nearly all of those who converted to Islam rose to high positions in the Turkish Empire and other Muslim countries and attained fame and wealth. Some even rose to the high positions of counsellors, viziers and pashas in the courts of the Muslim rulers. So there was a great attraction for those who came into contact with Muslim society to 'turn Turk' i.e. convert to Islam:

> . . . in Tunis and Tripoli (in the sixteenth and seventeenth centuries), the highest offices were exclusively available to Christian converts to Islam.[42]

In the 1660s King Charles II sent a Captain Hamilton to ransom some British sailors from the Barbary Coast but they refused to come back as they had already converted and were living there as respected and prosperous free men.[43] The charm of Islam was 'the rewards of honour and riches', especially for the poor and those who aspired to identify with a superior civilisation and a powerful empire. During the height of the Ottoman Empire from the fifteenth to seventeenth centuries, therefore, hundreds of thousands of European Christians converted to Islam of their own free will:

> Clearly, there was enterprise, reward and glory in converting to Islam and numerous Britons. . . seized the opportunity to 'take the turban'.[44]

In the early seventeenth century, just in the kingdom of Algiers, there were 200,000 Christians most of whom were 'Renegados or apostates'.[45] During the heyday of the Mughal Empire, in the seventeenth century, the same thing was happening in India, when many

---

[41] *Islam in Britain 1558-1685* p.36

[42] *ibid* p.50

[43] *ibid* p.37

[44] Blank, David p.51

[45] *Islam in Britain* p.16

British employees of the East India Company were converting to Islam.[46]

The lure of Islam was so great that sometimes, the Christians living in the Islamic lands had to be restrained by force by their co-religionists to prevent them from adopting the Muslim faith.[47] There is every probability therefore, that during the zenith of the Muslim power and especially during the sixteenth and seventeenth centuries hundreds and maybe thousands of Scots captives as well as freemen converted to Islam, achieved high position and wealth and settled in North Africa or other parts of the Muslim world. While in Britain, during those times, strict regulations were in force governing even the dress of subjects according to their social status, in the Islamic society, there were no distinctions or discrimination based on the social origin, status or colour of a person. Thus, whether a person came from Scotland or Swaziland, was a recent convert or a born Muslim, was black, white or yellow, in the Muslim society, if he had the means he could adorn whatever he liked and if he had the ability and aspiration he could rise to any position of influence and power irrespective of his race, colour or background. This equality, egalitarianism and the vast opportunities in the Islamic countries were perhaps the most important incentives to conversion, especially for the poor and those belonging to the lower class of British society, who had no chance of making good in their own country. Also, they found Islam a rational, simple and moderate religion without asceticism and rigidity that acknowledged Christianity and Judaism.

It was not just the captives and the poor freemen who out of convenience converted to Islam. Some high diplomats and learned members of the nobility found Islam attractive and joined its ranks with conviction. A general in the Ottoman armed forces known as *Inglis Mustapha* was actually a Campbell from Scotland. He had joined the Ottoman army after converting to Islam and taking the Islamic name *Mustapha*. In 1606, Benjamin Bishop, the English Consul in Egypt, embraced Islam, left his post and broke his connections with England. Thus, Islam lured the British with its superior and sophisticated culture and not by force.[48]

On their conversion to Islam, as the converts adopted Muslim

---

[46] Dalrymple, W. *White Mughals* p.24

[47] *Islam in Britain* p.41

[48] Dalrymple, William *White Mughals* pp.18-19

names and severed contacts with their families and their homelands, they disappeared from the records of their respective countries of origin. No records of European or any other converts were kept in the Muslim countries either. Thus, converts of all nations, colours or creeds assimilated in Muslim society without leaving any trace of their origin or race. There is an amazing case of a Scottish woman, probably from Bothwell, married to a Turkish officer and living in a town near Jerusalem in the sixteenth century:

> And here by occasion of this termination I am to craue the reader's patience for a little digression, to relate a thing wherof it hath giuen me remembrance. So it fel of late yeares that an English gentleman trauailing in Palestine. . . as he passed through a countrie town, he heard by chance a women, sitting at her door dandling her chyld, to sing: *Bothwell bank thou blumest faire,* the gentleman heer-at exceedingly wundered & forthwith in English saluted the woman, who joyfully answered him, and said she was right glad there to see a gentleman of our Ile, and told him that shee was a Scottish woman and came first from Scotland to Venice and from Venice thether where her fortune was to bee the wyf of an officer vnder the Turk, who being at the instant absent and very soon to returne, intreated the gentleman to stay there vntil his returne: the which he did, and she for countrie sake to shew her self the more kynd and bountifull vnto him, told her husband at his home-coming that the gentleman was her kinsmen: whereupon her husband entretayned him very friendly and at his departure gaue him diures things of good value.[49]

There is no information about how she ended up in the Holy Land or under what circumstances she married a Turkish officer. It is possible that she went there as a pilgrim or as a member of the family of a Scottish diplomat or trader, or perhaps she was sold as a slave to a Turk. Whatever the case, her story is very interesting.

A more astonishing case of a very important and royal connection between Scotland and Islam concerns a Scottish girl by the name of Helen Gloag, who became the Empress of Morocco.

---

[49] Vesrtegan, Richard *Restitution of Decayed Intelligence* pp.296-297

Helen was born in Perthshire, perhaps around the middle of the eighteenth century. She grew up to be a beautiful green-eyed girl. When 19, she ran away from home and boarded a ship to go to America. Moroccan pirates captured the ship and Helen became their captive. Eventually she was sold to a slave trader who presented her to the Sultan *Sidi Muhammad* of Morocco. With her charm, very soon Helen became the Sultan's favourite wife. In 1790, after the death of her husband, she seemingly appealed to the British government for help when she found her sons by the Sultan in danger from his heir *Mad Yazeed*. The British did not respond to her request. Her brother had become a trader who often went to Morocco and visited her. On one of his visits, she gave him presents to be delivered to her relatives and friends in Perthshire.[50]

During the fifteenth to eighteenth centuries when piracy was at its height in the Mediterranean, English Channel and all around Europe there would have been numerous Scottish girls who, like the above-mentioned woman in Palestine and Mary Gloag, would have ended up in the harems of North African Muslim aristocrats and forgotten forever.

Another influence of the Muslim/Turkish culture, that made its way into Britain in the mid seventeenth century, was coffee, the 'Mahometan berry' and the appearance of coffee houses first in London and then throughout the British Isles. Coffee was introduced to Britain, through diplomats, travellers and traders who drank it during their sojourns and travels in the Muslim lands and perhaps got so used to it that on their return they brought a sufficient quantity of the berry with them for their personal use. These personages, naturally, would have introduced it to their friends and family and thus the drinking of coffee spread to a wider circle, though at first, to the elite of society. The first coffee house in Britain opened in 1652 in London. To attract customers the enterprising owners of the coffee houses widely distributed handbills emphasising the medicinal benefits of drinking coffee, translated from Arabic. This was followed by the publication of many more translations from Arabic texts, some by very well known people, specifying the health benefits of coffee drinking. All this publicity led to coffee drinking becoming very popular within a few years and 'so fashionable that it rivalled the traditional ale'. Soon coffee

---

[50] (Calder, Angus, Ecosse, The Sunday Times, Sept. 28, 2003)

drinking took on a religious mantle. Its proponents argued that coffee made the drinker more active, more hard working, more productive and 'coffee was the drink of the Protestant work ethic because it stimulated the mind of the drinker'.[51] On the other side were the opponents of coffee drinking. They denounced it and maintained that it intoxicated the drinker and it possessed not Protestant but Muslim qualities and resulted not in Christian, but Turkish sobriety.[52] Some went even further and warned that it prepared Englishmen for conversion to Islam.

As the first English translation of the *Quran* by Alexander Ross, a Scotsman, and coffee were introduced in Britain, at the same time, the antagonists established an ominous link between these two events! They claimed that coffee followed the 'Alcoran', both introduced during the lax Cromwellian period, to induce Britons towards Islam. The donning of Turkish dress and turbans by the coffee housekeepers further exacerbated the issue. The fact that it was the recently admitted (also by Cromwell) Jews, who were opening or managing some of the coffee houses and importing the berry from the Ottoman Empire, added fuel to the fire. The antagonists claimed that the Jews, large communities of whom lived in the Ottoman Empire, were part of the conspiracy to bring British drinkers under 'the power of this Turkish spell' to spread Islam in Britain. They argued:

> that if coffee had mysterious potencies that could cure diseases, then it might also have mysterious powers to seduce Christians from their faith, coffee could be a Muslim agent to entice Englishmen away from their religion and turn them into renegades: coffee was as dangerous as 'Alcoran' because it threatened the fabric of England's Christian society.[53]

It is very strange that the introduction of coffee drinking generated so much controversy in Britain. It was especially paradoxical to blame the Jews for promoting Islam in Britain through coffee when almost at the same time these very same Jews were being 'prophesied' to destroy Islam and convert themselves to Protestant-

---

[51] *Islam in Britain* p.111

[52] *ibid* p.112

[53] *ibid* p.112

ism. However, when one reflects upon the dread of the Turk, the ever-extending influence of Islam in Europe and the anti-Islam atmosphere of that age, this confusion can be easily understood. It is obvious that its adversaries were not considering just the demerits of coffee drinking, it was more to do with coffee's links with the Turks that had caused their enmity against it and the associated controversy. They were afraid of the increasing Muslim influence that coffee was bringing with it.

However, in spite of all the opposition from the pulpit and the press this 'Turkish Enchantress' not only survived but also thrived in Britain. It reached Scotland eleven years after London when in 1673, Walter Whiteford, a retired Army Colonel, opened the first coffee house in Glasgow. In the same year, John Row opened one near the Parliament House in Edinburgh.[54] Thus, within about twenty years of its introduction in London and in spite of much opposition, the 'Mahometan berry' had become popular throughout Britain. By the seventeenth century, therefore, contacts between Islam and Scotland had become widespread and the Islamic influence in this country more significant.

Scholars and Travellers

The most positive source of contacts between Islam and the West during the Middle Ages was through learning and the intellectual acquisition by European scholars from highly knowledgeable Muslim academics, especially of Spain. Before embracing Islam in the early seventh century, the Arabs were a desert-dwelling, undisciplined and illiterate people. Within less than one hundred years of their conversion to Islam, they became well-educated, cultured and civilised. How this transformation came about is not a mystery but was a natural progression effected by their new faith.

Their religion induced them to seek knowledge, as numerous verses of the *Quran* enjoin Muslims to learn, to reflect upon and to contemplate God, His Creation and His Signs in this Universe. Islam puts great emphasis on *Ilm*, i.e. knowledge. The word *Ilm* and its derivations are mentioned 880 times in the *Quran*. There are verses that make it absolutely clear that in the sight of God, a person with knowledge is superior to one without it, e.g. *'Allah* will

---

[54] Ellis, Markman *The Coffee House* p.76

raise to high ranks those who have faith and knowledge among you.' (58, 11); and 'None save those who are endowed with knowledge truly fear *Allah*.' (35, 28) In addition, there were a number of sayings of the Prophet of Islam directing Muslims to acquire knowledge. These include the following: seeking knowledge is the sacred duty of every Muslim male and female; seek knowledge from the cradle to the grave; seek knowledge if even you have to travel to China. Islam went as far as conferring the sanctity of worship on learning and intellectual activity and made every area of intellectual exertion open to Muslim seekers of knowledge. No field of knowledge was barred to them and they were free to approach any people, anywhere, of whatever faith or race, and seek, acquire and borrow knowledge from them. Thus, there has been never a conflict between Islam and knowledge or science. *Muhammad Asad* (Leopold Weiss) the twentieth century Austrian philosopher states:

> . . . while there was always a conflict between Christianity and science – manifested, on the one hand, in. . . dogma, and on the other, in the most atrocious persecution of scientific thought and of scientists down to modern times – we are unable to discover the slightest trace of a conflict between Islam and science, be it in the teachings themselves or in the attitude of Muslim *Ummah* towards scientists.[55]

Hence, Muslims took learning as a religious duty and felt obliged to look for, learn and seek all and every kind of knowledge.

When the Muslim Arabs came into contact with the Greeks, in about the middle of the seventh century, they were fascinated with their well-developed culture and knowledge and became the devoted pupils of Greek scholars and scientists. Once they realised the true scope of Greek knowledge and wanted to learn more, they searched for and found old books and writings of the early Greek philosophers that had been discarded, banned or had missed being burned by the Christian Church. With the help of Greek and Jewish scholars, they translated them into Arabic. Indeed, by this very important timely action the Arab Muslims saved many of the works of Plato, Aristotle, Socrates and other famous Greek philosophers

---

[55] *Is Religion a Thing of the Past* p.20

and thinkers, considerably enhanced them and eventually transmitted them back to the West.

The Muslims further widened their search for knowledge and from the Persians, Egyptians, Indians and Chinese they learnt the sciences and arts pioneered and developed by them. From the synthesis of the knowledge borrowed from all those civilisations, they developed the fabric of their own learning. Their zeal for learning and promoting knowledge was so intense that within a century of their rise from the desert of Arabia they had taken their culture and knowledge to a highly advanced stage. Before the end of the eighth century, Baghdad had become the hub of learning with many schools, colleges and several libraries open to all seekers of knowledge. In 830, the Caliph *Al-Mamun* (813-33), who was a great patron of the arts and sciences, established his unique *Bayt al-Hikma* (House of Wisdom), containing an academy, an extensive library, astronomical observatories, and a translation bureau. Salaried Muslim, Christian and Jewish scholars were employed to translate the Greek, Coptic, Persian, Indian and Chinese manuscripts into Arabic.[56]

Cairo, Cordoba and Toledo followed Baghdad and also became great Muslim centres of learning. Seekers of knowledge flocked to these institutions from every corner of the world. Soon every major town in the vast Muslim Empire became an intellectual centre with its own schools, colleges and libraries offering learning facilities to all, irrespective of race, colour or creed:

> Education was a high priority in Muslim empires during this period. By the tenth century, there were thousands of schools at mosques, . . . including 300 in Baghdad alone. A number of libraries gathered manuscripts from around the world, and schools that would become universities were established. Under the Fatimide, a Cairo Mosque that opened for prayers in 972 eventually grew into the University of *Al-Azhar*, the oldest university in the Mediterranean.[57]

When the Arabs realised that they had acquired sufficient knowledge, they began to reflect upon nature, as they had been

---

[56] Rahman, H.U. *A Chronology of Islamic History 570-1000 CE*, p.166
[57] Carnegie Corporation of New York, Annual Report 2001 pp.15-16

directed by their faith, and investigate the natural phenomena around them. Their investigations resulted in the revelation of many secrets of nature. For example their research on the *Quranic* verse, 'We have created everything out of water' (21: 30) led the Muslim pioneers of science to study living organisms, and that in turn guided them to develop the science of biology. Other *Quranic* verses such as:

> He (God) it is who appointed the sun a splendour and the moon a light, and measured for her stages, that ye might know the number of the years, and the reckoning (10: 6); And He it is Who created the night and the day, the moon and the sun. They float, each in an orbit. (21: 33)

made them interested in the study and the development of the sciences of astronomy and mathematics and so on. To do that effectively they built the observatories in Baghdad and other major cities, invented telescope, compass and the pendulum. As regards the contribution of Muslims to the sciences, especially chemistry, suffice to say that the words chemistry, alcohol, alkali, alembicin etc. all originate from the Arabic language. In about 800 AD, to facilitate the promotion of knowledge throughout the Muslim Empire, the Caliph *Harun al-Rashid* ordered the building of a paper mill in Baghdad. From Baghdad, the use of paper spread westwards to North Africa and Spain and from Spain, it came to Europe in the twelfth century. However, paper mills were not introduced into Europe until the fourteenth century.[58]

Consequently, the Muslims developed an unrivalled sophisticated civilisation of their own in which sciences, arts, crafts and culture blossomed in a spectacular fashion. They did not draw any lines between religious and secular knowledge, they embraced all. Knowledge to them was the way to God. To comprehend the Creation and the Scheme of the Creator, God Almighty, they studied all – spiritual and temporal – with respect and with dedication. The result was that most of the early Muslim theologians were also renowned scientists and philosophers whose names are now household words the world over. They pioneered and for centuries led the world in all aspects of science and arts.

---

[58] Watt, W. M. *Influence of Islam on Medieval Europe* p.25

Before the end of the ninth century, Muslim culture had already produced several world famous astrologers, mathematicians, philosophers and scientists whose inventions, innovations and works became and remained authentic and cherished sources of learning in the West until well after the Renaissance. For example the introduction of Indian numerals and *sifr*, or zero by *Muhammad ibn Musa Al-Khwarzimi* (780-850), which were adopted into Latin by Adelard of Bath (c1090-1150), provided new easy solutions for complicated mathematical equations. The decimal system also was introduced by *Al-Khwarzimi,* who was using it during the ninth century. The word algorithm or algorism derives from his name. He also introduced Algebra and wrote the first ever book on it that was translated into Latin by Gerard of Cremona (1114-1187). This book was in use in the West up to the sixteenth century.[59]

Al-Razi (865-925) or Rhazes, as he is better known in the West, was the first to diagnose smallpox and measles and to use animal gut for sutures. This was just one of his achievements among many others in the field of medicine. *Ibn al-Nafis,* a Syrian discovered the fundamental principles of pulmonary circulation. *Hunayn ibn Ishaq* (809-873), a Syrian Christian was a famous teacher and translator at the Baghdad House of Wisdom. His greatest work though was in the science of optics especially, his ten treatises on the eye, which was, on this subject, the first systematic textbook with ophthalmologic diagrams. For several centuries, this book profoundly influenced the development of the science of optics.[60]

In medicine and surgery, Muslims also made ground-breaking discoveries. In Europe during the Middle Ages, the works of Muslim physicians and surgeons were a compulsory part of the course of medical studies. Until the late seventeenth century Avicenna's *(Abu Ali Al Hussain ibn Abdullah ibn Sina,* 980-1037) Canon was the only recognised textbook for European medical students. Moreover, the first ever free public hospital in the world was opened in Baghdad in the early ninth century and within a short period of that, every major town in the Muslim empire had its own hospital. These hospitals were also used as medical schools for the education and training of surgeons, physicians and pharmacists.[61]

---

[59] Rahman, H.U. p.188/9

[60] *ibid* p162

[61] *ibid* p163

The Muslim rulers of the Iberian Peninsula, once fully established, began attracting and employing Muslim, Christian and Jewish academics and scholars from the East and actively encouraged the learning and development of knowledge in their empire. Consequently, during the ninth and tenth centuries, while the rest of Europe still lived in ignorance and darkness, Spain and the rest of the Muslim world was experiencing the flourishing of advanced sciences, philosophy, arts and a highly sophisticated culture. The tenth and eleventh centuries produced a glittering civilisation in the Iberian Peninsula. The bilingual Muslims and Christians and the trilingual Jewish academics of Spain, all worked in complete harmony to develop this unique civilisation. Cordoba, the capital of Muslim Spain, became known as 'the Jewel of the world'. It had seventy public libraries with millions of books and numerous schools. Under the benevolent patronage of the Muslim rulers of Spain and in an atmosphere of tolerance and religious diversity Muslim, Jewish and Christian scholars and scientists came together, introduced new ideas and innovations in the fields of science, medicine, mathematics, astronomy, philosophy and architecture.

Soon the reputation of the sophisticated teachers and highly advanced learning institutions of Muslim Spain spread throughout Europe and European scholars realised that they had much to learn from this corpus of knowledge. Consequently, Western Christian students and scholars began to flock to those fountains of wisdom, the *Madrasssas*, i.e. the schools and colleges usually based in the Mosques in Cordoba, Seville, Toledo and other cities. This process accelerated after the capture of Toledo by Alphonso VI (r. 1065-1109) of Castile in 1084, who very wisely preserved the contents of the main mosque library of the city. He and the new Archbishop of Toledo encouraged the Muslim and Jewish scholars and scientists to remain in Toledo under Christian rule and carry on their work in their existing schools and seminaries. Consequently, from the end of the eleventh century, Toledo became the focus of learning for European scholars.

Hence, more and more Europeans began to travel to Spain for learning, especially to the city of Toledo, under its new rulers. From Britain, Adelard of Bath was one of the famous early scholars and seekers of knowledge who went on a learning odyssey to Muslim lands.

In the twelfth century, . . . all those who wanted scientific knowledge went to Spain and Adelard actually deserted the Greek for the Arabic linguistic area.[62]

He spent fifteen years, from 1110 to 1125 AD, travelling through Sicily, Syria, Palestine and Spain, learning Arabic and studying under Muslim and Jewish teachers. When he had become proficient in Arabic, he began translating scientific and philosophical books of the Arabs from Arabic into Latin. On his return to England, Adelard was appointed royal tutor to Duke Henry, the future King Henry II of England.

The most productive period of translations from Arabic and the study of the works of Muslim academics and intellectuals, began with the founding of a special school of translation in Toledo by Archbishop Raymond I (1126-52). This school attracted a considerable number of scholars from various countries until the middle of the fourteenth century, and during this period, most of the knowledge developed by the Muslims passed to European scholars.[63]

By the middle of the twelfth century, many Arabic manuscripts or Latin translations of them had become available in Britain and that began generating more interest in the studies of the Arabs. Daniel of Morley was another well-known scholar from the British Isles who went to Spain, in the later part of the twelfth century, to learn the Arabic language and then the Arabic sciences. He had gone at first to Paris for education but found the institutions of learning there staffed by ignorant people. He left Paris and went to Toledo to learn from 'the wisest philosophers in the world'. On his return, along with the knowledge he had acquired, he brought many translated and Arabic books from Toledo in order to pass on his knowledge, that was the *doctrina Arabum,* to others in Britain.[64]

The high estimation in which Muslim academics and their academies were held by some Christian scholars, as early as the eleventh century, is obvious from the following extract:

The story begins at the Benedictine monastery of Monte Cassino in Southern Italy, where in the middle years of the

---

[62] Daniel, Norman *The Arabs and Medieval Europe* p.280

[63] Rahman, H.U. p.190

[64] Daniel, Norman *ibid* p.277

eleventh century an inmate named Constantine 'the African' (because he was an immigrant from Tunisia) started to translate medical works from Arabic into Latin because, in his own words, 'among Latin books I could find no author who gave certain or reliable information'. This activity continued in the twelfth century in both Italy and Spain. . .[65]

From Scotland, Michael Scot (1175-1232), the famous philosopher, translator, mathematician and astrologer, better known as 'The Wizard' in Scotland, was the most renowned scholar who studied in Spain. He owed his intellect and his reputation to the Muslim scholars of Spain and the knowledge they had developed. Michael Scot was born at Balwearie Castle and later on lived at Aikwood Tower, Fifeshire. As a young student he went to Oxford and from there, at the beginning of the thirteenth century, he left for Spain to seek Arabic learning. He settled at Toledo where he began learning Arabic in order to study the major scientific works of the Arabs. Being a dedicated scholar he soon became proficient in that language and began translating Arabic works into Latin. During his stay in Spain and later in Sicily, he read and translated a considerable number of very important books and treatises of famous Muslim philosophers, scientists, mathematicians and astronomers. His most important translations were the works of *Ibn Sina* (Avicenna), *Al Ghazali* (Algazal), *Ibn Rushd* (Averroes), *Al-Farabi* (Apharabius) etc. In 1217, during its author's life, he translated *Kitab Al-Hai'a*, the well-known astronomical works of the famous Arab astronomer *Al Butrugi*. Among his other important works of translation from Arabic to Latin are: Aristotle's *Metaphysics, Physics, De cello et mundo, Hisotria Animalium, De Partibus Animalium* and *De generatiione Animalium,* the last two with the commentaries of *Ibn Rushd* (Averroes). He also wrote his own books, which dealt mainly with alchemy, astrology and the occult sciences.[66]

In the early 1120s, Michael Scot entered the service of Emperor Frederick of Sicily and Southern Italy. Soon he won the confidence of his master and became his constant companion. He accompanied his emperor to the Holy Land on Frederick's Crusade of 1228-29. There, as a scholar of Arabic and a confidant of Frederick, he played

---

[65] Fletcher, Richard *The Cross and the Crescent*, p.123

[66] Thorndike, Lynn *Michael Scot* pp.22-25

a very important role in the successful negotiations of Frederick with the Sultan *Al-Kamal* on the peaceful recovery of Jerusalem.[67] This was a feat, which, during the last nearly 150 years, various European Crusaders had failed to achieve with force and it is to the credit of this son of Scotland that he helped to achieve it though dialogue.

Michael Scot's knowledge of the Arabic language and the study of sciences and arts developed by Muslim scholars enabled him to become one of the most learned, influential and famous philosophers, medical practitioners, astronomers and astrologers of his age. By his trans-

The statue of Michael Scot in Muslim dress in Melrose Abbey

lations into Latin, he introduced to the West many important works of renowned Muslim scholars, philosophers and scientists. In fact he, as one the most influential medieval translators of Arabic works, played a significant part in the enlightenment of Europe and the development of Western civilisation, between the fourteenth and sixteenth centuries. His contemporaries who held him in great esteem regarded him as the leading intellectual of his age. Pope Honorius III was a great admirer of Michael Scot and called him 'singularly gifted in science among men of learning'.[68]

Scot died in 1232, most probably in Sicily, but according to some accounts in Scotland. He is buried in Melrose Abbey. I was intrigued to learn that in his statue on his tomb in Melrose Abbey, he is shown wearing Muslim dress with a trimmed beard and Arab head-dress. To verify this statement and in order to satisfy my curiosity I travelled to Melrose with my daughter Hanna. Melrose is a small market town, with a population of about 3,000. It is beautifully situated on the bank of the River Tweed surrounded by the Eildon hills, in the Scottish Borders region.

When we reached Melrose and were near the Abbey I asked a

[67] MacQuarrie, Allan *Thesis* p.116

[68] Thorndike, Lynn, p.1

number of people first in the street and then in the Abbey compound about the location of the tomb of Michael Scot. To my surprise no one seemed to know Michael Scot. After much disappointment I stopped two elderly gentlemen and asked them. One of them answered 'Michael Scot! Who is he? I don't know him'. Fortunately the other gentleman said, 'Oh aye, you mean the wizard, he is Michael Scot, isn't he?' But he did not know the location of his tomb or that he was buried here. Eventually we found the tomb but there was no tablet or any statue at or near it. I made some enquires and was told that for safekeeping and to avoid any damage, it had been removed and kept in the attached museum. Fortunately, we were allowed admission and an opportunity to examine the statue and my curiosity was satisfied to see that Michael Scot's statue did indeed have a Muslim style beard and a head-dress like an Arab scholar. Anyone looking at his statue would consider him a Muslim, an Arab, an oriental gentleman, but not a Christian.

Many European students who went to Spain for studies in those days normally adopted the Arab dress perhaps to conform to the local scene. During his academic life Michael Scot also wore the Arab dress and sported a Muslim style trimmed beard. He continued wearing the Arab dress at the court of Emperor Frederick who, like his predecessors, patronised many learned Arab courtiers and was himself fond of Arab dress and culture. Perhaps Michael Scot's statue was made with a beard and turban to present him as he was and to appreciate and emphasise the influence of Muslim culture upon him. Whatever the motive of those who were behind the designing of his statue, in the anti-Islam ambience of those days, it was a daring act, indeed it would have been considered blasphemy if such a statue had been put in a church or an abbey anywhere else in Europe. The clergy and the elders at Melrose of that time must have been very brave, indeed very broad minded, tolerant and enlightened people. However, it was very disappointing to learn that among the citizens of Scotland he is only known as 'The Wizard', and not as the famous philosopher. 'The Wizard' comes from his extensive knowledge and his writings on astrology, alchemy, occult sciences and of course his reputation: 'Throughout Europe, all the way back to Scotland, people believed he could see the future and part mountains'.[68]

---

[68] Bruce, Duncan A. *The Scottish One Hundred* p.293

He was considered a great magician and there are many tales of his magic feats:

> He used to feast his friends with dishes brought by spirits from the royal kitchens of France and Spain and other lands. On an embassy to France he brought the French monarch to his knees by the stampede of his horse's hoof, the first ringing the bells of Notre Dame and the second causing the towers of the palace to fall.[69]

It is probable that some other unknown Scottish students would also have gone to those famous educational institutions in Spain for studies before Michael Scot and returned with knowledge and Islamic influences. After Scot, however, there was another Scottish literary genius, John Duns Scotus (1265-1308) who came under the influence of Muslim philosophers. Born in Duns, Berwickshire, around 1265, Duns Scotus received his early education in Scotland and then like Michael Scot moved on to Oxford and from there to Paris. On his return after four years from Paris, he was ordained in the Church of St Andrew at Northampton. A couple of years later he went back to France where he studied in Paris under 'the master' Gonsalvus of Spain and received his doctorate in 1300.[70] Coming from Spain 'the master' Gunsalvus would have been a scholar of the sciences and philosophies expounded by the famous Muslim philosophers of his native land. It was under Gonsalvus of Spain, during his second term in Paris, that Duns Scotus studied the works of Muslim philosophers, especially of *Ibn Sina*, and became deeply influenced by him. In fact, no other European philosopher came under such profound influence of *Ibn Sina* as Duns Scotus. He admired every thing *Ibn Sina* had written except anything that he considered might conflict with his faith. Norman Daniel states:

> Scotus has also been said to separate philosophy from theology, in that, too, like *Ibn Sina*; and his well known emphasis on the will of God, as distinct from the natural law, can be seen as parallel to normal Islamic doctrine: 'There

---

[69] *Encyclopaedia Britannica* Vol.20 p.138
[70] Bruce, Duncan A. *The Scottish One Hundred* p.295

is no cause why the will (of God) wills (this particular thing) except that the will is the will.'[71]

Duns Scotus died at Cologne in 1308. In a rather short life of only forty three years, he became a renowned metaphysician, a great logician and a successful debater. On account of his dialectical ingenuity and wit he acquired the distinctive title of Doctor *Subtilis*. *Encyclopaedia Britannica* calls him 'the greatest medieval British philosopher and theologian'. He was beatified by Pope John Paul II in 1993 nearly seven hundred years after his death.[72]

By the beginning of the thirteen century, Arabic learning had become popular among some of the secular and spiritual elite in medieval Britain. Many academics believed that the mastery of Arabic was essential for the advancement of knowledge. Roger Bacon (1214-1294) had learned Arabic and his knowledge of Arabic texts was unparalleled by anyone outside Spain. He was so dazzled by the fathomless store of knowledge available in that language that he wanted to reform the current old and rigid curriculum of the schools not only in England but also throughout Christendom. One of the main things he wanted to be included in the new curriculum was the study of languages especially Arabic in order to make Arabic studies available to ordinary people in the schools. Roger Bacon sought the help of the Pope in this matter and pleaded with him to introduce Arabic language as part of the curriculum of education in Christendom.[73]

However, neither the Pope nor many in Britain took Roger Bacon seriously until the late sixteenth and seventeenth centuries, when academics suddenly realised that they had lagged behind the rest of Europe in the study of Arabic and Islam. Though the value of the Arabic legacy to some extent was acknowledged and the Arabic language was studied at Oxford and Cambridge, the importance that the learning of Arabic deserved was only recognised when in 1630, the chairs of Arabic were established in both these universities. From the beginning of the seventeenth century therefore, academics and scholars began to take much more interest in Arabic

---

[71] *The Arabs and Medieval Europe* p.304

[72] Bruce, Duncan A. *The Scottish One Hundred* p.295

[73] Burnett, Charles *The Introduction of Arabic Learning into England* pp.77&79

and Islamic studies. Some even began corresponding with their friends in Arabic. The interest to learn Arabic spread also among the common people and a grocer in London is reported to have learnt Arabic and become quite proficient in reading and writing it. Edward Pococke (1604-1691) wrote poems in Arabic to celebrate the Restoration of Charles II in 1660 and to mourn the death of Prince Henry in the same year.[74] Pococke also translated some important Arabic works of Muslim philosophers. A complete edition of the Arabic history of Barhebraeus (*Abu'l-Faraj*, 1226-1286) was his masterpiece. His son Edward Pococke Jr translated the twelfth century famous allegorical tale *Hayy ibn Yazqan,* by the Spanish Muslim scholar *Ibn Tufayl,* under the title *The Self taught Philosopher*, which became a bestseller in seventeenth century Europe.

William Bedwell (1563-1632) wrote the first book ever to be published in Britain on the *Quran*. It was only a list of the chapters of the *Quran,* but it was a beginning. The title of the Book was: *Index Assuratarum Muhammedici Alkorani, That is, A Catalogue of the Chapters of the Turkish Alkoran*. That was followed by the translation of the full text of the *Quran* in English, in 1649, by a Scotsman, Alexander Ross (1592-1654): *The Alcoran of Mahomet, Translated out of Arabique into French; By the Sieur Du Ryer, Lord of Malezair, and Resident for the King of France, at Alexandria*. This was the first ever translation of the *Quran* in English, though rather poor, available to the British readers until the translation by George Sale in 1734.[75] These developments stimulated more interest in the legacy of Arabic not only among academics and in the universities but also in the ordinary people of Britain, some of whom became interested in learning the language.

> Meanwhile the writings of Rosicrucians, alchemists and astrologers, as well as in the controversies of English and Scottish clerics and in the curriculum of pupils. . . Arabic texts, names and cultural imports continually appeared.[76]

In the sixteenth and seventeenth centuries, Scottish and English academics valued the benefits of Arabic learning to traders, travel-

---

[74] Matar, Nabil *Islam in Britain* pp.84-85

[75] *ibid* p.73

[76] *ibid* p.84

lers, statesmen and scholars alike. The sixteenth century academic Robert Wakefield applauding Muslim philosophers and scientists and emphasising the importance of the knowledge contained in the Arabic language states:

> There were wonders in Arabic. . . only by mastering Arabic could Christians penetrate the secrets of Aramaeans and the Arabs.[77]

Arguably it was the knowledge acquired from the Arabs that contributed to and brought about the European Renaissance. However, few Western scholars have acknowledged or given due credit to the Arabs/Muslims for their tremendous contribution towards the awakening of Europe. The renowned Scottish scholar Prof. the Rev. William Montgomery Watt states:

> In speaking of Arab achievements in science and philosophy the important question to ask is: how far were the Arabs mere transmitters of what the Greeks had discovered and how far did they make original contribution? Many European scholars seem to approach the subject with some prejudice against the Arabs. Even those who praise them do so grudgingly. The writer of the chapter on 'Astronomy and Mathematics' in *The Legacy of Islam* (Barron Cara de Vaux) felt compelled to begin by disparaging the Arabs. A moment later, however, he goes on to . . . conclude that 'the Arabs have really achieved great things in science; they taught the use of ciphers (sc. Arabic numerals), although they did not invent them, and thus became the founders of the arithmetic of the everyday life; they made algebra an exact science and developed it considerably and laid the foundations of analytical geometry; they were indisputably the founders of plain and spherical trigonometry, which, properly speaking, did not exist among the Greeks. In astronomy they made a number of valuable observations.[78]

Over and above acquiring scientific and other knowledge from Muslims, Europeans also learnt a lot about architecture, in gracious living, in music and many other fields. The ideas of using carpets for home insulation, providing public baths and public libraries,

[77] *ibid* p.83

[78] Watt, W.M. *Influence of Islam on Medieval Europe* p.30

the concepts of making cameras and flying with wings and rockets all came from the Muslim world. Muslims introduced many improvements and refinements in building techniques in Europe and many words used today in the art of architecture are of Arabic origin. The order of different courses followed and dishes served even today in banquets at most formal occasions come from Muslim Spain. In music the Muslims especially of Spain, invented and improved many music instruments.

> Seville was noted for the production of musical instruments and Arabic names of lute, guitar, rebec and naker suggest that these came to Europe from the Arabs.[79]

From the second half of the fourteenth century, as most of the Arabic sciences and literature had been translated into Latin and other European languages and more and more opportunities to learn in their own countries became available, the traffic of scholars from other European countries to Spain and other Muslim countries slowed down. The Scots also from then on, instead of going to Spain to satisfy their thirst for knowledge, went to universities in England, and some even further afield to France and Italy. However, this state of affairs led to certain concerns among the Scottish Church leaders who were afraid that Scottish students might pick up 'certain heresies' from those foreign universities. Therefore, 'as a means of preventing Scottish students being contaminated by the heresies, the first Scottish university was established at St Andrews in 1413. This was followed by the founding of Glasgow University in 1451 and King's College Aberdeen in 1495.[80]

At this time, there were still some adventurers who were keen enough to travel into Muslim lands to look and learn. In the mid-sixteenth century James Bonaventure Hepburn, a Scot, travelled through the vast Turkish and Persian Empires. On his return, on account of his knowledge of oriental people and their languages, he was appointed the librarian of the extensive Vatican collection of Arabic and other oriental books and manuscripts. It appears that unfortunately he did not leave any record of his travels. In the

---

[79] Watt, W.M. *ibid* pp.24-25

[80] Donnachie, Ian and Hewitt, George *Dictionary of Scottish History* p.343

early seventeenth century, another Scottish intellectual George Strachan of the Mearns went on a journey seeking knowledge and learning languages to Turkey, Syria, Lebanon and the Holy Land. He first went to Istanbul in late 1613. In August 1614 he left Istanbul for the Levant. He stayed in the Holy Land for about six years where he not only learnt the languages but also collected many books, presumably in Arabic. Unfortunately he did not return to Scotland as he died during his sojourn in the Holy Land.[81] Most probably, his collection of books did arrive in Scotland.

William Lithgow was another Scottish adventurous traveller of the seventeenth century, who visited many Muslim countries bringing back information that he recorded as *The Total Discourse of the Rare Adventures and Painful Peregrinations of Long Nineteen Years from Scotland to the Most Famous Kingdoms in Europe, Asia and Africa*. He was born in Lanark, in about 1582. His father was a burgess of Lanark. He was educated at the local grammar school and trained as a tailor. According to some reports he was forced to embark upon his peregrinations because of his fears for his safety arising from a feud he had developed with a powerful local family. He began his travels from the Shetlands and Orkney islands. That was followed in 1608, by his journey to the Netherlands, Germany and France. From France in March 1609, he set out for the Muslim lands of Turkey, Syria, Palestine and Egypt, via Italy and Greece. From Egypt, he travelled to North African countries from where he returned to Scotland by way of Malta, Italy and Eastern Europe. He states that during his travels through the Muslim lands he wore Muslim dress and donned a turban as is obvious from the engraving that is included in the account of his journey.

William Lithgow's last journey was to be in quest of the legendary Emperor Prestor John in Abyssinia, but on his way, the Spanish police detained and arrested him at Malaga, as a suspected British spy. The Spanish Inquisition tormented and tortured him breaking many of his bones leaving his left arm useless. He was released with the mediation of the British Ambassador in Madrid and this once very strong and courageous adventurer came back home as a broken man. King Charles I sent him to Bath to recuperate. He published his *Rare Adventures and Painful Peregrinations* in 1632. After many other lesser adventures and publications, he died in 1654, according

---

[81] McRoberts, David *Scottish Pilgrims to the Holy Land* p.102

to local tradition at his place of birth, Lanark. He was a Protestant partisan, but a courageous man and a resourceful and an ardent traveller.

He had begun his travels to the Muslim countries from European Turkey. In his *Peregrinations*, he makes some revealing remarks about the religious tolerance and freedom for all, hospitality and civility, and lofty culture of the Turks and other Muslim nations he visited. On his way to Istanbul, he stayed for five days at Thessalonica, a town in Macedonia that he states was wholly populated and governed by the Jews – a kind of a semi autonomous Jewish state in Europe within the Turkish Empire. This was at a time when the Inquisition was raging in Spain and some other parts of Europe, where Jews were being forcibly converted to Christianity or burnt alive. Their autonomy in a city-state and freedom to practise and promote their religion was yet another example of Muslim tolerance towards other faiths. Lithgow describes this little Jewish haven as follows:

> Thessalonica is a pleasant, large and magnificent city; full of all sorts of merchandise, and it is nothing inferior in all things unto Naples in Italy. . . This city is now converted in a university for the Jews, and they are absolute signiors thereof under the great Turk, with a large territory lying without and about them. It hath been ever in their hands since Selman [Suleiman I] took in Buda in Hungary, anon 1516, They speak here the Hebrew tongue, man, woman and child. All their priests are bred here, and from hence dispersed to their several stations.[82]

From Macedonia and Greece, he went to Crete that was then under the Venetians. He observed that the Venetians employed 12,000 well armed soldiers on that island to defend it from the Turks and also to prevent the inhabitants from rebelling against their rule. He states that this was because the people of Crete preferred Turkish rule to living under the Venetians, as they levied heavy taxes upon them and imposed many restrictions on their freedom. They considered that under the Turkish rule they will

---

[82] Phelps, Gilbert ed. *The Rare Adventures and Painful Peregrinations of William Lithgow* p.76

'have more liberty, and (be) less taxed under the infidel than now they are under the Christian'.[83]

Lithgow stayed in Istanbul for three months with the British Ambassador Sir Thomas Glover. He states that the secretary of the Ambassador in Istanbul was one of his compatriots, a Scot named Master James Rollock. He describes with some accuracy some of the religious and cultural customs and tradition of the Turks that he witnessed during his stay. However, his account of Islam and the life of the Prophet of Islam is blatantly pejorative based on the biased and totally false representations current in Europe since the time of the Crusades. During his stay in Turkey and other Muslim countries, he observed the religious and social ways of the Muslims and recorded them as he saw them but he did not bother to enquire deeper into the beliefs and practices of Islam or read about them. Hence, he repeats many common European myths such as that Muslims 'worship Mahomet' etc. However, he brought back some useful new information pertaining to the Islamic world and he asserts that all and everyone living under the 'Great Turk' is free to follow his particular religion.

He is very appreciative and grateful for the Turkish hospitality offered to him everywhere he went and applauds the policy of religious tolerance practised throughout the Turkish Empire. During his sojourn in the Levant, he visited Tripoli, Aleppo, Damascus, Nazareth, and Jerusalem. He was impressed at what he witnessed in Aleppo and amazed at finding out about their 'airmail' i.e. pigeon post:

> The city is called Aleppo of Alep, which signifieth milk, whereof there is a great plenty here. There are pigeons brought up here as after an incredible manner, who will fly between Aleppo and Baghdad, being thirty days' journey distant in forty-eight hours, carrying letters and news, which are tied about their necks, to merchants of both towns and from one to another, who only are employed in the time of hasty and needful intendements (undertakings). There education to this tractable expedition is admirable, the flights and arrivals of which I have often seen in the time of my

---

[83] *ibid* p.58

[84] *ibid* pp.119-120

wintering in Aleppo, which was the second winter after my departure from Christendom.[84]

Having visited all the holy sites in the Holy Land William Lithgow left for Cairo on Palm Sunday 1612. He shows great stamina, physical strength and courage during his journeys. Lithgow was robbed and beaten up many times by robbers and brigands on the roads in the Levant countries and in Europe. Nonetheless, where most of his companions succumbed to diseases and attacks from brigands, he survived. Also, he was honest enough to admit that whenever an occasion arose he did not desist from robbing others, dead or alive but mostly dead, i.e. his French companions on the road to Cairo and the two dead Italian barons, who had killed themselves in a duel. Writing about Cairo he says: 'This incorporate world of Grand Cairo, is the most admirable and greatest city seen upon the earth'.[85] The city, he says, is 28 miles in length and 14 miles in width and it is thrice as large as Constantinople and similarly so populous. Writing about the River Nile, he wanders off into the legend of Prestor John and states that to stop that monarch from blocking the flow of water in the river that runs through his country of Ethiopia, 'the Great Turk is enforced to pay yearly the tribute of fifty thousand sultans of gold to Prestor John'.[86]

After staying in Cairo for twelve days Lithgow moved on to Alexandria and from there to Malta where he met his compatriot William Douglas (already mentioned in a previous chapter), a Knight of the Hospitallers. From Malta he travelled to Sicily and then to Naples, where he met another two of his countrymen, the Earl of Bothwell and Captain George Hepburn. His next stop was Rome, from where he went to Paris and from Paris he came back to London where he presented many relics he brought from the Holy Land to King Charles and Queen Anne.

On his second peregrination, Lithgow first travelled through various countries of Europe and arrived in Malta from where he took a ship to Tunis. In Tunis, he met with many expatriate Scots and Englishmen, who had converted to Islam, including Captain Ward, once a great British commander and pirate at sea. Ward had embraced Islam, as mentioned earlier, and joined the Turkish fleet

---

[85] *ibid* p.170

[86] *ibid* pp.177-178

fighting against the Venetians and the Knights of Malta. The Turks had endowed upon him honours and riches. In 1615, Lithgow visited him in his palatial home in Tunis. Lithgow developed a friendship with Ward and was impressed by his status, his riches and his lifestyle as a Muslim in Tunis. From Tunis Lithgow travelled to Algiers in twelve days where he observed the women wearing 'abundance of bracelets on their arms and rings in their ears'. They coloured the nails of their hands and feet red with henna. The Berber men he found to be the best archers and equestrians in all of Africa, who take 'great pleasure in breeding of their barbs (Barbary horses)'.

From Algiers, accompanied by a French traveller, in seven days Lithgow travelled to Fez in Morocco. Morocco was not part of the Turkish Empire but he is immensely impressed by the advanced civilisation of Morocco where he was received with as much kindness, respect and hospitality as anywhere in the Turkish Empire. About Fez he remarks:

> Truly this is a world for a city, and may rather second Grand Cairo. . . The citizens here are very modest and zealous at their divine services, but great dancers and revellers on their solemn festival days. . . The Moors in time past of Fez and Morocco had diverse excellent personages, well learned and very civil, for among the kings Mahometans one cannot praise too much Kings Almansor, Maunon and Hucceph, being more excellent men in their superstition, in whose time flourished the most famous medicines and philosophers that were among the pagans: as Avicenna, Rasis, Albmazar, Averroes etc., with other great numbers maintained by the kings of Morocco, that then were masters of all Barbry and Spain – as in Spain may be seen yet (though now fallen in decay) a great number of colleges, showing they were great lovers of their religion and doctrine, and are so to this day. . .[87]

He singles out the four Muslim cities of Constantinople, Cairo, Aleppo and Fez, as the best and the finest he has seen in his lifetime. After seventeen days stay at Fez, Lithgow left for further adventure into the Sahara. Wandering in the Sahara for some days and

---

[87] *ibid* p.211

suffering from heat, hunger and thirst he came back to Tunis from where he went to Malta and then Sicily in August 1616. At Messina in Sicily he met another of his countrymen, Mr Wood. Here he also met Sir Francis Verney of an old and distinguished family of Buckinghamshire who had converted to Islam. Lithgow in his narration is vile to 'Papists' as well as, sometimes, to Muslims. From Italy and through Eastern Europe, satisfying his curiosities for visiting as many places as possible, holy as well as mundane, he went to Austria, Hungary, Poland where he met another countryman William Bailey from Clydesdale, a merchant who brought Lithgow to Danzig in a wagon. From Danzig he went to London via Stockholm. He says he had been drinking coffee during his travels in the Muslim World and on his return, he describes with zest the pleasure of coffee drinking. He must have been one of the first Britons to consume and get used to coffee, as coffee was not introduced into England until 1643. In Tunis, he had witnessed the artificial incubation of eggs and brought back this new and important information to Britain and Europe. All the information he brought back, especially about the Scots and Englishmen converted to Islam and living in Muslim countries, the coffee drinking, the pigeon post, the artificial incubation of eggs etc., must have been of much interest to people in Britain. However, his thirst for travel and his longing to satisfy his curiosity about the strange and far-off lands made him embark upon his third but fatal peregrination.

On his last voyage, William Lithgow intended to unravel the secrets of the legendary domain of Prester John, who had been occupying the imagination of European Christians since about the twelfth century. This legendary figure was supposed to be a powerful Christian sovereign of a vast empire somewhere in the East, who was going to come to the aid of European Christian rulers against the Muslims. At first it was presumed that his empire was in India, then it was in central Asia and in the thirteenth century it was moved to Africa. As Ethiopia was the only country in Africa known to be Christian it was presumed in Europe that Prester John was its ruler. This legend was circulating in Europe for about the last three to four centuries and William Lithgow was determined to unravel it. This time he begins his journey from Ireland. He berates the Irish and their religion and departs for Spain where he visits Granada and praises the citadel and Alhambra 'excelling far any modern industry whatsoever'. He moves on to Malaga, where as mentioned before, he is arrested, imprisoned, tortured and after a much suffering released. He returns home in a bad state with many bones crushed and one arm broken. That was the end of the Peregrinations of William Lithgow and perhaps a blessing in disguise.

He was saved from a huge disappointment, because the legendary Prester John and his kingdom in Ethiopia was a myth without any historical existence whatsoever. It is possible though that this myth was woven round a Mongol prince who was rumoured in Europe, to have embraced Christianity in the mid thirteenth century. This was the time when the Crusaders were under immense pressure from the Turks in the Holy Land and it was hoped that this Christian prince would come to the aid of the Crusaders. Perhaps, like many other myths created by the Christian clerics during the Crusades period, this also was fabricated to give the hope of help to the Crusaders against the Muslims, and to raise the morale of the Christian masses, in order to motivate them to join the Crusades.

Another British traveller Henry Blount, who travelled through the Levant and Egypt, about twenty years after Lithgow, also eulogises the sophisticated culture and customs of the Muslim people. He too, emphasises the tolerance, courtesy, friendliness and religious devotion of the Turks and Muslims in general. About the population and size of 'Grand Cairo', he confirms Lithgow's observations that the circumference of city was about thirty five to forty miles and its population was enormous. He adds that he, with a Venetian companion, wandered in the major streets of the city, found its buildings majestic and its streets thronged with people.[88]

Blount also in his travelogue, like Lithgow, narrates many similar misconceptions and fictitious tales about the Muslim religion. Nonetheless, concerning their respect and politeness towards strangers he says that he had never come across people more civil and courteous than the Turks. When they meet someone on the road, may it be a friend or a stranger, they 'bow down and putting their right hand upon their chest salute that person by saying *Salaum Aleek*' [The usual Muslim salutation meaning peace be with you]. About the behaviour of Muslim seamen, Blount travelled with, he records:

---

[88] Blount, Henry *A Voyage into the Levant* pp.40&43

The strangest thing I found among the Turkish Mariners, was their incredible civilitie; I who had often proved the *Barbarisme* of other nations at Sea, and above all others, our owne, supposed myself amongst, till by experience, I found the contrary; and that not only in ordinary civility, but with so ready service, such a patience, so sweet and gentle a way, generally through them all, as made me doubt, whether, it was a dreame, or real; if at any time I stood in their way, or encombred their ropes, they call me with a Janum, or Benum. [dearest] Terms of most affection, and that with an encline, a voyce and gesture so respective, as assured me, their other words (which I understood not were of the same straine. . .[89]

There were certainly many more Scottish travellers, traders, soldiers and sailors, especially in the sixteenth and seventeenth centuries, who during their respective careers and adventures lived in or visited Muslim countries but who have not left any records. Nonetheless, the fact remains that since the seventh century the Scots have had varied contacts with Muslims and Islamic culture and many Scots, males and females, especially in the Middle Ages, ended up in the Muslim countries. Strangely, though, during the same period, there are no records, no tales, and not even any myths about Muslim traders, adventurers, diplomats or even slaves coming to or visiting Scotland, although there would have been some.

Although Turkish and North African travel activity did reach Scotland. . . there are no records of Muslim refugees, merchants or Ambassadors.[90]

Also, while there are records of many British women, including Scottish, living in Muslim countries, not only through slavery and piracy but also through marriage, no Muslim women appears to have ever come to or been brought to Britain, especially Scotland until the nineteenth century. The Scots throughout the Middle Ages, through the factual and fictitious tales of their returning pilgrims, crusaders and adventurers, were aware of Muslim culture and the

---

[89] Blount, Henry p.75

[90] Matar, Nabil *Turks Moors and Englishmen in the Age of Discovery* p.39

Muslim world. On the other hand, as there were no obvious Muslim visitors to Scotland, the Muslim world, except the academics and scholars, during the Middle Ages, would have remained somewhat ignorant about the Scots and Scottish culture, excepting of course, the tidbits they would have heard from Scottish traders, captives or converts.

However, the age of Europeans learning from the Islamic sources had come to a close. The lure of Islamic civilisation, the charm of its culture, the splendour of its cities like Cairo, Istanbul, Fez and Granada was diminishing fast. By the fifteenth century, the Islamic civilisation and its knowledge, having reached its zenith, had turned into a state of stagnation. Muslim domination of the world was approaching its final stages. The reason for this downward trend was that the Muslims had forgotten their religious duty of the quest for knowledge. They were less open and they had withdrawn from intellectual receptivity. They were not even updating the sciences and knowledge their ancestors had developed and bestowed upon them. They were not keeping up with the times. They had become too confident and too proud of their heritage. Their knowledge and especially their domination of the world and their wealth had made them complacent and arrogant. They were not as humble, as tolerant and as broad minded now, as were their forefathers, who had the hunger and humility to go to and sit at the feet of Greek, Persian, Chinese, and Indian scholars, wherever they found them, to seek knowledge and avidly learn from them. On the contrary, the myopic Muslim theologians from the fifteenth century onwards began to discourage Muslims from learning European languages or even seeking knowledge outwith the Islamic world. Some of them, like the Christian clerics of the early Middle Ages, became so narrow minded that they began deterring Muslims from pursuing any knowledge that was outside the ambit of their religion.

> In the fifteenth and sixteenth centuries. . . there was a reluctance to embrace novelty, a sort of cultural failure of nerve. This withdrawal from intellectual receptivity is the more curious because it was coincident with the immense burst of confidence born of military triumph and political expansion, not only the West of the Dar al-Islam, but also. . .

to the East in the shape of the Mogul Empire in India. Why was it that the scholars and scientists of the Ottoman period were less open, less adventurous, than their counterpart of the Abbasid age? It is a question that has never convincingly been answered.[90]

Hence, along with the loss of knowledge they also lost their concepts of values. Such narrow minded and indeed, un-Islamic attitudes brought about the stagnation of the Muslim power and civilisation followed by its deterioration and eventual collapse before the end of the eighteenth century. Europeans on the other hand, after learning from the Muslims, were now updating, refining and advancing that knowledge far beyond the bounds of the Muslim scientists and scholars. By the end of the seventeenth century, therefore the Europeans had revolutionised their sciences and technology. All this became a catalyst for the great Industrial Revolution that in the eighteenth and nineteenth centuries led to the domination of Europe first over the Muslim Empires of the Turks, the Persians and the Mughals and then the whole Muslim world.

The Europeans had got all they needed from the Muslims by the end of the fourteenth century. The roles had reversed by the seventeenth century. The European learners by now had turned into the learned and the flow of learners was bound to adjust in due course from the Muslim East to the Christian West, as it did in the nineteenth century. Henceforth, it was not the European students who travelled to and through the Muslim world to seek knowledge and experience its splendour. It was, first the European traders and then, the soldiers and sailors who went to seek conquests, occupy and dominate the Muslim lands. As long as knowledge was the high agenda of the Muslims they dominated the world, especially Europe, but when they neglected knowledge they became dominated by more knowledgeable Europeans.

---

[90] Fletcher, Richard *The Crescent and the Cross* p.151

Abdul Karim arrived from India at Balmoral in 1877, recruited perhaps to give a touch of India to the royal household after the proclamation of Queen Victoria as the Empress of India. He was educated and intelligent and began as a waiter to the Queen who was so impressed by him that she promoted him to be her *munshi*, i.e. teacher of the Hindustani language. The Queen became so fond of her Muslim teacher, that in 1890 she engaged Von Angeli, the famous painter of the period to paint his portrait. In 1894, *Abdul Karim* was promoted to the office of Indian Secretary to the Queen and soon after made a Companion of the Order of the Indian Empire. To reward her trusted Indian Secretary even more Her Majesty wrote to her Viceroy in India to make a suitable grant of land to him.

However, the honours and high social status granted to an Indian created jealously and ill will towards him in royal circles and the India Office. In that atmosphere of racial superiority and rampant racism, during the heyday of the Empire, British courtiers and high ranking civil servants could not tolerate a black man from a subject race being given the same status in the royal court and treated as equal. (see p 191ff)

CHAPTER 4

British Empire and Islam

T HE spread of British influence in the world, especially the Muslim world, beginning with the seventeenth century, increased the contacts between Scotland and Islam and the Muslims.

By the end of the seventeenth century, the Muslim empires that had dominated the world, were in a state of decadence. They had closed their eyes and ears to the progress of the outside world. The Europeans were now surpassing them in every field of endeavour. Their erstwhile superiority complex was preventing Muslims from even noticing the advances being made by Europeans in all fields of human activity. Having dominated them for centuries, in their arrogance, they considered the Europeans and their knowledge inferior to theirs. They were unwilling to bend with the wind of change and learn and adopt new ideas, innovations and inventions. For example, when in the late fifteenth century the printing press was introduced into Europe, Muslims of the Ottoman Empire were forbidden to learn or adopt that beneficial and efficacious technology. The Ottoman religious leaders decreed that printing the *Quranic* text on a printing press would be a blasphemy and on their recommendations, the Ottoman Sultan Selim I (r 1512-1521) 'issued a decree which threatened any Muslim who attempted to learn the science of printing with the death penalty'.[1]

Similarly, in India, when the British were building their Empire on the ruins of the Mughal Empire during the eighteenth century and encouraging Indians to learn English, the Muslim religious leaders decreed that for a Muslim to learn the English language would be a profanity, a sacrilegious act. When in the nineteenth century a Muslim reformer *Syed Ahmed Khan* actively promoted the learning of English language and Western knowledge and sciences some Muslim religious leaders declared him an apostate. Thus,

---

[1] Fletcher, Richard *The Cross and the Crescent* p.150

the Muslims during these crucial times ignored the fact that their ancestors, who had laid the foundations of their excellence in knowledge and their resulting greatness, had acquired that knowledge from the Christian Greeks, the Syrian Jews, the fire worshipping Persians and the Hindu Indians. Indeed, Muslims of the late Medieval Age and later period disregarded and ignored the numerous exhortations of the *Quran* and their Prophet concerning the seeking of knowledge.

The result of this absurd pride and negligence or complacency was that Muslims began to suffer from military and intellectual decline and within a couple of hundred years lost their influence and their ascendancy of the world. On the other side, the Western nations that had learned from the Muslims were moving forward at a fast pace and continually adding to their intellectual and military might. By the end of the eighteenth century, therefore, European influence and domination had spread to all the disintegrating Muslim Empires in the world. The once mighty empires of the Mughals in India, *Safvis* in Persia, and the Ottomans in the Middle East and Europe were fast falling under the might of the British, the Dutch, the Portuguese and the French armies and adventurers.

As British influence spread so did the involvement of Scots in the Muslim world. British colonial rule in the Muslim countries beginning in the eighteenth century provided many opportunities for the Scots as traders and administrators but mostly as soldiers in the British forces of conquest and occupation.

> Within the imperial relationship the Scots could feel that they were the peers of the English. Not only that, but the Scots had been conspicuously successful as Empire builders.[2]

Indeed, it was mostly Scottish regiments that were in the forefront of subjugating Egypt, Sudan, Kenya, Zanzibar, Nigeria, Ghana, India, Malaya, all Muslim countries. Thus as the saying goes, the Scots conquered the Empire and the English ruled it. The Scots therefore, at this stage began their everyday contacts with Islam and the Muslim people in all those countries.

The most important and lasting contacts however, were those between the Scots and the Muslims of India. That was where the

---

[2] Devine, T.M. *The Scottish Nation, 1700-2000* pp.289-90

Scots came across the rich and sophisticated culture of the Muslim nobility and the fading rulers of the decaying vast Indian Mughal Empire. These connections had commenced as early as the beginning of the seventeenth century when in 1603, a couple of years after the founding of the East India Company, the Union of the Crowns of Scotland and England came into effect and widened the scope for broader Scottish international contacts. To protect the trading interests of Britain King James IV of Scotland, who under the Union of Crowns was now also James I of England, established diplomatic relations with Mughal rulers of India, in 1615. Sir Thomas Row was appointed the first resident Ambassador of Britain at the court of Mughal Emperor Jahangir (r. 1605-1627) at Agra. This was most probably, the first official or diplomatic contact between Scotland and the Indian sub continent that was to lead to a long and eventful relationship between the two countries with different cultures and diverse customs.

This initial contact led many British soldiers, adventurers and traders, English and Scottish, to India, which at that time was famous for its fabulous riches. The Mughal Emperors welcomed the European gunners into their armies and especially those who knew the art of casting guns. The Emperors Shah Jahan (r. 1627-58) and Aurangzeb (r. 1659-1707) each had over one hundred European gunners in their service. The name of one of the master gunners was Reuben Smith; he may have been a Scotsman. The personal guard of the Emperor Muhammad Shah (r. 1719-48) consisted of seventy Europeans.[3]

Under the British flag, Scottish ships began to venture beyond the countries with which they so far had been dealing and trading. Noticing the success of the East India Company that was an English concern with no shareholders from Scotland and no commitment to employ Scots, some Scottish businessmen in the early part of the seventeenth century tried to set up a rival Scottish East India Company. However, under severe opposition from London, this idea was abandoned and the Scots began to cement their connections with the East India Company. The situation changed after the Treaty of Union in 1707, when more and more Scots, highborn and lowborn, began to seek employment for service in India as civil servants, soldiers, or clerks with the East India Company. The

---

[3] Grey, C. *European Adventurer in Northern India* pp.3-4

wages of the soldiers and other minor employees were very low, about £1.50 a month. Even this rather meagre wage attracted many poor Scots, and those with no prospects at home, to join the Company's service. 'Most recruits were drawn from distressed areas of Britain, Scotland and the countryside of England. . .'[4]

The poor wages of the soldiers however, more than often, were compensated with their share of plunder and booty after battles and wars in which British forces, with few exceptions, always had an upper hand. The number of Scots in the service of the East India Company, therefore, began to grow fast and by the middle of the eighteenth century, they had secured far more jobs than their fair share:

> That the Union should bear such tangible results was anyway a concern of the Prime Minister, Sir Robert Walpole. He put a fair share of Indian appointments the Scots way. Given their clannishness, it soon became better than a fair share. By 1750, they took up to 30 percent of posts in Bengal, later under Warren Hastings sometimes more. Henry Dundas, presiding over Indian administration at the end of the century, may even out of political prudence have cut the number somewhat.[5]

By the last quarter of the eighteenth century, the proportion of Scots in the service of the East India Company in India had increased to nearly 50 per cent. In the province of Bengal, the richest of the Company's possessions, in the 1770s and 1780s, 47 per cent of the Writers, 49 per cent of the officer cadets and more than 50 per cent of the assistant surgeons were Scots. In Madras, in the first half of the eighteenth century, all the Principal Medical Officers were Scots. The Scots dominated the armed forces of the Company and the royal army in India.

Scottish businessmen also did very well in India. Even before the Treaty of Union, under the patronage of the East India Company, some of them were successfully engaged in local trade. However, their progress in commercial activities during the eighteenth century was enviable and by the end of that century,

---

[4] Hawes, Christopher p.12

[5] Fry, Michael *The Scottish Empire* p.85

Scots merchants dominated the most powerful merchant houses in Bengal and Bombay.[6] Their rivals, the English and others, denounced them for 'their clannish instincts, which, they alleged, helped them to engross the business'.[7] Hence, from the early eighteenth century, India had become the 'promised land' for the Scots where they found great opportunities and where some of them made their fortunes. Sir Walter Scot acknowledging this reality when in a letter to Lord Montague in 1821, he wrote that India was the corn chest for Scotland where the poor Scottish gentry must send their young sons as they send their black cattle to the south.[8]

In India, during the seventeenth and eighteenth centuries, the East India Company encouraged its high ranking as well as minor employees to establish contacts with the local nobility and common people. To its employees and soldiers, who could not themselves afford to bring their wives from Britain, they not only allowed but also induced to marry or establish relationships with Indian women. This was to save the Company expense for the passage of wives from Britain for their lower rank British employees and also, to develop better relations with the people of the host country, in order to get better treatment in their trade dealings.[9] Even the British Army condoned and even encouraged such liaisons of their soldiers in India.[10]

Most of the East India Company employees and soldiers therefore entered into relationships of one sort or another with any women they liked, of whatever faith or status. However, they were not allowed to take their wives or concubines and even their children back to Britain. The Scots in higher ranks and senior positions in India, who had wider social contacts with the Muslim nobles of the Mughal Empire, became enamoured with the sophisticated Mughal culture and customs. Many of them became completely 'Indianised'. They studied Persian and Urdu, the languages of the Mughal elite and adopted local customs and developed local tastes. They dressed like the Muslim nobles, smoked the *hookah* (the *hubble bubble*), enjoyed local dance and music, chewed *pan* and

---

[6] Devine, T.M. *Scotland's Empire* p.251

[7] Devine, T.M. *The Scottish Nation* p.120

[8] Cain, Alex. M. *The Corn Chest for Scotland* p.7

[9] Hawes, Christopher *Poor Relations* p.3

[10] Hawes, Christopher *ibid* p.14

betel nut, pursued sports like cock fighting, pigeon racing, hawking and hunting, drank *Ark* (Indian spirit) and enjoyed the Mughal cuisine. Some even married into noble Muslim families and converted to Islam, as conversion was a precondition for marrying into a Muslim family. These conversions with a few exceptions however, were merely as a ruse to fulfil the condition to marry into a Muslim family. On their return to Britain, most of them left their wives and their new religion behind in India. However, some brought over their children with them or managed to send them over before their return. Such children, born to Muslim mothers and brought up as Muslims during their early life in India, were baptised as soon as they arrived in Britain and brought up as Christians. To make them forget their background, their religion and ancestry from their mother's side they were denied any contact and communication with their mothers in India. All of them with rare exceptions were of very pale or very light brown colour, because their Muslim mothers, being of Turkish, Afghan or Persian origins, were themselves very pale skinned.

Thus, these children outwardly easily assimilated and soon became absorbed in the indigenous population, but mentally they would have been very disturbed or confused during and even after this traumatic transformation. The descendents of these mixed race children must be numerous in Scotland and most of them probably have no idea that they have Muslim ancestry and Muslim blood in their veins.

The first noteworthy Scot in the service of the East India Company in India was the surgeon William Hamilton of Dalzell who went there in 1711. From 1711 to 1714 he was a member of the Embassy to the court of the Mughal Muslim Emperor at Delhi. During his stay at Delhi, Hamilton successfully treated the Mughal Emperor *Farukh Siyar* for a serious infection. The Emperor was so pleased with him that he rewarded Hamilton with an elephant, a horse, five thousand rupees, two diamond rings, a jewelled aigrette, a set of gold buttons and models of all his instruments in gold. The Emperor also granted the East India Company the very profitable right of free trade in Bengal, Bihar and Orissa, the most populous and richest provinces of the Mughal Empire. Most importantly, however, the Emperor made a grant of thirty eight villages around

---

[11] Cain, A.M. *The Corn Chest for Scotland* pp.12-13

Calcutta to the Company.[11] In India, this was the first piece of land, spread over more than four hundred square miles with a population of thousands, that came under the direct possession of the East India Company. This indeed was laying the foundation stone of the building of the future British Empire in India and ironically, this foundation stone was laid by the Mughal Emperor of India himself. Thus, this Scots surgeon, William Hamilton, proved to be the greatest benefactor of his country and the Company in India, by achieving more than anyone else had until then.

From the beginning of the eighteenth century, the number of Scots in India had begun to increase at a faster rate and by the 1750s, proportionately more Scots than English were serving as army and civilian officers in India.[12] In their respective sphere of influence, they were developing friendly relationships with the Muslim nobility and contributing to the interests of the East India Company in various fields.

John McPherson, a civil servant at Madras, who was the son of a Scottish minister and a fluent speaker of Hindustani languages, acted as the ambassador of *Nawab Muhammad Ali* to King George III (r. 1760-1820) and secured for the Nawab the recognition as the lawful ruler of the rich province of Carnatic.[13]

The victor at the battle of Buxar, fought in 1764, between the Mughal Emperor *Shah Alam* and the forces of the East India Company, General Sir Hector Munroe, was from Scotland. By this significant victory, this Scotsman, in addition to other lucrative benefits, brought the Muslim Emperor of India under the direct influence of the British and the East India Company. Sir Hector was a native of Novar in Ross-shire. He returned to Scotland after making his fortune and became the Member of Parliament for Inverness. Like General Monroe many other Scots soldiers, administrators and traders made their fortunes, especially in the eighteenth century, and returned to Scotland with their riches.

After their victory at Buxar, the power and the influence of the East India Company and its employees had increased tremendously. They had absolute power over the resources and millions of people of the very populous and very prosperous areas now under their control. However, many of them abused their power, exploited the

---

[12] Devine, T.M. *The Scottish Nation* p.26

[13] Buddle, Ann *The Tiger and the Thistle* pp.12-13

local princes, oppressed the common people and extorted from them as much money as they could.

> There followed an era of scandalous oppression and exploitation of helpless natives, rich and poor, high and low. It was also a period of unscrupulous corruption and graft. With rare exceptions, everyone, from the lowly clerk to the Governor General, from the planter to the trader, and from the freebooter to the regular soldier, tried to amass as much wealth as they could by very little fair and mostly foul means.[14]

For example, John Johnstone of Westerhall and the founder of the House of Johnstone of Alva returned from India in 1765, with a fortune of £300,000, equal to perhaps more than £300 million of today. He used this wealth to buy three estates and a parliamentary seat. Peter Murray (Macgregor of Glencarnaik) brought over £200,000 and William Young (the natural son of Lord Elibank) came back with over £100,000.[15] John Faquhar topped the list of the Scots who abused power and made their fortunes in India. He grasped so much that on his return to Scotland he became one of the richest men of nineteenth century Britain and was worth £1.5 million when he died in 1826.[16] The wealth brought back from India had a rejuvenating effect on the economy of Scotland and of course Britain. This wealth played a significant role in bringing about and propelling the industrial revolution. Such was the impact of these riches that: 'A Glasgow banker believed, after the Scottish banking crisis of 1772, that . . . were two or three *nabobs* (lords) to take up their residence amongst [us] matters would soon revive.'[17]

By the late eighteenth century, Scots as soldiers, administrators and traders had become well involved in the affairs of the East India Company. More and more of the Scottish gentry were now seeking employment in India or sending their sons to carve out their futures and fortunes. Boys as young as twelve and thirteen years old were recruited as cadets and clerks and shipped to India. Many of these young cadets and clerks rose to become high-ranking

---

[14] Maan, Bashir *The New Scots* p.40

[15] Cain, A.M. *The Corn Chest for Scotland* p.14

[16] Devine, T.M. *Scotland's Empire* p.253

[17] Bryant, G.J. *The Scottish Historical Review* April 1985

soldiers and administrators. David Baird of Newbyth was one of these young Scottish boys who reached the rank of Major General and became famous as the victor of Seringapatam in 1799, and the fall of *Tipu Sultan*. Earlier, during the defeat of the British army at the battle of Pollilur in 1780, *Tipu Sultan* had captured and imprisoned him at Seringapatam. He was released from imprisonment in March 1784, under the conditions of the treaty of Mangalore, after *Tipu* had once again defeated the British forces. Nonetheless, during the fourth Mysore war in 1799, it was General Baird who with his Scottish regiments captured Seringapatam and killed *Tipu Sultan*, the most formidable and much feared enemy of the British in India.

Tipu was an innovative and ambitious Muslim ruler of Mysore, an extensive and rich state in southern India. For forty years *Tipu* and his father *Haidar Ali* had seriously undermined the British domination of India. They were the only local rulers who the British could not intimidate or tame to their advantage. *Tipu* had ascended the throne in 1782 after the death of his father and like his father, he became a serious danger to British supremacy in India. He had earned such high regard of his compatriots and the Europeans for his military power and his administrative skills that he became a legend during his lifetime. He was dreaded by his neighbouring Indian rulers as well as the British and was obsessed with maintaining his independence, protecting his dominion and destroying the dominance of British in India.[18] With his death on 4th May 1799, during the Scottish regiments' assault on Seringapatam this last obstacle to the British ascendancy in India was removed. Indeed, *Tipu* was such a formidable barrier against the British conquest of India that on seeing his dead body Lord Wellesley is reported to have shouted in exhilaration, 'today India is ours'.

In India as well as in Britain there was great rejoicing and many celebrations at the defeat and death of *Tipu Sultan* and the end of this powerful independent Muslim state of Mysore. Scotland also rejoiced, as it was the Scots soldiers who had played the most significant part in this great victory. The Scottish press of the time triumphantly reported this 'glorious victory'. In its edition of September 1799, *The Scots Magazine* published the full text of the letter of General Harris, the commander in chief of the forces fighting *Tipu Sultan*, to the Governor General of India giving him

---

[18] Buddle, Ann *The Tiger and the Thistle* p.39

details of the assault on Seringapatam and the death of *Tipu*. The same magazine in its edition of March 1800 published poems on the Ornaments of *Tipu Sultan's* throne.

However, the British press did not report the death of over 10,000 soldiers and civilians during and after the British siege and assault on Seringapatam. Nor did it report the atrocities committed upon the residents of the fallen city by the British forces and the immense plunder seized by them following their victory. The royal palace was systematically pillaged, all the jewels, every precious ornament and artefact of *Tipu Sultan* was expropriated by the victors. The commander in chief of the victorious British army, General Harris, received £150,000 as his share of the booty from Seringapatam.[19] The ornaments and artefacts looted from the palace of *Tipu Sultan* are now proudly exhibited in various Museums from Edinburgh to London and in the royal apartments at Windsor Castle. The victory at Seringapatam and especially the death of *Tipu Sultan* made a huge impact on British literature, arts and drama. Numerous paintings of the Sultan, his palaces, his treasures, the storming of Seringapatam etc., were produced and the contemporary newspapers were filled with articles about him and narratives of the Mysore wars. In drama, the impact was so great that as late as Easter Monday, April 20th 1829, this 'final triumph of British power in India' was being celebrated and staged as a theatrical drama 'Storming of Seringapatam or the Death of Tippoo Saib' in Ashley's Royal Amphitheatre, London.

Indeed, Scotland is still relishing the famous fall of Seringapatam as was evident from the celebrations in 1999, of the two hundredth anniversary of this historic victory. Part of the celebrations in Edinburgh, was an extensive exhibition displaying numerous memorabilia of *Tipu Sultan* and of the Scottish victors with many large and small paintings of the Sultan and his palaces, the assault on Seringapatam, the discovery of the body of *Tipu* and the rest. To mark this two hundredth anniversary the National Library of Scotland published a book *The Tiger and the Thistle* by Ann Buddle. This beautifully illustrated book contains the history of *Hyder Ali* and *Tipu Sultan*, but especially, the account of the fall of Seringapatam and the characters involved in it.

Some Scots like Thomas Munro, a Glasgow man, John Malcolm,

---

[19] Devine, T.M. *Scotland's Empire* p.259

son of a Borders farmer, Mountstuart Elphinstone, son of Lord Elphinstone of Elphnistone, Stirlingshire were not only good soldiers, administrators or diplomats in India but also scholars of Persian and other Indian languages. They integrated into Indian society and in their spheres of influence patronised oriental learning and Muslim traditions thus learning from and contributing to Muslim culture.

However, there were certain Scots who not only became integrated but also fully assimilated into the Muslim culture in India. Most of them married into noble Muslim families and converted to Islam because conversion and circumcision for a male were prerequisites to marrying into a Muslim family. Conversion to Islam was nothing new for the British and the other Europeans – they had been doing that since they first came into contact with Islam in the Levant and the Mediterranean. However, the fifteenth to seventeenth centuries, as has been mentioned in the previous chapter, witnessed literally thousands of Britons 'turning Turk' i.e. embracing Islam especially in the North African countries. For instance, by early 1626, there were about seven thousand British captives in just two North African cities, Algiers and Sali and the British government was busy making desperate arrangements to secure their release before they followed the example of many of their compatriots and converted to Islam.[20]

James Achilles Kirkpatrick was one of those Scots who, during his service in India, adopted the Islamic faith and went through circumcision in order to marry into a noble Muslim family of Hyderabad, Deccan. The account of his marriage and his children, born to their Muslim mother, is worth a look in some detail as it provides an in-depth study of the life style and attitudes of the British employees of East India Company in India, during the eighteenth and early nineteenth centuries. James Achilles' Jacobite grandfather was a native of Closeburn, Dumfriesshire who, after the defeat of the Jacobites in 1715, fled to Charleston, South Carolina. James' father was James Kirkpatrick who retired in 1769, as a Colonel in the Madras Cavalry of the East India Company. On his return to Britain after his retirement, the Colonel went to Hollydale, in Kent, where his father had settled in the middle of the eighteenth century after selling his plantation in Charleston.

---

[20] Dalrymple, William *White Mughals* pp.17-18

During his service in India, the colonel had married Katherine Munro a British woman and James Achilles was born to her in India on 22nd August 1764. When James Achilles was only a year and a half old his mother Katherine died and from then on Indian *Ayahs* (nurses) looked after him and his elder half brother William Kirkpatrick. William's mother was an Indian woman, with whom the colonel James Kirkpatrick had a relationship before he married Katherine Monroe. The colonel on his return from India in 1769 brought his two sons with him to Hollydale.

When James Achilles was fifteen years old, like his father, he also joined the East India Company Madras Army as a cadet and left for India. During his service in India, he learnt Persian, the Mughal court language and Urdu or Hindustani, the *lingua franca* of India. He also was fluent in Tamil, the language of his childhood *Ayahs* (nurses), and the major South Indian language. In India, like many other British officers he had developed a relationship with a *bibi*, i.e. an Indian mistress or concubine, from whom he had a son. In 1791, he came to Britain on a holiday and brought his son over to leave him with his father. His half brother William had already left his two Anglo Indian children, from an Indian *bibi*, with his father to be brought up in Britain.

James' career took a sudden turn for the better soon after William his half-brother was appointed the British Resident in Hyderabad in 1793. Hyderabad was a vast country as big as France, under a Muslim ruler *Nizam Ali Khan*. After the decline of the Mughal court at Delhi, Hyderabad, by the end of the eighteenth century, had become a powerful independent Muslim State and the repository of Muslim culture in India. It was one of the most important, if not the most important power in India with which the East India Company wanted to have good relations. Thus, for William Kirkpatrick, it was a prestigious and influential appointment. Realising James' proficiency in Persian and other Indian languages, and the fact that he was not progressing well in his career in the Army, William wrote to James inviting him to join him in Hyderabad. After nearly fifteen years of service in the army James Achilles was still a Lieutenant with no prospects of further promotion in the near future. He therefore, gladly accepted this invitation, obtained his transfer from the army to diplomatic service and in early 1795 joined the staff of his brother.

Promotion was unexpectedly rapid for James in his diplomatic career in Hyderabad. Within one year of his appointment at the Residency, he was promoted to the post of Deputy Resident after the sudden death of the incumbent of that office. In 1797, James was made the Acting Resident in place of his brother William who had resigned because of ill health. Thus, in just two years James had risen from an ordinary member of staff to the head of that very important British Mission. In Hyderabad during these two years, James had also done rather well diplomatically. He had developed close friendships with the local nobles and most importantly had won the confidence of the ruler who began to call him 'beloved son'. His sound knowledge of Persian and Urdu, his pleasant manner, his friendly disposition and his fondness for Muslim culture had made him very popular with the Hyderabadi aristocracy.

In Hyderabad, like many other Europeans in India, James had begun wearing Muslim dress and had adopted many other traits of the local Muslim nobles like smoking the *hookah* and dyeing his hands with *henna* (herbal red dye). He had also developed the oriental custom of visiting friends in the evening, where he played chess, or enjoyed recitation of poetry from renowned poets and indulged in idle talk. He participated in the Muslim festivals and visited and supported by donations the *Sufi* shrines of Hyderabad. He attended cockfights, flew pigeons and became fully integrated within the Muslim society of Hyderabad. Whether he had formally converted to Islam yet or not, most of the Hyderabadis considered him a practising Muslim. His friendships with the nobles of the realm and above all his adoption of their culture enhanced his trustworthiness at the court and brought many benefits to the East India Company and to Britain. The *Nizam* treated him as one of his nobles and bestowed upon him the grand titles of *Mutamin ul Mulk, Hushmut Jung* (Guardian of the State, Formidable in Battle) and *Nawab Fakhr-ud-Dowla Bahadur* (Lord Courageous Pride of the State). In Hyderabad, therefore James Achilles was better known by his title *Hushmut Jung Sahib*.

Through his close connections with the noble families of Hyderabad, James Kilparick heard about the exceptional beauty of a young girl named *Khair-un-Nisa Begum* daughter of a Muslim family, with whom he had good relations. Then on the occasion of the wedding celebrations of another lady of the same family, James and the young beauty somehow came face to face, and instantly fell in love with each other. The young lady however, was already engaged to the son of a Muslim noble of the city and that posed difficulties and many complications. To make things worse, with the connivance of her mother perhaps, but against all the norms and conventions of Muslim society, the young lady began to see James regularly. This created an unprecedented scandal in Hyderabad that immensely humiliated and shamed the family of the girl and the male members of the family became vehemently opposed to this liaison. It also led to difficulties for James Achilles, hitherto a very popular and successful British Resident in Hyderabad and in Calcutta, the seat of the Governor General of the territories of the East India Company in India. Nevertheless, such was his love for the girl and hers for him that he resolved to marry her. Though the family of the girl were very unhappy about the situation, the girl's determination to marry James eventually convinced them, or more appropriately, forced them to sanction the marriage.

However, the marriage was still impossible, as James as yet, had not formally converted to Islam and according to Islamic law until he did that he could not marry a Muslim woman. James surmounted this final hurdle by embracing Islam before a Muslim cleric in 1801 and going through his circumcision. He sent his certificate of conversion to the family of *Khair un-Nisa,* and the family gave their approval of the marriage. Then on a pre-arranged evening, James Achilles went to the house of the mother of his bride to be, and there discretely went through the Islamic ceremony of marriage with *Khair-un-Nisa Begum.* Soon after a son was born to them.

> James was in the house for the birth, and the note he wrote that night on a tiny scrap of paper still survives in the private archives of their descendants. It reads as follows: On Wednesday the 4th of March, 1801 answering to ye 10th *Shuwaul* AH 1215, at about four o' clock in the morning a son was born to me in the city of Hyderabad. His mother from a Dream she had, wishes him to be named *Meer Goolam Ali*, to which I mean to add that of *Saheb Aallum* [Lord of the World].[21]

---

[21] Dalrymple, William *White Mughals* p.259

Thirteen months later *Khair-un-Nisa* gave birth to a daughter who was named *Noor oon Nisa-Saheb Begum* (The Lady of High lineage). Both the children were brought up as Muslims, suckled by wet nurses and attended by serving girls speaking Urdu and Persian. James and his wife also conversed in Persian or perhaps Urdu, as *Khair-un-Nisa* did not know English. Thus the children grew up speaking Persian and Urdu.

However while James was enjoying the bliss of his love marriage and the delight of the company of his two young children there were ominous developments looming around him at Hyderabad and in far-off Calcutta. The Governor General and many others in the establishment naturally did not like or approve of the rumours of James' conversion to Islam, his serious liaison with a Muslim lady and his fondness of Muslim culture. Scurrilous stories began circulating in Calcutta about the Resident at Hyderabad. He was being regarded a renegade, a turncoat and his loyalty to the Company and Britain became suspect. Some of his own staff at Hyderabad, and especially the British soldiers attached to the Residency, on occasions became discourteous to him. A secret enquiry was initiated by the Governor General Lord Wellesley to investigate his conduct and his affair with *Khair-un-Nisa*. The investigation confirmed that James had married the lady in question who was living as his wife at the Residency. This was a very difficult time for James. However, considering his unprecedented diplomatic successes and achievements and his very close relations with the nobles and especially the ruler of Hyderabad, the Governor General reluctantly kept him in his job.

Nonetheless, by the middle of 1805, when he was only about forty years old James Achilles was a sick man. Perhaps the worry he suffered following the scandal about his liaison with *Khair-un Nisa*, the ugly rumours that tarnished his reputation, the investigation against him and of course the oppressive weather of Hyderabad, all added up to badly damaging his health. His doctor advised him to go on a holiday to recuperate possibly on a sea voyage. Considering the uncertain state of his health and following the trend set by his compatriots of sending their Anglo-Indian children to Britain, to be educated and brought up there, James decided to send his children to his father in Kent. Accordingly, in September 1805, against the wishes of his wife and in spite of her cries, tears and torment, James despatched aboard *Hawkesbury*, four and half years old *Meer Goolam Ali Saheb Allum* and about three and half year old *Noor oon-Nisa Saheb Begum* to his father in Britain. *Hawkesbury* sailed from Madras for England, on 9 September 1805.

The two children were travelling on the ship under their new names as Master William George Kirkpatrick and Miss Katherine Kirkpatrick. The children must have been very confused, to begin with, by suddenly being called Master William and Miss Katherine, the names they would never have heard before, in place of *Saheb Alum* and *Saheb Begum*, the names they were used to. However, without realising,

> The Lady of High lineage and the little Lord of the World
> had shed their Muslim identities as finally and conclusively
> as a snake sheds its first skin.[22]

In Calcutta there had been some changes that would prove favourable to James Achilles. Lord Wellesley had been replaced by Lord Cornwallis who upon hearing about James' in-depth knowledge of Hyderabad, summoned him to Calcutta for an urgent meeting. James left for Calcutta immediately. However, en route his health deteriorated. By the end of the journey, he was so ill that he had to be carried ashore when his ship docked on 7 October 1805. Cornwallis, the Governor General, was not in Calcutta but somewhere in Bengal where he had suddenly died.

James now seriously ill, lingered on in Calcutta for a week and on 15 October, the eighth day of his arrival, he died while in a coma. In Hyderabad, *Khair-un-Nisa* had no idea of these developments. She was still going through the torment of the separation of her dear young children. The tragic news of James' death reached her eighteeen days later.[23] Within two months, at the age of only nineteen, she had lost her children and her husband. How she took this devastating news in her already miserable condition and how she reacted to this monumental blow cannot even be imagined.

Khair-un-Nisa Begum mourned the untimely and devastating death of her beloved husband for six months with her mother in the latter's mansion,. Not emotionally satisfied with that she resolved to go and mourn at the grave of James Achilles in Calcutta.

[22] Dalrymple, William *ibid* p.396
[23] Dalrymple, William *ibid* pp.399-400

Accompanied by her mother, an educated male attendant and her ladies-in-waiting, after an arduous and long journey, the grieving widow arrived in Calcutta in May 1806. During her first two months in Calcutta, she spent most of her time wailing and weeping at the grave of her husband. Though exhausted by grief and harsh weather, in time she developed a friendship with Henry Russell. Russell had come from the Hyderabad Residency just before *Khair-un-Nisa* to perform his duties as one of the executors of James Achilles' will. Russell was a good friend of James and in Calcutta he helped and looked after *Khair-un-Nisa Begum* and her mother. As time passed *Begum* and Russell became friends and their friendship developed into intimacy. By the end of the year when Russell and *Begum* left Calcutta to return to Hyderabad, they had developed a close relationship and most probably had married.

The news of the relationship between *Khair un Nisa* and Russell, unfortunately for them, had reached Hyderabad long before their arrival. The reaction of the family of *Khair un Nisa*, the Hyderabadi nobility and the new Resident was as expected, very hostile towards both of them. The Resident, Thomas Sydenham made it explicitly clear to Russell that while in Hyderabad, he would not be allowed to have any contact with *Khair-un-Nisa*. The family felt humiliated and dishonoured by her conduct. The new Prime Minister of the State *Meer Allum*, a cousin of *Khair-un-Nisa.*, was so furious that he banned her entry into Hyderabad. With Hyderabad out of bounds for *Khair un Nisa*, Russell arranged for her to live at Masulipatam, a seaport on the eastern coast of Southern India, outside the dominions of Hyderabad, where he visited her regularly.

A little later Russell left Hyderabad, as he was posted at Madras, from where he also kept in contact with *Khair-un-Nisa* at Masulipatam. However, a year or so later Russell married an Anglo-Indian girl at Madras and ended his relationship with *Khair un Nisa*. In 1810, Russell became the Resident at Hyderabad. *Khair-un-Nisa* and her mother had come back to Hyderabad in 1809, after the death of *Meer Allum*, the Prime Minister who had denied them entry. *Khair un Nisa* and Russell did not renew their relationship or even see each other in Hyderabad. However, a couple of years later when *Khair-un-Nisa* was seriously ill, she did write to him to inform him of her imminent death. Russell arranged for her to be brought to the Residency to pass her last few days in the surroundings where, in her tragic short life, she had experienced a few years of happiness in the company of her loving husband and her two beloved, beautiful little children. These familiar surroundings with the memories of good old days would have added to her misery, as soon after moving to the Residency, she died there in September 1813, aged only 27 years. There was no obvious cause of her death. The death of her husband, no news of and no contact with her two young children made her so despairing that she gave up her miserable life.

Khair-un-Nisa's two little children had safely reached their grandfather in February 1806, about five months after leaving Madras. During their long journey to England, they would have not known that in India, their father had died. They would have learned the sad news from their grandfather, whenever he thought it fit to inform them. *Khair un Nisa*, during her short life, wrote regularly to them and their grandfather without ever receiving any reply or acknowledgement in return, as the children were strictly forbidden to correspond with their mother or her family. It would also have been harrowing for the children to find themselves in a totally alien culture, unfamiliar surroundings and being abruptly cut off from their parents at such a tender age. Nevertheless, they appear to have survived through this trauma and received their education under the affection and care of their grandfather. At age eleven a serious accident left William George disabled with at least one of his limbs requiring amputation. Nonetheless, being still active and attractive he got married at age twenty and had three girls before he died at the young age of 27.

Katherine known as Kitty Kirkpatrick grew up as a talented and beautiful girl. In 1829, when she was aged 27 years, she married a young Captain. In 1841, Kitty had a very pleasant surprise. She received news of her grandmother *Sharaf un-Nisa* (mother of *Khair-un-Nisa)* through Henry Russell who had retired from service and was now living in England. Having come to know, 28 years after her mother's death and 36 years after she had left India, that *Sharaf un-Nisa* was still alive in Hyderabad, her childhood memories came alive and she established contact with her and then: 'There followed a remarkable and extremely emotional correspondence between the two women.'[24]

---

[24] Dalrymple, William *ibid* p.490

In one of her letters, perhaps the first ever to her grandmother, apologising for not maintaining contact with her Kitty tells her about her husband, her house, her children, their ages and that her son looks exactly like her late father. Then she becomes very emotional and pores out her inner feelings, which had been suppressed for so long. For the reader to experience the true feelings of Kitty and indeed through her of many other young children of mixed marriages, separated from their mothers and brought over to Britain from India during those times, a few excerpts from her letter to her grandmother are given under:

> I often think of you and remember you and my dear mother. I often dream that I am with you in India and that I see you both in the room you used to sit in. No day of my life has ever passed without my thinking of my dear mother. I can remember the veranda and the place where the tailors worked and a place on the house top where my mother used to let me sit down and slide.

> When I dream of my mother I am in such joy to have found her again that I awake, or else am pained in finding that she cannot understand the English I speak. I can well recollect her cries when we left her and I can now see the place where she sat when we parted, and her tearing her long hair – what worlds would I give to possess one lock of that beautiful and much loved hair! How dreadful to think that so many, many years have passed when it would have done my heart so good to think that you loved me & when I longed to write to you & tell you these feelings that I was never able to express, a letter which I am sure would have been detained & now how wonderful it is that after 35 years I am able for the first time to hear that you think of me, and love me and have perhaps wondered why I did not write to you, and that you have thought me cold and insensible to such near dear ties. I thank God that he has opened for me a way of making the feelings of my heart known to you.

> Will this reach you & will you care for the letter of your grandchild? My own heart tells me you will. May God bless you my own dear Grandmother. [25]

[25] Dalrymple, William *ibid* p.491

Sharaf un-Nisa, who had at last found her long-lost grand-daughter, on receiving Kitty's letter, naturally was ecstatic. She replied promptly, with even deeper emotion and far greater delight. With her reply she also sent to Kitty a lock of the hair of *Khair un-Nisa* that Kitty had asked for and that *Sharaf un-Nisa* had kept since the death of her daughter. 'Dictating in Persian to a scribe who wrote in English on paper sprinkled with gold dust and enclosed in a *kharita* (silk bag),' in her reply she expresses her feelings as follows:

> Fresh vigour was instilled in my deadened heart and such immeasurable joy was attained by that it cannot be brought within the compass of being written or recounted. My Child, the Light of my Eyes the solace of my soul, may God grant you long life.

> After offering up my prayers that your days may be length-ened and your dignity increased, let it be known to you that at this moment, by the mercy of God, my health is excellent, and I am at all seasons praying for her welfare at the Threshold of the Almighty. Night and day my eyes are directed to my child. In compliance with what my child has written, the wife of Captain Duncan Malcolm invited me to her house and told me of the welfare of my child, and of the children of my child. Night and day my eyes are directed to my child. The letter written to me by you is pressed by me sometimes to my head and sometimes to my eyes. . . If I can procure a female artist I will send you my child my portrait. My child must send me her likeness and those of her children.

Such emotional and passionate correspondence between Kitty and her grandmother continued for about six years. Many presents, mementoes and pictures were exchanged before *Sharaf un-Nisa* died in 1847 and this tragic chapter came to an end at least for her.[26]

There are many more fascinating but not so tragic tales of love and marital affairs between the Scottish men and Muslim women

---

[26] Most of the material to write this tragic account of James Achilles Kirkpatrick and Khair-un-Nisa has been gratefully drawn from William Dalrymple's *White Mughals*

in India during the eighteenth and nineteenth centuries that can fill volumes. The tragic tale of James Achilles Kirkpatrick and *Khair-un-Nisa Begum* is only one of the many well-known cases.

Another Scot, William Gardner, a freebooter, was married to *Mah Munzel-un-Nisa Begum*, the daughter of the Muslim Nawab of Cambay. During one of his diplomatic assignments, Gardner had accidentally briefly seen the young princess and fell in love with her. He asked for her hand in marriage and after much persuasion and against the reservations of some of her relations, he succeeded in marrying her. He lived a successful and happy long life with *Mah Munzel-un-Nisa Begum* in India and one of his sons, who were brought up as Muslims, married a niece of the Mughal Emperor.[27]

Hamish McGregor McPherson turned a freebooter after deserting his Scottish regiment and in around 1829, entered the service of the Muslim ruler of Bahawalpur, a sizable state in the southwest of Punjab. There he trained and commanded a regiment of the Bahawalpur army numbering about one thousand. After converting to Islam in Bahawalpur, he married *Begum Murad Bakhsh*, the daughter of a Muslim noble of that State. There is no information about his children if he had any. He was killed in 1848, near Multan, while commanding his regiment engaged in a battle along with the East India Company forces against the Sikhs. His tomb that still exists at the village of Ahmedpur near Multan, was built by his wife, who lies beside him, and it bears the following inscription:

> Hamish McGregor McPherson of Scotland, killed in battle
> at the head of his regiment, while fighting against the Dewan
> Mool Raj, at Soddhoosam, near Multan, on the 1st July,
> 1848.[28]

Alexander Houghton Campbell Gardiner was an adventurer who left Scotland to go to the East by land. After roaming through Egypt, Palestine, Syria, Turkey and Iran, in 1808 he arrived in Afghanistan, where he entered the service of *Habibullah Khan* the former king of that country. Here he converted, married a Muslim lady and assumed the name of *Arb Khan*. After spending some years

[27] Dalrymple, William *ibid* pp.119-120

[28] Grey, C. *European Adventures of Northern India* pp.292-295

in Afghanistan and having lost his wife and son in the turbulence there, he parted from Habibullah and came to Peshawar, where he entered the service of the local chief *Sultan Muhammad Khan*, 'to whom in six months he taught the art and craft of artillery practice'. In 1832, he appeared at Lahore, at the court of *Ranjit Singh* the ruler of the Punjab and joined his armed forces as a Colonel. Here he married a Kashmiri woman and after the death of *Ranjit Singh* and the collapse of the Sikh kingdom settled in Kashmir where he died on 22 January 1877.[29]

Sir David Ochterlony, a native of Angus, was a Scot who fully assimilated into the Muslim culture of India. After a distinguished army career, he was appointed Resident at the debilitated court of the titular Mughal Emperor at Delhi. Sir David lived like and adopted all the ways of Muslim nobles. He dressed like them, smoked the *hookah* and loved the performance of the *nautch* (Indian dancing) girls. He probably had three to four wives and also kept a few concubines to each of whom he provided an elephant for transport and as a symbol of status – like a Rolls Royce in the present age. The Mughal Emperor bestowed upon him the grand title of *Nasir-ud-Dowla* (Defender of the State), that Sir David relished. He did not send his children to Scotland nor did he return himself. He died at Delhi in 1825 and is buried there.

William Fraser, a young soldier, diplomat and a Persian scholar joined Sir David Ochterlony in 1805, as his Assistant in the British Residency at Delhi. He was from the Frasers of Reelick in Inverness-shire. He became so immersed in the Muslim/ Mughal culture that he felt at ease only in the company of the Mughal nobles and scholars of Delhi and 'found . . . the bores of the European community intolerable.' The influence of the company of Muslim scholars and poets so affected him that he also began composing Persian poetry and became a reasonably good poet. The greatest ever Urdu poet *Mirza Ghalib*, who composed also in Persian, was one of his close friends. William Fraser is reputed to have had seven wives and many children from them. In 1833, he became the British Resident in Delhi. Soon after, he got 'involved in the violent inheritance dispute' between the sons of his late Mughal friend *Nawab Ahmed Baksh Khan* who had recently died. Ironically, in 1835, one of the disputants, who had been a ward of William and had

---

[29] Grey, C. p.274

lived with him for some time, feeling aggrieved and insulted by his treatment in connection with the inheritance dispute, had him killed.[30]

Lieutenant Colonel James Dalrymple of the British army in India married *Moti Begum* the daughter of the Muslim Nawab of Masulipatam. He sent his four sons back to Scotland to be brought up as Christians and educated by his family in East Lothian while his wife kept their only daughter in India. The daughter was raised as a Muslim and she married *Sadue Beig*, a Muslim *Pathan* army officer under her father.

There were many more children born to Indian women who were brought to Scotland by their fathers but not many can be traced as no official specific records of such children were kept in this country. In school and university records however, the place of birth or country of origin of all students was recorded and those born outside Scotland can be identified from those records. In the records of Edinburgh University, for the session 1850-51, I found thirty students born in India but all bearing Scottish names. It is certain that before and after that session, there were similar numbers in Edinburgh University and more in the other three Scottish universities of that period. Many of them, especially in the first half of the nineteenth century, would have been born of Muslim Indian women. However, it is impossible to identify them, because on their departure from India, their Muslim or Indian names were changed to Christian, which they bore for the rest of their lives and there is no reference anywhere to their mixed parentage.

There are a few cases though, where reference to the colour or parentage of some of them was made in Scotland for a specific reason and from that, they could be identified as of mixed parentage. One of such cases was of a girl by the name of Jane Cumming Gordon. She was the daughter of George Cumming of Altyre, a young army officer of the East India Company, who following the tradition of his family had joined the army and gone to India, in 1792. In India, he married or developed a liaison with a woman who gave birth to his daughter Jane. George Cumming died aged twenty six, but before his death, he had informed his mother about his little daughter. In 1803, his mother, Lady Helen Cumming Gordon, arranged for her granddaughter to be brought over to

---

[30] Dalrymple, William *City of Djinns* pp.114-115

Scotland. She kept the child with her for some time at her mansion at Gordonston and then in 1804 sent her to a boarding school at Elgin. In 1809, the family moved to Edinburgh and Jane was placed in a local girls' school of the city. During her studies at that school, Jane and a couple of her fellow students accused their two female teachers of an indecent relationship. This accusation turned into a big public scandal and Jane and her grandmother became involved in a law suit. It was during this scandal that Jane Cumming was reported as 'a dark skinned girl, a native of India' and her mixed parentage revealed.[31]

Some Scottish academics made positive contributions to Islamic culture in India. John Baillie from Inverness was a professor of Arabic and Persian at Fort William College, Calcutta. John Borthwick Gilchrist, a lowland Scot, probably did not marry into a noble Muslim family, instead he was wedded to *Urdu* the new and upcoming language of Northern India. He considered *Urdu* as 'the equivalent of English in the British Isles'. The *Urdu* language had developed during the fifteenth to eighteenth centuries through the infusion of Muslim and Hindu cultures and the languages of Persian, Arabic, Turkish and Hindu soldiers, living in the cantonments of the Muslim rulers of India. As this new language was rather coarse during its early development, attempts were being made, from the mid-eighteenth century, by some Indian Muslim literati to refine and formalise it. In the early nineteenth century John Gilchrist, himself a scholar of Persian and *Urdu*, joined these attempts and played a significant role in bringing *Urdu* to its purification and perfection for the benefit of the British and the common Indian people. In 1823, he produced his Urdu medical dialogues titled *Hindoostani Dialogues* for the use of British doctors, among who were many Scots working with the Indians. For the use of the British administrators and soldiers in India, he produced the *Principles of Urdu Philology* in Roman script.

> The British 'discovery of Urdu' has always been associated with the name of John Gilchrist. His status as the 'father' of the language has been challenged... Gilchrist was nevertheless important in recognising the significance of Urdu.[32]

---

[31] Faderman, Lillian *Scotch Verdict* pp.28-38

[32] Bayly, C.A. *Empire and Information* p.270

Gilchrist's recognition of the significance of *Urdu* in the early nineteenth century was indeed prophetic and he deserves credit for his foresight. During the mid-nineteenth to mid-twentieth century *Urdu* had become the cultural language of Indians especially Muslims and after independence and the division of India *Urdu* became the official language of the Islamic Republic of Pakistan.

Many other Scots went to India, or deserted their service once in India to become freebooters or traders in the tumultuous India of the late eighteenth and early nineteenth centuries. The breakdown of the Mughal Empire attracted and encouraged local and foreign adventurers to try their luck in sharing the spoils of that rich crumbling Empire. Most of the Europeans did well and some amassed immense riches in that chaotic environment.

After achieving good positions in the service of Indian feudal lords, who at that time numbered thousands in that vast but troubled country, many converted to Islam and married, in most cases, into noble Muslim families. These marriages brought them many benefits and broadened their chances of doing even better, thus they entered such arrangements with enthusiasm. Their conversions however, in most cases, were of convenience and not of conviction as nearly all of them who returned to their countries of origin reverted to their former religions. The history books of that period are full of such European freebooters, many with Scottish names. The women they married, in most cases, were educated, liberal and from influential families. Writing about the liberal lifestyle and high status of Muslim Indian women in those days and especially those whom they married, Lester Hutchinson reveals:

> Within the limits of the *zenana* (women's quarters) women were free enough, and in some respects more emancipated than their European sisters were. They indulged in sports such as polo, which the contemporary ladies in Europe would have condemned as hoydenish and would have been terrified to imitate. Many of them took a shrewd interest in politics, supporting one faction or another, and sometimes paying the supreme penalty for their mistakes or defeats.[33]

From the beginning of the nineteenth century, when the British

---

[33] Hutchinson, Lester *European Freebooters in Mogul India* p.51

had progressed from being traders to conquerors and rulers, the liaison between British men and Indian women began to be looked down upon and indeed actively discouraged. When they were humble traders, this liaison was considered very beneficial to British men as well as the East India Company and the Company as well as the British Army high command in India encouraged it. However, when the British became conquerors and rulers, such close relationships with the subject people were considered undesirable and dangerous for the Raj, hence discouraged and indeed forbidden. Even the remnants of the mutual trust and understanding, that had developed over the previous two hundred years, between the Muslims and the British in India, suddenly evaporated after the War of Independence in 1857, or the Mutiny as it was called by the British. After their capture of Delhi, the British army massacred most of the Muslim nobility and demolished their beautiful palaces and mansions. With the destruction of Delhi, that had been the centre of Muslim power in India for the past eight hundred years, Muslim culture also was obliterated.

> With the British victory, and the genocidal spate of hangings and executions that followed it, the entire top rank of the Mughal aristocracy was swept away and British culture was unapologetically imposed on India; at the same time the wholesale arrival of the *memsahibs*, the rise of Evangelical Christianity and moral certainties it brought with it ended all sexual contact between the two nations. [34]

Nonetheless, by then in India there were thousands of children of the liaisons between Indian women and British men, many with distinctive Scottish names. The lucky ones of these, who in India were publicly called 'country born', Eurasians or half-castes, and privately with many derogatory names, ended up in England or Scotland, where they received good education and did well in their lives. The not so well-off Britons in India did not send their offspring of mixed marriages to Britain, as they could not afford the expense of their upkeep and education. Many of them did not return home and died in India. Their children grew up in India, mostly in the religion of their mothers. These mixed race children had a hard

---

[34] Dalrymple, William *White Mughals* p.498

life; they faced racial prejudice and discrimination from the British. Their prejudiced white British cousins barred them from higher army and civil offices. The only careers open to them were such as lower rank Army officers or junior clerks in government offices and later on as train drivers and train conductors in the various Indian Railways.

Many of the male and even some female children of mixed marriages of the rich, who were brought over to Britain, after their education again ended up in India as members of the British Indian armed forces, civil servants and as wives of the British officers serving in India. However, most of them returned to Britain after their retirements. Such products of these mixed marriages, because of their fair skin colour, were soon absorbed into Scottish society without any trace. Consequently, there would be now probably thousands of Scots and a far greater number of English, who without realising have Muslim ancestry. The marks left by those British soldiers, administrators and adventurers are therefore, still visible in the Muslim lands they operated in and as well as in Scotland and England.

> And so they passed, this sometimes brilliant sometimes shabby company of adventurers, as the times that gave rise to them passed. Professional soldiers, runaway sailors, army deserters, pastry cooks, scullions, clerks and unsuccessful traders, they played their part in history. Some reached lasting fame, some made immense fortunes and retired to live in their native lands, but the majority never saw their homes again and lived in relative poverty until they filled unremembered graves, their children adding to the growing Eurasian population.
>
> They were not entirely without virtue. They were not burdened with colour prejudice; indeed few were in the eighteenth century. . . They were, of course, predatory, but not more so than the princes and the Company officials. . . A few committed atrocities. . . As is always the case, the sufferers were the simple and the poor, the peasant mass. . .
>
> So it was then, so it was before then, and so it will always be until man becomes a rational animal.[35]

[35] Hutchinson, Lester *ibid* pp.183-184

One of the most important and lasting aspects of the Empire and especially of the role played by the Scots in India is the presence of about 50,000 Muslims in present day Scotland. The returning Scots brought over their Indian servants with them and the Scottish merchants ships recruited and brought over the Indian seamen to Scotland. Most of these servants and seamen were Muslims. After their retirement, a number of them stayed on in Scotland and looked for alternative means of earning a living. When they felt well settled here, they invited their relatives and friends from India and Pakistan. That was the beginning of the settlement in Scotland of the Muslim community, which is now an integral part of the Scottish society.

The two children are Master William George Kirkpatrick and Miss
Katherine Kirkpatrick – they must have been very confused by these
names they would never have heard before, in place of *Saheb Alum* and
Saheb Begum. They were the offspring of James Kirkpatrick and
Khair-un-Nisa Begum (see p.168ff)

John Yehya-en-Nasr Parkinson was born in Kilwinning and was deeply influenced by Islam

James Achilles Kirkpatrick dressed as a Muslin noble

CHAPTER 5

Islam in Scotland

THE influence of Islam had reached Scotland by the early eighth century, through Scotland's trading links with the Muslim countries of North Africa and through the *De Locus Sanctis*, written in the late seventh century based on the observations of a Frankish pilgrim to the Holy Land. Pilgrims to the Holy Land from Scotland and England before the Crusades, and the visits of the Muslim traders to England beginning with the mid-eighth century, would have added to that influence. The Scottish Crusaders, who had been present in the Levant and Egypt, during the three centuries of the Crusades period and were interacting with Muslims and experiencing their culture, would have further enhanced that influence on their return home.

However, outside Europe, in the early Middle Ages, Scotland was considered to be at the fringe of the world, 'where the sun sets' and had very limited impact in the Muslim world. Muslim traders of North Africa and Spain knew of Scotland only through their trading links with this country, and the Muslim intellectuals knew Scotland through their wide knowledge of the topography of the then known world.

In his work *The Book of Marvels*, the famous Muslim geographer *Masudi* (871-937), mentions a prosperous island in the Atlantic with flourishing towns engaged in commerce and trade. *Idrisi* (1099-1155), the well-known Muslim geographer in his book, *Nuzhat al Mushtaq fi'khtiraq al-afaq*, (known in the West as the *Book of Roger* or *Al-Rojori*, after his patron Roger the Norman monarch of Sicily), identifies this island with Scotland and some modern scholars are also of the same opinion. *Al-Rajori* contains seventy maps, two of which show the island of Scotland connected with the island of England. *Idrisi* mentions that Scotland stretches for one hundred and fifty miles to the North of the larger island of England. He

185

states that the ravages of civil wars in the country have destroyed the commerce and trade and many of the cities and villages are in ruins. His information about Scotland is sketchy and may have been collected from travellers who had some knowledge of Scotland. Nonetheless, in Europe, during the Middle Ages, *Al-Rajori* or the Book of Roger became the most reliable source of accurate topography of the known world. To prepare his book *Idrisi* learnt from the works of previous geographers, obtained information from travellers to Sicily about their respective countries and travelled widely from Asia to the west coast of England. The Muslim geographers such as *Idrisi* were further advanced in knowledge than the Europeans and it was from the Muslims, especially of Spain, that Europeans learnt the advanced and accurate geographical knowledge. The Europeans' knowledge of geography was so limited that until the mid-twelfth century, they believed that the whole world except most of Europe belonged to the Muslims.[1]

It is possible that *Idrisi* obtained information about Scotland during his visit to England around the mid-twelfth century. There are only a few surviving versions of *The Book of Roger* and owing to the possible loss of some original material and pages and the carelessness of the copiers, they differ in their contents. It is very likely that *Idrisi* visited Denmark during his travels as he gives accurate and detailed information about that country and its people. Denmark had good communications and certainly well-established trade relations with the Muslim world. Many records of these connections and of the presence of Arab traders and other dignitaries in Denmark have survived until today.[2] The fact that, as early as the ninth century, Scotland is mentioned in the works of Muslim geographers confirms that in the early Middle Ages Scotland was known to academics and geographers in the Islamic world. However, in spite of the presence of Scots, as traders and pilgrims in the Muslim countries and the visits of the Muslim traders to England since the eighth century, there is no evidence of the presence of any Muslim in Scotland during the Middle Ages.

In his Traveller's Log, the medieval traveller, Sir John Mandeville, records that Muslim rulers sent out their spies disguised as travellers and traders to various countries of Europe, including

---

[1] Watt, W.M. *Influence of Islam on Medieval Europe* p.21

[2] *The Arabian Journey* Moesgard Museum, 1996, pp.1-2

Britain. He claims that he received this information from the Sultan of Egypt during an audience with him. He states that during his audience the Sultan ordered everybody present to leave the chamber, 'for he would speak with me in counsel. And there he asked me how the Christian men governed them in our country.' On Mandville's reply 'Right well, thanked be God', the Sultan disagreed and told him about the bad ways and evil deeds of the Christian rulers. Amazed at the Sultan's correct response Mandeville asked the Sultan how he knew all that. The Sultan replied that he knew 'by his messengers that he sent to all lands, in manner as they were merchants. . . for to know the manner of every country among Christian men'. After this conversation the Sultan called in all his courtiers and pointed four of them to Mandeville. Those four nobles spoke to Mandeville in fluent French and told him about Britain and many other Christian countries, 'as well as they had been of the same country'.[3]

It is, therefore, probable that one of the spies or a genuine Muslim diplomat, trader or traveller from Syria, Spain or North Africa might have visited Scotland in medieval times. As mentioned before, Scottish merchants kept a hostel at Alexandria (Egypt) in the twelfth century. That implies that they were often travelling to Egypt and other South Mediterranean countries, where they had links with Muslim traders and where they stayed for considerable periods to buy and sell their merchandise. There is every probability therefore, that in response to the Scots, the Egyptian, North African or Andalusian Muslim traders would have come to Scotland to buy and sell their goods. Further, there is plenty of evidence of the presence of Scottish soldiers, sailors and slaves in Muslim lands during the Middle Ages. Hence, it is reasonable to expect or presume that some Muslim friend or colleague of a Scottish soldier or sailor would have accompanied him on his return to Scotland to see this country and its people. However, there is no recorded evidence of any such visitor and according to reliable available information a Turk named *Ismael Bashaw* (about whom there will be more in the following pages) was the first Muslim visitor to Scotland. *Bashaw* came to Scotland from England in the eighteenth century and stayed here for a few months.[4]

---

[3] *The Travels of Sir John Mandville* pp.92-93-94

[4] Matar, Nabil *Turks Moors and Englishmen in the Age of Discovery* p.73

Nonetheless, there is circumstantial evidence that points to the possible presence of Muslims in Scotland from at least the late fifteenth century. There are many entries in *The Lord High Treasurer's Accounts,* relating to the presence of 'Black Mores' (Moors from North Africa who most probably were Muslims) at the court of James IV (r.1488-1513) of Scotland and his successors. They first appear in 1504, in the household of King James IV, as musicians and entertainers. They were not slaves but freemen, employed by the royal household, who received similar wages, lodgings, fees and treatment to other royal servants of the same status.[5] One of those Moors, who was a drummer and choreographer, is reported to have been a favourite of the King. There was also a 'Black Lady' (a Moor) at the court of the King who took part in jousting tournaments held in 1507 and 1508 at Edinburgh. William Dunbar wrote poems about her, which are rather derogatory of her appearance and flagrantly racist. *The Accounts of the Lord High Treasurer of Scotland (1505-1508)* contain vivid details of the 'Black Lady's gown of damask, floured with gold'. Further *The Accounts of the Lord High Treasurer of Scotland* for the years 1567 and 1569 reveal that clothes were bought for '*Nagier* the More'. There is also the mention of a 'Black More' who in 1594, participated in a pageant to celebrate the baptism of Henry Frederick, eldest son of James VI of Scotland, in Edinburgh.[6] Another important event on this auspicious occasion was an 'action' held near the castle in which four teams were to take part. However, on the time appointed only three teams, each consisting of three Christians, three Turks, and three Amazons, appeared. The missing team was to be three Moors, which was omitted because it was not certain whether it would be present.[7]

The Islamic and oriental influence at the Scottish court is obvious from these celebrations. Further, it is reported that in 1679, six black trumpeters were attached to the Scottish Life Guards. In the eighteenth and nineteenth centuries also, we find black musicians (Moors) attached to the Scottish regiments. There are eyewitness accounts of their impressive performances during regimental parades, etc., and there are records of money spent on

---

[5] Bawcut, Priscilla ed. *The Poems of William Dunbar* p.350

[6] Fryer, P. *Black People in the British Empire* p.4

[7] Chew, Samuel, C. *The Crescent and the Rose* p.457

their boots and turbans. The Coldstream Guards retained their black musicians until about 1840.[8]

There is no mention of the religion of these Mores or Moors but in the Middle Ages especially, and in some cases even now, the people of Morocco are called Moors and they were Muslims then as they are now. It is therefore certain that those Moors at the court of Scottish sovereigns in the sixteenth and seventeenth centuries, and the Black musicians (Moors) attached to the Scottish regiments until the middle of the nineteenth century were Muslims from Morocco. The mention above of the name 'Nagier the More' confirms this assertion as *Nagier*, *Nageer* or *Nazeer* in its various forms is a common Muslim name. The continuous presence of those Moors in Scotland, especially at the Scottish court, means that since the Middle Ages there have been regular contacts between Muslims of Morocco and Scotland.

However, the first recorded account of the presence of a Muslim in Scotland is that of *Ishmael Bashaw* who came to Britain in the late eighteenth century. He was a Turk born in 1735, in Istanbul. When he grew up, he joined a Turkish merchant ship. During a voyage on his ship in the Mediterranean Sea, he was captured by Spanish pirates and imprisoned in Spain. He escaped from the prison and found refuge in the house of the British Consul in Lisbon, where he stayed hidden for three years until he was able to escape to Britain. In his Turkish dress and turban, he wandered from village to village in England enduring much ridicule, abuse and violence. Eventually he arrived in Scotland, where at Dalkeith, he was befriended by the Duke of Buccleuch. The Duke treated him with kindness and unsuccessfully tried to convert him to Christianity. After a few months stay in Scotland he went back to England. On his way back, he was robbed and abused as a Turk – 'To be a Turk in England and Scotland, he discovered, was to be an object of Christian ridicule, persecution and violence.'

In Richmond, Yorkshire, he met a woman; they fell in love and married. The minister who performed their marriage ceremony was a Scot from Edinburgh. He tried without success to dissuade the women from marrying a Muslim Turk. Eventually *Bashaw* embraced Christianity. The Minister who baptised him clipped his long and twisted moustache, took off his turban and gave him

---

[8] P. Fryer pp.81, 82, 85

English clothes to replace his Turkish dress. With a new name, his English dress and English wife, *Bashaw* tried to assimilate into British society. However, his suffering did not end with his change of lifestyle or religion. With his wife at his side, he continued to wander from city to city, 'sometimes eking out a living, at other times, relying on the charity and kindness of people, especially the Quakers'.[9]

It is very strange to note that British Christian people instead of showing any respect or regard ridiculed and abused a convert to Christianity. This is totally against the Islamic tradition where a convert, from whichever race and religion, immediately becomes a more respected member of the community. This was one of the reasons why so many Europeans, as referred to above, converted to Islam in the late Middle Ages in North African countries. However, in Britain of those days:

> Neither conversion nor Anglicisation could effect his integration into the Christian society of England and Scotland. Bashaw was an Other, defeated, impoverished, and alterised.[10]

The second half of the eighteenth century and the nineteenth century saw a steady flow of Muslim servants and seamen coming to Scotland. The servants accompanied their employers returning home after serving in the Muslim areas of the British Empire and the seamen were employed on British merchant ships. The English and Scottish merchant ships began recruiting Muslim seamen from East Africa, Yemen, and India during the seventeenth century because they were cheaper to hire and maintain on sailing ships. They were paid only a quarter of the wages paid to the British seamen and their upkeep on the ships was a fraction of the money spent on the maintenance of the indigenous British seamen. Hence, the British merchant ships began recruiting more and more of the Muslim seamen and bringing them to various ports in Britain.

The East India Company officials and army officers who spent some years in the Empire, especially India, became used to luxurious lifestyles and the cheap and obsequious services of their local

---

[9] Matar, Nabil *Turks Moors and Englishmen in the Age of Discovery* pp.173-75

[10] *ibid* p.175

servants. In India, for example, most of the British during their stay had numerous servants. These servants did everything for them, even dressed and undressed them. Describing just the morning routine of their lifestyle Percival Spears states:

> The moment the master throws his legs out of his bed, the whole force [of servants] is waiting to rush into his room, each making three salaams. . . In about half an hour after undoing and taking off his long drawers, a clean shirt, breeches, stockings and slippers are put upon his body, thighs, legs and feet, without any exertion on his own part as he was a statue. The barber enters, shaves him, cuts his nails, and cleanse his ears. The *chillumjee* (basin) and ewer are brought by a servant whose duty it is, who pours water upon his hands and face, and presents a towel. The superior then walks in state to his breakfasting parlour in his waistcoat; is seated, the *consumah* (butler) makes and pours out his tea, and presents him with a plate of bread or toast. The hairdresser comes behind, and begins his operation, while the *houccaburdar* (hooka attendant) slips the upper end of the snake or ivory tube of the *houcca* [the hubble bubble] into his hand, while the hairdresser is doing his duty the gentleman is eating, sipping and smoking by turns. By and by his banian treasurer presents himself with humble salaams and advances somewhat more forward than the other attendants.[11]

Thus, most British army officers, civil servants and businessmen, especially those who had amassed enough wealth in the service of the East India Company in India, on their return brought with them some of their Indian servants to maintain their luxurious lifestyle in Britain and show of their wealth. For example, Warren Hastings, the first Governor General (1773-1785) of British India, on his return in 1785, brought over two Indian footmen and four maids.[12] A great majority of these servants would have been Muslims. Not many Hindus would have come during that conservative period, because their religion prevented them from crossing the seas and from eating or serving meat of any kind especially of the cow, which

---

[11] *The Nabobs* p.43

[12] Hecht, J. *Continental and Colonial Servants in the Eighteenth Century* p.50

they worship as a goddess. Some returning Britons even brought servants or perhaps slaves from India to sell them in Britain. In 1709, 'A black Indian boy, twelve years of age, fit to wait on a gentleman,' was advertised for sale in London.[13]

There are many references and accounts of the presence of Indian servants in England during the eighteenth and nineteenth centuries, but in Scotland, surprisingly such accounts are very rare. However, as it was the trend in those days for the rich and the noble to bring some of their hordes of servants with them on their return, there would be many who were brought over to Scotland. Joseph Salter, an evangelist who targeted Indian servants and seamen throughout Britain, writing in 1870, states:

> Even in Scotland Asiatics are to be found. . . They have been met and spoken to at Dundee, Glasgow, Perth, Greenock and Edinburgh. . . From this Scotch Town [Dumbarton] my tour commenced in search of the wandering Asiatics. Passing a short time in Glasgow, Stirling, Leith and Edinburgh I passed on to Suderland... On this journey I met and spoke to 81 Asiatics. At Stirling I had an interesting conversation with a native who had come from Aberdeen, where he had seen others. [14]

There were therefore, quite a number of Asians, i.e. Indians in Scotland in the nineteenth century. Some of them would have been seamen or *Lascars,* as they were commonly known, and others servants and abandoned or retired servants. Some may have married Scottish women and settled here. Salter mentions *Roshan Khan* who with his Scottish wife and five children lived in Edinburgh. As a profession: 'He has long enjoyed the fame of supplying savoury pipes to the lovers of smoke. . .' that he sold in the High Street every Friday.[15] Salter further records: 'At Edinburgh and Leith I found *Shaik Roshan* and *Meer Jan,* and two others'.[16] As mentioned above, the seamen, servants and other lower status Indians in Britain were subjected to evangelism and persuaded to convert to Christian-

---

[13] Hecht, J. *ibid* p.51

[14] *The Asiatics in England* p.234

[15] *ibid* p.235

[16] *ibid* p.236

ity. Some did convert and Salter mentions two, *Jhulee Khan*, who came as a *Lascar* in 1841 and *Jumal Din* who had married here and had two daughter who were 'dressed in Indian costume'. However, except for a few, they all retained their faith and lived here or went back to India.

The two best-known Muslim servants arrived from India at Balmoral in 1877. They were brought to join the team of servants of the royal household. *Abdul Karim* and *Muhammed Bakhsh* were recruited perhaps to give a touch of India to the royal household after the proclamation of Queen Victoria as the Empress of India. The Queen's secretary, Sir Henry Posonby, stated that Her Majesty 'was excited about them as a child would be with a new toy.'

Abdul Karim was an educated and intelligent 24-year-old with a pleasant but serious countenance. In the royal household, he began as a waiter to the Queen standing motionless behind her wherever she happened to be. The Queen was so impressed by him that she promoted him to be her *munshi*, i.e. teacher of the Hindustani language. She took her learning seriously and was soon able to write a little and speak a few sentences of Hindustani with her Indian servants and to greet the visiting Indian princes and nobles. The Queen, in due course, became so fond of her Muslim teacher, *Abdul Karim*, that in 1890 she engaged Von Angeli, the famous painter of the period to paint his portrait. In 1894, *Abdul Karim* was promoted to the office of Indian Secretary to the Queen and soon after made a Companion of the Order of the Indian Empire. To reward her trusted Indian Secretary even more Her Majesty wrote to her Viceroy in India to make a suitable grant of land to her excellent secretary.

However, the honours and high social status granted to an Indian in the royal court and the Queen's excessive favours and patronage of *Abdul Karim*, created jealously and ill will towards him in the royal circles and the India Office. In that atmosphere of racial superiority and rampant racism, during the heyday of the Empire, British courtiers and high ranking civil servants could not tolerate a black man from a subject race being given the same status in the royal court and treated as equal to them. Hence, they began a vicious campaign to discredit *Abdul Karim* in the eyes of the Queen and to influence Her Majesty to dismiss him or put him in his proper place of being an ordinary household servant. *Abdul Karim* began to be snubbed and humiliated at every turn by the court officials.

They sought discriminatory and damning information about him from the relevant British official in India, who realising the situation readily concocted and sent it in all haste to London. This was then presented to the Queen. Consequently, *Abdul Karim* lost his status and prestige in the court. Thus, by deceiving their sovereign with false information, the detractors succeeded in their ploy. Soon after, though the Queen died in 1901 and a disgraced and humiliated *Abdul Karim* returned to India. Before he departed all his papers relating to the Queen or the royal court were burnt on the orders of the new King George IV. *Abdul Karim* died in 1909, at Agra, his hometown. After his death, the Indian Government officials visited his Widow and demanded all his papers relating to his stay in the UK. Those with any reference to Queen Victoria or her Court were taken away and the rest returned to her.[17]

In 1960, while visiting my family and friends in my ancestral village in Pakistan, I met an old man named *Sundhi Din*, who had come to Scotland from India, as a servant, at the beginning of the twentieth century. He had accompanied his employer, a Scottish army Colonel. *Sundhi* was an illiterate and a rather quiet man. He did not volunteer much information about his journey to and from and his sojourn in Scotland and unfortunately, not realising at that time the importance of the information he possessed, I did not encourage him to give me a more expansive and detailed account. However, what he did reveal was that he had been a cook to the Colonel in India. On his retirement from the British Indian army, the colonel asked *Sundhi* to accompany him to Scotland. *Sundhi* agreed and they came to Scotland about four or five years before World War I. The Colonel died a few years later and *Sundhi* went to live first in the *Lascar* colony in the Anderston area of Glasgow and then rented a house in the Port Dundas area of the city. To earn a living, to begin with, he worked as a hawker in the city streets and in the mid-1920s, he turned to peddling in the rural areas surrounding Glasgow. In 1930, he went back to India from where he migrated to Pakistan in 1947 and settled in my ancestral village.

In the late 1980s when I was involved in the research for my book *The New Scots*, I remembered about *Sundhi*, and I discovered that according to Glasgow City Council records, *Sundhi* had tenanted a house, from 1925 to 1930, at 56 Water Street, Port

---

[17] Visram, Rosina *Ayahs, Lascars and Princes* pp.30-33

Dundas, Glasgow. This confirmed the information he had given me. However, except for the mention of his name in the Glasgow City Valuation Roles as a tenant of one of the houses in the city, there is no other record of his arrival, stay or departure from Scotland and nobody knew or knows that an Indian Muslim named *Sundhi Din* came as a servant to Scotland. In other words had he not rented a house in Glasgow there would be no record at all of his presence in this country. This was owing to the fact that the subject people of the British Empire were treated as British citizens and those with a proper passport or travel documents had the right to come and go from Britain without any records or restrictions. Hence, there are scarcely any government or other records of Muslim servants, and there were literally hundreds, maybe thousands of them, who were brought from India by their returning employers during the eighteenth and nineteenth centuries. Some of them, on their retirement, went back to India; others lived and died here and were forgotten. A few of them, who during the eighteenth and nineteenth centuries came under the pressure of the evangelists like Joseph Salter and others, who were constantly targeting the Indian servants and sailors, converted to Christianity. The converts were given new Christian names in place of their Muslim names and thus they lost their real identity and eventually with their deaths their memory also disappeared from society.

Over and above the seamen and servants, from the middle of the nineteenth century, Muslim students had begun to come to Scotland, to pursue higher education in Scottish universities. The records of their presence in Scotland have survived in the various university archives. The first Muslim student to come to Scotland was *Asyri Bey* from Egypt, who is registered as a medical student in the records of the University of Edinburgh for the years 1854 to 1863. *Wazir Beg* from India was the next who came in 1857 and studied medicine at the University of Edinburgh from 1857 to 1861. The numbers of Muslim students increased steadily during the last quarter of the nineteenth century and by its close had gone up to about one hundred in the various universities of Scotland.

Until about 1920, Scottish universities received comparatively far more students from India than England. This was owing to the wider involvement of the Scots in the education field in India. They outnumbered the English as teachers in the educational institutions of India and also actively promoted the education of Indians by opening new schools and colleges. This resulted in proportionately more Indian students preferring the Scottish universities, where their teachers had been educated. Thus, during the opening years of the twentieth century there were, on average, about 300 Indian students in the various Scottish colleges and universities, out of about 700 in the whole of the United Kingdom. In addition, Muslim students came to Scotland from other Muslim countries like Malaya, the Middle East and Egypt. As a result, their numbers in Scotland kept steadily growing until the 1930s.

By the late nineteenth century, some passage migrants had already become settlers. The Indian seamen, for example had developed their own colonies (the *Lascar* colonies) in all port cities of Britain where the transient or dismissed seamen and abandoned or retired Indian servants sought refuge. In some cases, port authorities also had provided homes and hostels for Indian seamen coming on merchant ships to their ports. In Scotland, such facilities existed in Glasgow, Leith and Dundee. Most of the seamen and servants however, congregated in Glasgow in their own *Lascar* colony in the Anderston area where they could eat their own food and live among their own people. The abandoned servants and seamen were often unemployed. Under prevalent racism and extreme prejudice against black and coloured people in Scotland in those colonial days, it was difficult for them to find permanent employment. To survive, they tried to earn a meagre living as unskilled labourers doing odd jobs, whenever they could get any, or as hawkers in the streets of the major cities of Scotland, and some unfortunate ones by begging.

By the beginning of the twentieth century, their numbers had increased especially in Glasgow and some had rented cheap dilapidated houses where they lived in groups of four to twelve, depending on the size of the house. When World War I began and every hand was needed to contribute to the war effort they all found jobs, some in the merchant navy, some in the armed forces and the rest were made to work in the munitions factories. Nonetheless, soon after the War ended, they were all dismissed from wherever they were working, as their jobs were required to accommodate the demobbed Scottish soldiers and sailors of the British Army and Royal Navy. Thus again becoming unemployed they all came back to their old haunt, the *Lascar* colony and once more began eking out a living by doing odd jobs and by hawking in the city streets.

In the mid-1920s, some of them, on the advice of a Jewish gentleman, created their own jobs by starting peddling children's, ladies' and men's clothing in the housing schemes and small villages around Glasgow. In this profession, hard work, unsocial hours and vagaries of the inclement weather were involved but having no other choice they accepted it and persevered in it. They sold their goods on credit to the poor people of the rural areas who were glad to patronise the dark strangers, as they could not afford to pay cash to buy their and their children's clothes from the city shops. The peddlers worked very hard and some of them did reasonably well. The success of the pioneers in this trade encouraged other ex-seamen and servants to join them and soon every one of the Muslims and other Indians in Scotland, except the students of course, had become a peddler.

Peddling proved to be the catalyst for the settlement of Muslims in Scotland. It was a profession that according to the local standards, provided them with less than a reasonable income, but it was more than good enough for them according to their standards of living, as they did not indulge in drinking, gambling, dancing or any other such expensive pursuits. Once they had saved enough money, they left the *Lascar* colonies and rented or bought cheap houses in the poorer slum areas of Port Dundas and Gorbals, Glasgow. When the news of their success in peddling spread to the *Lascar* colonies in England, many of their unemployed compatriots from there, made their way to Scotland and joined them. Realising the potential of doing well in their trade some of the Muslim peddlers invited their poor relatives and friends from India to join them and share with them the benefits of working as peddlers in Scotland. Thus, their numbers began to grow steadily and doubled from about 50 in 1925 to over 100 in 1930. At this stage, Glasgow was becoming a little overcrowded with the Indian peddlers and competition among them began to hurt some of them. Therefore, during the late 1920s, a few of them had gone to Edinburgh and a few to Dundee to try their luck in the rural areas around these cites. This was the beginning of the dispersal of the Muslim community in Scotland.

It is relevant to mention here that most Muslims in Scotland, at that time, were from a small area around both banks of the River

Sutluj in India, and were either related to or friends of each other. In 1930s, when word spread among their families and relatives back home that they were doing well in Scotland, many more from there came over to join them. Consequently their numbers began to grow fast and to avoid overcrowding in Glasgow some of them began to spread out to the Highlands and the North East of Scotland. By 1935, a few of them had even appeared in the Outer Hebrides. Thus, before the beginning of World War II in 1939, there were about ten to fifteen of them in Edinburgh and about five to ten each in Dundee, Aberdeen, Lossiemouth, Inverness and Stornoway. Their base however, was Glasgow, where they returned every few weeks to see their friends, to obtain news about their families back home, and of course to buy the goods of their trade. To begin with, they bought their trade goods from Jewish and other Scottish whole-salers in the city. However, when in the thirties their numbers had begun to grow, a couple of Muslim entrepreneurs, who had done better than others in peddling, opened wholesale outlets in Glasgow to supply their compatriots and co-religionists. By 1939 therefore, the Muslim community had grown to about 300 and had spread to all the major Scottish cities and even some rural and Highland areas.

World War II interrupted their trade and temporarily changed their way of life. Most of the factories that manufactured the goods of their trade closed down during the war and imports into the UK were also hindered. The government introduced rationing and it became very difficult for them to get their supplies. Most of them were forced to abandon peddling. Those who had gone to the North and the Hebrides came back to Glasgow. As during World War I, again there were jobs available. Some were taken into the armed forces and the rest began working in armament and munitions factories in and around Glasgow.

During this period, living together and leading a relatively settled life they were able to give attention to their religious rites and requirements. In about 1931, in London, a Muslim organisation called *Jamiat ul Muslimin* (The Muslim Association) was founded to look after the religious interests of the Muslim community in Britain. In about 1933, a branch of that Association was set up in Glasgow. This was the first Muslim organisation or society in Scotland. The Muslims performed their daily prayers mostly in their respective houses but for their Friday congregational prayer their Association had made specific arrangements in a suitable house, in Hospital Street, Gorbals, owned by one of its members. During World War II when everyone came back to Glasgow, their numbers increased and more space was required for their congregational Friday prayers and their gatherings to celebrate religious festivals. Therefore, in 1940, the Muslim Association began hiring a hall in Gorbals Street around which most of them lived. (It was a strange coincidence that 44 years later, in 1984, a site on the opposite side of Gorbals Street, became the location of the first purpose-built mosque in Scotland, the beautiful Glasgow Central Mosque.) However, this arrangement did not prove satisfactory and the Association resolved to acquire their own premises, big enough to be turned into a mosque and a community hall. In 1943, they found a suitable building in Oxford Street, Gorbals, Glasgow and got it converted to suit their purposes. Thus, in early 1944, the first mosque, on the soil of Scotland, was ready for prayers.

After the War when the munitions factories closed down and the industrial sector began to function again, most Muslims reverted to peddling. For the first few years after the War, the community remained static. There were few new arrivals from India as the sub-continent was going through the throes of partition and independence. By late 1948, the mass migration process of population between India and Pakistan had nearly ended and the situation began to stabilise. All the Muslim families whose members were in Scotland had by then migrated from India to Pakistan and had settled down in their new environment. Most of these refugees were in a dire state as they had lost all their belongings and money during their flight from India and there were no jobs, yet, for them in Pakistan. Hence, to provide for their families, they began joining their relatives and friends in Scotland.

The Muslim community in Scotland, therefore, began to grow again and by 1950, their numbers had gone up to about four hundred. The 1950s saw many more coming from Pakistan and a few also from India. In the mid-fifties when the industrial expansion in Scotland had created more jobs in the factories, in the business sector and in service industries many Scottish people left their jobs with unsocial hours or hard and dirty work to take up better jobs. There were, therefore, many vacancies in the Transport Departments of the major Scottish local authorities, bakeries, chemical and jute factories etc. The employers in those sectors, desperate for labour but realising that they would not be able to fill vacancies with the indigenous workers, set aside their racial prejudice and reluctantly began to employ Muslims and other Asians. Most of the recent arrivals and those who could not persevere and progress in peddling gladly took up those jobs.

The industrial boom of the early 1950s in Britain had turned into recession by 1955. In England many factories, especially textile mills, began to close down and those remaining resorted to reducing their workforce. In Yorkshire and the Midlands, the immigrant workers from the Indian sub-continent and the West Indies were the mainstay of the textile mills and other industries, but on account of their colour, they were the first to lose their jobs. The redundant Muslim immigrants of Bradford and Birmingham, where they were in hundreds, somehow heard that there were jobs available in Scotland and many of them made their way to Glasgow, Edinburgh and Dundee. Those with enough education to be able to pass the required entrance tests joined the respective transport departments of the above cities as bus conductors and drivers and others sought employment as unskilled labourers in various factories and works. In addition, many more relatives and friends of those already here, and others, were coming over from Pakistan and joining the transport departments or the bakeries and the chemical factories in Scotland.

In addition, some who had been living here for many years brought over their families from Pakistan and India. Until 1950, most of them in this country, whether married are not, were living alone with the idea of making some money and going back home. However, their thinking began to change in the mid-1950s and instead of going back themselves to their families, they began bringing their families to this country. Thus, throughout the 1950s, the number of Muslims in Scotland kept growing at a steady rate and according to a rough estimate, by 1960 it had gone up to about 3,000.

Since the end of World War II, thousands of immigrants from the West Indies, the Indian sub-continent and other British colonies had been coming to Britain. The racist elements in the country were becoming concerned at the growing number of black and

Asians settlers in the UK. Therefore, for some considerable time, voices were being raised especially in the Conservative Party, to restrict the entry of Commonwealth citizens to the UK. Early in 1961, it became clear that in the near future, the Conservative government intended to introduce legislation to that effect. This realisation started a panic in the Indian sub-continent and the West Indies. Hence, to beat the ban an unremitting flow of immigrants from these countries began to disembark every day at Heathrow and other air and seaports.

This process continued until legislation banning the unrestricted entry of immigrants to Britain came into force in 1962. Once this rush was over, afraid of further restriction being imposed on the entry of the dependents of those who were here, many immigrants including Muslims began to bring over their families. In addition, in the early 1960s quite a number of Muslims came from Birmingham and Bradford to Dundee where the jute industry, while doing rather well, was facing a labour shortage. The indigenous workers were not taking those jobs, as the work in the jute mills was unpleasant, required hard labour, and unsocial hours. The newly arrived Muslims who had been idle in England were glad to take up those jobs and rescue the jute industry. In the mid-1960s, a large number of Asians arrived from the newly independent African countries of Kenya, Malawi and Uganda. They had British citizenship and a considerable number of them were Muslims. Some of these Muslims also came to settle in Scotland. Thus, all through the 1960s, the number of Muslims kept growing at a fast rate and by 1970, the total population of Muslims in Scotland had increased five fold to about 15,000.

The pattern of life of the Muslim community had changed during the 1960s. A few of them had already abandoned peddling in the late 1950s and bought corner shops in Glasgow and other Scottish cities. In the early 1960s, this trend gathered pace and more Muslims, especially those in Glasgow and Edinburgh, left peddling and began going into small businesses. Consequently, by the end of the 1960s, not many were left engaged in their old profession of peddling. Those who had done rather well in peddling or corner shops and saved enough were venturing into bigger businesses such as wholesaling, manufacturing and import and export.

In 1962, the Edinburgh Muslim community, that numbered only a couple of hundred at that stage, bought a house in Laurieston Place and converted it into a mosque. This was the second mosque in Scotland. In the late 60s, the Dundee Muslim community also acquired a suitable property and converted it into a mosque. The Muslim community was now planting its roots, becoming confident and adventurous and looking forward to its future in Scotland. Most of them were living in their own houses with their families and very few were in council houses. The idea of returning to their homeland was disappearing as more and more wives and children were coming over to join their husbands and fathers in Scotland.

Some who had done well in business were leaving their ghettoes and moving out to the better and more affluent housing areas. Their children were going to local schools and growing up with Scottish children. Their religious organisations in Glasgow, Edinburgh and Dundee were providing evening and weekend classes for the children in the mosques to teach them their religion. The children who were attending these classes grew up learning their religion and traditions. In 1968, only fifteen years after my arrival in Scotland, I was appointed a Justice of the Peace, the first ever from the black or ethnic minority in Scotland. This was the first indication of the acceptance of the Muslim community in Scotland and a sign of their integration into Scottish society.

The Muslim community in the UK, especially until the 1980s, had been mobile and closely interconnected. In the 1970s, when those in England became aware that most of the Muslims in Scotland were in businesses and doing well, the adventurous and resourceful among them began to head for Scotland. My unexpected but very welcome victory in the Glasgow Corporation local authority elections of 1970, bestowed upon me the honour of becoming the first Muslim city councillor in the UK, and gave Scotland the reputation of being a less prejudiced and a tolerant country. Further, my selection as the first Asian Labour Party Parliamentary candidate in 1972, and my contesting the East Fife constituency in the February 1974 Parliamentary elections, evoked political awareness among immigrants throughout Britain and enhanced the reputation of Scots as a friendly and tolerant nation. It motivated many Muslims, in Scotland as well as in England, to join political parties and seek nominations as candidates for local councils and Parliament. It raised the morale of not only the Muslim community but also of all black and ethnic minorities in Scotland.

In 1973, Mr Nazir Choudhry, an active community worker in Glasgow, was made a Justice of the Peace, the second Muslim in five years to achieve this distinction. These achievements and the comparative prosperity of the Scottish Muslim community spread tales among the ethnic minorities in England that there was less prejudice and little racism in Scotland and hence there were better chances of succeeding in life. All this resulted in many more Muslims and some other Asians from England, coming to Scotland and buying or starting up small businesses. That resulted in the internal migration of quite a few hundred families from England to Scotland. The relatives and families from Pakistan and some from India and Bangladesh were still arriving to join their breadwinners in Scotland. All this was adding to the Scottish Muslim population. With the rapid increase in their numbers, they began to disperse all over, buying shops and opening restaurants in every town.

And with the continuous growth and spread of the community, more mosques were needed. The Muslim communities of Aberdeen and Motherwell acquired suitable premises in the late 1970s and turned them into mosques. In Glasgow and Edinburgh, owing to the wider spread of the community more mosques were appearing to cater for the religious needs of the local Muslim groups. By 1980, the community had grown to about 25,000 and their presence had become noticeable in all major cities and towns of Scotland.

The 1980s saw further diversification and innovation in their businesses and dispersal of the Muslim community. Over and above the wholesale, retail and manufacturing businesses, they were now entering the motor repair and service industry and taking over petrol stations. They were also becoming involved in property, DIY, computer technology, catering, and various other sectors. The small businesses were becoming big and the big were getting bigger and better. Scottish-born and educated young Muslim men and women were entering varied professions and getting involved in all occupations. By 1980, the number of mosques in Scotland had risen to nine – four in Glasgow, two in Edinburgh and one each in Dundee, Aberdeen and Motherwell and more were being planned.

The community was dispersing fast and slowly integrating into Scottish society. Many Muslims had become involved in politics, community work and were actively contributing towards the betterment of the Scottish society. Others through hard work and innovation in their businesses were contributing to the economy of the country. It was encouraging to note that the services of more of them began to be recognised. In early 1980s, Mr M.T. Shaheen, a committed community activist, generous person and successful businessman and the late Mr F.M. Sharif, a selfless and sincere community worker were each awarded an MBE for services to the community. The late Mr Yaqub Ali, a highly successful business-person and philanthropist, was awarded an OBE for services to commerce and industry.

Nonetheless, where there was success and affluence there was also failure and poverty. With recognitions and honours, there was also prejudice and discrimination. A small section of the Muslim community neither had the means to enter any trade or business nor the ability to find suitable jobs to earn an honourable living. In addition, there were those who were caught up in the trap of self-employment and were continuing with their non-profitable trades knowing that if they gave up their business it would be difficult for them to find a job to feed their families. Institutional and covert racism still existed in Scotland. They were therefore resigned to live in relative poverty with self-respect than to suffer the indignity of unemployment and social security benefits. Thus, not everything was rosy, though fortunately, most of the Muslim community were doing well.

During this period, many more Muslims arrived in Scotland from the Middle East, Turkey, Iran, Afghanistan, North Africa, Malaysia etc. Some of them were asylum seekers and refugees who were fleeing oppressive regimes and poverty in their homelands. However, many were entrepreneurs and professionals who came to take up specialist jobs. The increase in their numbers and especially their dispersal throughout Scotland required the provision of religious facilities in more towns and areas. Consequently, by the end of the 1990s the number of mosques in Scotland had increased to twenty-five. There was now a mosque in nearly every sizable town in Western, Central and North Eastern Scotland. These mosques served not only as places of worship but also as community centres and evening and weekend schools for the religious education of the Muslim children. All the mosques in Scotland so far were made in altered dwelling houses, halls or abandoned churches. The first purpose-built mosque was built in Glasgow in the early 1980s at a cost of nearly £3 million. It took over twenty years of planning and six years of construction work to complete. It is both spacious and beautiful, a fine example of the synthesis of Islamic and Western architecture and it can hold about 1500 worshippers. The Imam of *Kaabah* – the Holy Mosque in *Makkah* – officially opened it on May 19 1984, in the presence of many dignitaries, leaders, and adherents of the Christian, Jewish, Hindu, Sikh and all other religions in Scotland.

By 1990 there were very few places left in Scotland that did not have a Muslim family living among them. Shops, restaurants and take-aways operated by Muslims could be found now in the remotest corners of Scotland. All families by now had been reunited and the Muslim population of Scotland had increased to about 35,000.

The Muslim community had become well involved in politics by the 1990s and in all other fields of life in Scotland. When, after Iraq's occupation of Kuwait in 1990, the Gulf crisis erupted and it became obvious that the USA, UK and some other countries were planning to attack Iraq, the Scottish churches and most of the Scottish people opposed that dangerous course of action. The Scottish Muslim community also was against any military action against Iraq; they thought that it would bring more suffering to the Iraqi people and unsettle the whole of Middle East. Some churchmen took the initiative of calling a meeting of the representative of all churches and mosques to discuss a course of action to deal with that ominous situation. At that meeting, it was decided to set up a Gulf Reconciliation Committee consisting of members from both the Christian and Muslim faiths (I was one of the Muslim members of the Committee). The object of this committee was to make the government aware of the anti-war feelings of all religious bodies and of the majority of the Scottish people and to urge them to solve this problem through negotiations and diplomacy.

Nonetheless, Iraq was invaded by the coalition forces and Kuwait was 'liberated' by force. After this 'victory', the government decided to hold the National Gulf War Memorial Service not in St Paul's London or in Canterbury Cathedral but in St Giles Edinburgh. The Scottish Churches and the Gulf Reconciliation Committee opposed this Memorial Service and suggested that it should be a service for repentance, for adding to the misery of the people of Iraq, and not a celebration. Hence, the Churches and most of the Scottish people boycotted the Memorial Service held on 4th May 1991. The Gulf Reconciliation Group then resolved to hold two Repentance Services one in the Glasgow Central Mosque and the second in St Giles Cathedral Edinburgh. The Glasgow Service was attended by at least 500 representatives of Christian churches from all over Scotland and a large number from the Muslim community. The St Giles Service of Repentance was held on 20th October 1991.

The St Giles Cathedral Service would be remembered as one unique in the history of Christian-Muslim relations. The Service was scheduled to begin at 6.00 pm, however the Muslim attendees had to perform their evening prayers at 6.15 pm. They therefore had requested to be allowed to leave at 6.10 pm and to be provided with a separate room where they could observe their rituals. However, the Minister of St Giles Rev. Gilleasbuig Macmillan had a far more generous and imaginative idea in his mind. He decided to stop the Service a couple of minutes before 6.15 pm and invited the Muslims to perform their prayers in the Cathedral, where next to the altar enough space had been made available for them. The Muslim call for prayer was made from the pulpit of the Cathedral and the prayers were performed in the midst of a Christian congregation of over one thousand. I am certain that this was the first occasion ever in the history of the Christian Church that it allowed the Muslims to make their call for prayer and perform their prayers not only within a church but also next to the altar. The prayers were over in about ten minutes after which the service resumed. Such an unprecedented and noble gesture could only have come about in Scotland, where tolerance and benevolence in some quarters of the society sometimes exceed expectations. This is the kind of relationship and understanding that had developed between Muslims and Christians, in Scotland, by the 1990s and especially before and after the first Gulf War.

During the last decade of the twentieth century Muslim candidates from all major political parties participated in all local and Parliamentary elections. In the 1995 local authority elections, four Muslim councillors were elected to Glasgow City Council. In the 1997 general election, Muhammad Sarwar was elected a Member of Parliament from the Glasgow Govan constituency. Sarwar was the first Muslim Member of Parliament in Britain and it was to the credit of the people of Scotland that they elected him, as in 1970 they had elected me as the first Muslim city councillor in Britain. Also in 1997, a well-known Glasgow Muslim philanthropist the late Mr. Yaqub Ali donated £500,000 to Strathclyde University, to set up the Pakistan 50th Anniversary Scholarship Fund. The purpose of this fund was to provide bursaries for deserving students from Pakistan, for higher studies at this University. This was the largest single donation ever made to Strathclyde University.

On Friday, 31 July 1998, H.R.H. Prince Abdul Aziz of Saudi Arabia opened a beautiful purpose-built mosque and Islamic centre in Edinburgh, that was funded by the government of Saudi Arabia. This mosque is a fine specimen of Islamic architecture. In 2000, a new large purpose built mosque was opened in Dundee. By the end of the century, nearly a dozen Scottish Muslims had been honoured by the Queen in the honours list for their services to the nation. More and more of the second and third generation Muslims were joining various professions and serving the nation as doctors, dentists, pharmacists, teachers, lawyers, accountants and engineers. They were now to be seen in the media, as reporters, feature writers and television newscasters. Perhaps soon, we would see on the screen a Muslim girl, wearing hijab, presenting the news. They were in the police forces, the fire services and the armed forces of the nation. They were playing their part in the nation's affairs by being involved in politics and by serving on the boards of the various government and voluntary sector bodies. In sports also, they had made their mark, especially in cricket and hockey. They had well-established and effective religious, charitable, cultural and welfare associations in every city and town. These were clear signs of the integration of the Muslim community into Scottish society and proof of their political, social and philanthropic involvement in the mainstream of life in Scotland. By the close of the century, there were over 46,000 Muslims and 40 mosques in Scotland. The Muslim community had become a recognised part of Scottish society and Islam the second religion after Christianity.

The increase in the population of Muslims, during the last decade of the twentieth century, was mainly due to natural growth, the affianced coming from Asian countries, internal migration and the arrival of more Muslim refugees. The 2001 census gave a figure of 42,600 for the population of Muslims in Scotland. However, this figure is not accurate because many Muslims did not answer the question on religion in the census form. In addition, many Muslims, being careless or not proficient in English, did not complete or return the census forms and hence were not included in the figures. According to the official statistics, over four million people (about 7% of the total population of Britain) did not answer the question on religion. Therefore, if all those Muslims who did not answer the religion question or did not return the forms are added to the official figure, an estimation of over 46,000 Muslims in Scotland in the beginning of the new millennium looks more accurate. The majority of these, about 38,000, were of Pakistani origin and the remaining in descending order, Bangladeshis, Arabs, Turks, Iraqis, Iranians, Afghans, Kurds, North Africans, Palestinians, Somalis, Nigerians, Lebanese, Bosnians and Albanians. There were also about 500 indigenous converts to Islam in Scotland. *Sufi* Islam is becoming popular in the West and attracting many educated people to Islam. There is indeed, a large academics' group of indigenous *Sufis* in Edinburgh, most of them associated with the universities and other academic fields.

Scots have been converting to Islam not only in India during the Raj but also in Scotland long before the settlement of Muslims in Scotland. For example, *Yahya En-Nasr* was born in Kilwinning, Ayrshire on February 17, 1874 and his parents named him John Parkinson. He studied astronomy and biology and achieved distinction in both these fields. Then he became interested in philosophy that led him to investigate the field of religion. The study of Islam deeply influenced him and he converted in around 1901. He wrote books and many articles praising and promoting Islam. However, he achieved fame as a gifted poet and his poetry also is mostly dedicated to the cause of Islam. He died in 1918 at the young age of 42.[18]

Sir Thomas Lauder Brunton (1844-1916) from Hiltonshill, Roxburghshire was another Scot who embraced Islam in the late nineteenth century.[19] Sir Thomas studied medicine at Edinburgh

---

[18] *The Islamic Review* February 1914 pp.64-65 and April 1919 pp.149-152

[19] *1000 years of Islam in Britain* p.12

University and later moved to London where he established his reputation as a medical researcher and clinical pharmacologist. He was knighted in 1900.

Sir Abdullah Archibald Hamilton Bart, formerly Sir Charles Edward Archibald Watkins Hamilton (1876-1939) embraced Islam on 20th December 1923. Being a direct descendent of the Duke of Abercorn, baron Hamilton of Paisley and his wife Mary, a daughter of King James II of Scotland, Sir Abdullah was of royal descent.[20]

Yaqub Zaki was born in Greenock on 3 September 1944 and named James Dickie. The story of his conversion is remarkable. When asked how and when he converted he told me that during his early age he read some books on Islam in a library in Greenock and became interested. One day, when he was fifteen, he saw a copy of the English translation of the *Quran* in a bookshop, and bought it. He read it, and became very impressed by its contents. A few months later, in 1960 he came to Glasgow, found out where the mosque was, went there, saw the Imam and told him that he wanted to become a Muslim. The Imam was very surprised to see a teenage boy coming on his own and asking to be converted. After many arguments and searching question, realising the determination of the young man the Imam told him to repeat after him the *shahada* – the declaration of faith – 'I bear witness that there is no god but God and I bear witness that Muhammad is the messenger of God'. Having embraced Islam he came home and told his school friends that he had become a Muslim. When it became common knowledge in his school that he had converted his troubles began and he suffered much harassment and discrimination from fellow students and teachers. After leaving the school, he attended Glasgow university. In the university he experienced trouble and after two years' suffering left Glasgow for Granada in Spain. From there he went to Cairo to study Arabic. He returned to Spain and joined Barcelona university to study Semitic Philology. He got his Doctorate in Arabic Literature from Granada University in 1968. He has written books in English, Spanish and Arabic on Islamic topics, has made many contributions to symposia published in various countries and written numerous articles for the press. He has also been involved in producing many documentary films on various Islamic subjects. He is married to a Tajik Muslim woman and is still very busy writing

---

[20] *The Islamic Review* June 1939

and attending conferences home and abroad. When in Britain he divides his time between London and Greenock.

Another notable Scot to embrace Islam in the twentieth century is *Shaykh Abdul Qadir as-Sufi al-Murabit*. His Christian name was Ian Dallas. He was born in Ayr, in 1930, of a Highland family whose history goes back to 1279, and was educated at Ayr Academy, the oldest school in Scotland. For his further studies, he attended the Royal Academy of Dramatic Art and then the University of London. He began his career as a dramatist and wrote many plays, which were presented at theatres and broadcast by BBC television.[21] In spite of his early success in life he was, like many of his generation, disillusioned with materialistic Western culture. In search of solace, he travelled to Muslim countries.[22] In 1963, during his stay in Morocco he embraced Islam and changed his name to *Abd al-Qadir*. He then became a student and follower of a well-known Moroccan *Sufi, Shaykh Muhammad ibn al-Habib,* who conferred on him the title of *as-Sufi.* With his *Shaykh* (teacher/master), he travelled extensively in Morocco, Algeria and Libya and received further instructions in *Sufism* from some other famous teachers.[23]

After perfecting his knowledge of Islam, he returned to Britain with a mission to call people to Islam. In the mid-1970s, he set up his headquarters in Bristol Gardens, West London and soon had attracted a group of 20 to 30 disillusioned young British and American converts around him. The number of his followers grew fast and 'the whole street was taken over by tens of people in green turbans and Moroccan robes'. During the summer of 1976, *Abd al-Qadir as-Sufi* with his group held their midday prayers in Hyde Park, in order to draw the attention of British people to Islam. From London, the group, now increased to about 200 families, moved to an old mansion outside Norwich with the aim of setting up 'a self-sufficient Muslim village'. However, soon serious differences arose between *Abdul-Qadir* and his followers. He was accused of authoritarianism. Some of the members became disaffected and the group disintegrated within a couple of years, but the remnants of the group, about twenty families, still live in Norwich and are active in promoting Islam. *Abd al-Qadir* then moved to Granada in

[21] whttp://en.wikipedia.org/wiki/Abdalqadir as-Sufi al Murabit

[22] Ali, Kose *Conversion to Islam* pp.175/176

[23] whttp://en.wikipedia.org/wiki/Abdalqadir as-Sufi al Murabit

Spain, where a group of his followers had been functioning since the mid-1970s.[24] In Granada, with financial help from the King of Morocco, he played an important role in building the first mosque in that city since the expulsion of Muslims from there in 1492 and the destruction of all places of Muslim worship. In the early 1990s, he moved back to Scotland and settled in a mansion in a country estate near Inverness.

In late 1990s *Abd al-Qadir* moved again and this time to South Africa, where he still lives. In 2004, he founded Dallas College in Cape Town to educate and train future Muslim leaders. He has been a prolific writer since the early 1970s and so far has written about a dozen books and numerous articles on various Islamic topics. He has become well-known throughout the Muslim world and is often in demand to address meetings and conferences. He has followers and students, some quite well-known and highly educated, throughout the western world who are carrying on his mission of calling people to Islam in every country and writing books to propagate and preach Islam. His movement is unique in the sense that it has been begun, led and developed by European converts. It has been reasonably successful in attracting Western non-Muslims to Islam all over Europe and the Americas, many of whom are now active in the propagation of Islam. As founder of this movement this Scotsman, who was Ian Dallas at his birth, became *Abd al-Qadir* in his youth and is now known as *Shaykh Abd al-Qadir as-Sufi al-Murabit*, with hundreds of followers all over the world, has done much to promote Islam in the West in recent times.

The new millennium began with about a dozen Scottish Muslim businessmen having made the millionaires' list. All of them are the sons of those who came here in the 1930s and 1950s and began as peddlers. The credit for this success goes to those first generation pioneers, their patience, perseverance, aspiration and hard work. When they arrived in Scotland there were no jobs for them, nobody would employ them. The only way they could survive here and support their families back home was to engage in peddling and that was a very demanding vocation. They suffered with patience the abuse of racists, the humiliation of slammed doors, the mockery and banter of children in the streets, the discomfort of Scottish weather while carrying a heavy suitcase full of their wares and

---

[24] Ali, Kose *ibid* pp.176-180

knocking doors in rain, sleet and snow. In addition, even inside their houses, they had to put up with abuse from their neighbours for the 'smell of their cooking', 'speaking loudly' or making even the slightest noise. They had a hard life and their road to success was not easy. Nonetheless, their progress and success against all odds is remarkable especially when one realises that, in their early years in this country, they were denied jobs and now they were offering jobs to thousands of people and contributing millions to the economy of the country. They, their children and their Muslim community have now become an integral part of the Scottish society. They have firmly planted their roots in Scotland; they have adopted Scotland as their new country and they consider themselves Scots. Their second and third generations know no other country, they are born and bred Scots, to them Scotland is their only country.

The new millennium also saw the arrival in Scotland of over six thousands asylum seekers and a number of refugees. Most of these unfortunate people were Muslims from Iran, Iraq, Kosovo, Pakistan, Somalia, Turkey and many other Muslim countries. They, if given leave to stay – and it is hoped that many of them would be – will further raise the number of Muslims in Scotland. Thus, the Muslim community, that fifty years ago in 1955 was about 500 in Scotland, would be over 50,000 by the end of the first decade of the twenty first century. As regards the distribution of their population in Scotland, the bulk of them, that is about 30,000, reside in and around Glasgow. The rest are scattered all over the country: about 8,000 in Edinburgh and East Lothian; about 3,000 in Central Scotland and Fife, about 4,000 in Dundee and Tayside, about 2,000 in Aberdeen and Grampian, and the remainder in Dumfries and Galloway and the Highland and Islands.

During a visit to Orkney and Shetland in the early 1990s, as a member of the BBC's Scottish Advisory Council, I was pleasantly surprised to learn that some Muslims have settled in even these remotest parts of Scotland. After a meeting in Shetland, I asked one of the local councillors if there were any Muslims living on the island. He pointed towards a row of shops in the main street of Lerwick and said, 'All those belong to Pakistanis.' When in Orkney I asked the same question to a prominent resident of Kirkwall, his answer was, 'You see this hotel we are sitting in; it was designed by a Bangladeshi Muslim architect who lives in Kirkwall.'

By the beginning of the new millennium therefore, the Muslim community was well settled in Scotland and in general doing rather well. Their comparative contentment however, was disturbed by the atrocity committed on 9/11/2001 in the USA. Suddenly Muslims the world over became suspects as possible terrorists and Islamophobia seized the Western world. Like other Muslim minorities in the West, this tragedy also undermined the confidence of the Scottish Muslim community. They were hurt to learn that as Muslims all of them had become suspects in the eyes of the general population. However, the community stood up to this challenge and made every effort to lessen the damage done as quickly as possible. Communications were widened with other religious bodies, political parties, police, local authorities, other community groups and organisations in order to repair the damage done and restore their confidence in the Muslim community. These efforts proved successful and slowly the situation began to improve.

In the 2003 Scottish local authority elections there were eleven Muslim candidates, representing all major political parties; eight of them were elected as councillors, five in Glasgow and three in other local authorities. One of Glasgow's newly elected councillors was Mrs. Halima Malik, the first female Muslim city councillor in Scotland. In October 2004, in Mossend near Motherwell, the construction of a new beautiful purpose-built mosque was completed. It was built by the Lanarkshire Muslim Society at a cost of approximately £2 million for the use of the 2,500 Muslims living in that area.

Unfortunately, as the community was beginning to emerge with optimism from the aftermath of 9/11, the tragedy of 7/7 in London left them shattered and depressed once again. Again, they became suspects in their adopted country. To make thing worse the new terror laws, introduced in the wake of 7/7, generated more despair and dismay among the older generation and alienation among some young Muslims. The indiscriminate and insensitive use of these laws in England, especially in the Forest Gate episode, further bruised their confidence and made life difficult for them. Some of the first and second generations have already begun contemplating returning to their countries of origin and if the situation were to deteriorate, they would certainly do so. That would be detrimental to the interests of both the Muslim community and Scotland.

It is hoped that, learning lessons from England, the Scottish police, if need be, would use the new legislation with consideration and proper prudence. It is hoped that the use of anti-terrorism laws does not contravene the norms of traditional British justice and fair play. It is hoped that nobody is treated as guilty until proven so and that sense would prevail and the label of terrorist would not be applied to every Muslim in this country. Muslims are a responsible and law-abiding integral part of the Scottish society and labelling a segment of the society as terrorist would be a slight on the whole society.

Postscript: I have narrated the twentieth century history of the settlement of the Muslim community in Scotland, mainly from my own observations and recollections through my long involvement in their affairs. I came to Scotland in 1953, when this small, mostly illiterate community, numbering only about 300 was struggling to earn a living and survive in an atmosphere of rampant discrimination and racial prejudice. Being an educated person, I soon became involved in helping them with their various problems and looking after their interests. In the late 1960s, for a local publication, I interviewed most of who were still available from those who had come to Scotland between the two World Wars and earlier. My recollections and observations therefore are first hand and authentic. The numeration of the Muslims in Scotland, before 1990, mentioned in various places in this book are approximations based on my previous research and knowledge of the settlement of the community in Scotland. For a wider account and other details of the arrival and settlement of the Muslims in Scotland in the twentieth century and earlier, see Maan, B. *The New Scots*, [Edinburgh, 1992].

CHAPTER 6
What is Islam?

ISLAM is one of the most misunderstood religions in the world. Myths and misconceptions abound in the West about Islam. The irony is that not many people in the West even know that it is one of the three Abrahamic faiths and that Muslims believe in Jesus, Moses Abraham, their Books and all other prophets mentioned in the Old and New Testaments. Since 9/11, followed by 7/7, the misunderstandings and controversy about Islam has increased many fold and it has also become the most maligned faith especially in the West. This brief explanation of Islam is intended to correct some of those falsities and fictions and help bring about a better understanding of this faith leading to a better relationship between the Scottish Muslims and other communities.

The Arabic word Islam means submission, total surrender and also peace. Submission and total surrender to the will of *Allah* (*Allah* in Arabic means God Almighty, the One and Only, the Infinite, the Creator and the Sustainer of this Universe). It implies absolute compliance with the guidance of God as revealed through His prophets. Peace – implies to be at peace with oneself and with the world around one through peace with God, by submitting to His guidance and His providence. This involves bringing one's attitude, conduct, likes and dislikes and indeed the whole discipline of one's life in harmony with the Divine guidance. A Muslim therefore, is one who believes in God and submits and unequivocally surrenders to His guidance, and follows that guidance in word and in deed throughout his/her life.

Thus, Islam is not just a religion but also a complete and comprehensive way of life that covers the spiritual as well as the secular aspects of the life of its adherents. It regulates the private, social, family, religious, financial, commercial, professional, political and every other possible facet of the life of a Muslim. Hence whatever a Muslim does or says ought to be in consonance with the Divine Code and the Divine guidance.

Islam is not a new or a strange religion but is the continuation and indeed the culmination of the Divine religion revealed by God All-Mighty through His various prophets and messengers from Noah to Jesus. According to the Divine scheme, prophets or messengers have been coming throughout human history to every nation or people in all parts of the world. However, only some of them have been mentioned by name in the various scriptures. Islam teaches that basically all prophets and messengers have preached the same message that there is only One God, Omniscient, Omnipresent and Omnipotent. God gave books to certain of His prophets and inspired others to guide human beings to live charitable, chaste, honest, responsible and pious lives and that there is another world and another life after death in which all souls will be rewarded according to their deeds in this life. The good deeds in this world will earn the bounties of God in this as well as the next world and the evil deeds will earn His wrath here and in the hereafter.

Muslims believe in and revere, not only Muhammad as the Prophet of God and the *Quran* the Book revealed to him but also, all the other prophets, raised by God throughout human history, and their Books. The Islamic Article of Faith makes this obligation very clear as it reads:

> I believe in God Almighty (Allah), His Angels, (all) His Books,
> (all) His Messengers and the Last Day (the Day of Judgment).
> I believe in Destiny, the good of it and the bad of it.

Muslims therefore are obliged to believe in all the Prophets especially those mentioned in the *Torah*, the Bible and the *Quran*, from Noah down to Abraham, Isaac, Ishmael, Jacob, Moses, David, John the Baptist, Jesus and the last Prophet Muhammad and their Books. *Quran*, the Holy Book of Islam emphases this decree as under:

> Say (O Muslims): We believe in Allah and that which is
> revealed unto us, and that which was revealed unto Abraham
> and Ishmael, and Isaac and Jacob, and the tribes and that

which Moses and Jesus received, and that which the Prophets received from their Lord. We make no distinction between any of them, and unto Him have we surrendered. (2:136)

He hath revealed unto thee (Muhammad) the scripture with truth, confirming that which was (revealed) before it, even as He revealed the *Torah* and the Gospel aforetime, for a guidance to mankind: and hath revealed the criterion (of right and wrong). (3: 3-4)

He has ordained for you that religion which He commended to Noah, and that which We inspire in thee (Muhammad), and that which We commended to Abraham and Moses and Jesus, saying: Establish the religion, and be not divided therein. (42: 13)

With reference to this sacred connection among Jews, Christians and Muslims the well-known Scottish academic, theologian and author the Rev. Prof. William Montgomery Watt says:

Christians should thus recognise a deep truth in the Quranic claim to be following the religion of Abraham. Jews, Christians and Muslims all have a faith which goes back to that of Abraham, by whatever name it is called.[1]

Thus, Christianity, Judaism and Islam go back to the Prophet and Patriarch Abraham who about 4,000 years ago, established the settlement that, over the millennia, has developed into the present-day city of *Makkah* where Muhammad was born. In that settlement the Patriarch and his son Ishmael built a sacred house – *the Kaabah* – for the worship of One God. This house, according to the Muslim tradition, was the first to be built on earth for the worship of God and is the most sacred place of worship in Islam, where Muslims go to perform the pilgrimage and towards which all Muslims, throughout the world, turn while praying.

There is a considerable number of references to Jesus and Mary in the *Quran*. Indeed, there are more references to Mary in the *Quran* than in the Bible and chapter XIX of the *Quran* is entitled

---

[1] *Muslim Christian Encounters* p.29

'Mary' in honour of the mother of Jesus. The *Quran* confirms the virgin birth and indeed bestows a unique status upon Mary declaring her to be the best women of the creation:

> Allah has chosen you. He has made you pure and exalted you above all women of creation. (3: 42)

Such a unique and highly exalted position has not been granted to any other female in this world, not even to the mother, any of the wives or daughters of the Prophet Muhammad. The *Quran*, in its chapters II, III, IV, XIX, XLII, XXIII, XLIII, LVII, LXI and LXVI gives many details about Mary, Jesus, the virgin birth of Jesus, his ministry, his Ascension and much more. Just to cite one example of the material in the *Quran* about Jesus and Mary, the following is what *Quran* says about the virgin birth:

> (And remember) when the Angel said: O Mary! Lo! Allah giveth thee glad tidings of a Word from Him, whose name is the Messiah, Jesus, son of Mary, illustrious in the world and the Hereafter, and one of those brought near (to Allah). He will speak unto mankind in his cradle and in his manhood, and he is of the righteous. She said: My Lord! How can I have a child when no man hath touched me? He said: So (it will be). Allah createth what He will. If He decreath a thing, He saith unto it only: Be! And it is. And He will teach him the Scripture and wisdom, and the *Torah* and the Gospel. And make him a messenger unto the children of Israel, (saying): I come unto you with a sign from your Lord. Lo! I fashion for you out of clay the likeness of a bird, and I breathe into it and it is a bird, by Allah's leave. I heal him who was born blind, and the leper, and I raise the dead, by Allah's leave. And I announce unto you what ye eat and what ye store up in your houses. Lo! Herein verily is a portent for you, if ye are to be believers. (Trans. M.M. Pickthall, 3: 45-49)

Muslims believe that Islam is the culmination, in its comprehensive, complete, and final form, of the same Divine religion that was revealed to all prophets throughout the ages. It is the final universal message that is not confined to a particular community, area or generation. Earlier messages were limited to certain communities and certain periods until the appearance of a new messenger with new revelations. Humankind made certain limited progress in the light of those messages and the Divine guidance contained in them. Every new message incorporated certain modifications of the Divine law that took into account relative human progress. The final message in the form of the *Quran* is complete and perfect in essence. However, it leaves room for flexibility, according to the progressive human advancement, in the implementation of its details. It was revealed when human faculties had matured. Hence, it is meant for all humankind for all times and according to Islam there will be no subsequent messengers, Divine messages or revelations. This final Divine message therefore supersedes all previous messages.

The *Quran*, The Holy Book of Islam

According to Islam, the *Quran* is the final Holy Book containing the Divine revelations. It is the primary source of the Islamic faith. It was revealed, incrementally over a period of twenty three years, to the Prophet Muhammad in his mother tongue, Arabic. Prophet Muhammad was a descendent of Abraham through Ishmael his first-born. Whenever the Prophet received a revelation, it was impressed upon his memory and he would right away dictate it, in the same Divine words, to the scribes who wrote it down. Thus, before his death each and every Divine word revealed to the Prophet had been meticulously written down under his supervision.

In addition, some of his companions memorised the revelations when he pronounced or dictated them and a considerable number of them had memorised the whole *Quran* during the life of the Prophet. The memorisation of the *Quran*, since then, has been a common and indeed cherished practice among Muslims, and today there are millions of Muslims in the world who know the whole *Quran* by heart. In Scotland, in 1986, a seven-year-old Glasgow Muslim boy, Jamil Mughal, successfully memorised the entire *Quran* and caused a considerable stir in media in Britain and throughout the West.

The written down and the memorised text of the *Quran* has guaranteed its authenticity and uniformity since the time of the Prophet Muhammad. Since its revelation, fourteen centuries ago, no additions, deletions or distortions have happened in the *Quran*.

Its text is still in Arabic the language it was revealed in and not a single dot has been added to or deleted from it. Therefore, in every Muslim house, in every Mosque, in every library, whether it is in Indonesia or in America, it is the same *Quran* in the Arabic language, exactly as it was revealed to the Prophet Muhammad, which the faithful read, revere, and try to follow:

> Islam is the faith of a single sacred text; Christianity, by contrast, of many texts. This contrast between mono-textual and multi-textual faiths has had very far-reaching consequences in the world's history. The sacred text of Islam is the Koran, revealed by God to his Prophet Muhammad. . .[2]

Muslims believe that the *Quran* is addressed to the entire human race and is for all times. It contains the fundamentals of religion and ethics as well as prescriptive legislation for everyday living. It is a guidance for all people and the confirmation and summation, in a single sacred text, of all that was revealed before it. There are certain revelations in the *Quran* that contain subtle and sophisticated ideas that were only properly understood in the twentieth century. The truth contained in these revelations, in many cases, has been scientifically established in recent times. To cite two examples, the *Quran* states:

> We first created man from an essence of clay; then placed him, a living germ in a safe enclosure (the womb). The germ We made a clot of blood, and the clot a lump of flesh. This We fashioned into bones, then clothed the bones with flesh, thus bringing forth another creation. Blessed be Allah the noblest of creators. (23: 12-14).

And:

> Have not those who disbelieve known that the heavens and the earth were joined together as one united piece, then We parted them. . . (21: 30)?

---

[2] Fletcher, Richard *The Cross and the Crescent* p.1

In the first example, the description of the development of the human embryo in the Quranic verses was confirmed to be correct by prominent anatomists and embryologists including Dr Keith L. Moore, Professor Emeritus of Anatomy and Cell Biology at the University of Toronto, Canada:

> In 1981, during the Seventh Medical Conference in Dammam, Saudi Arabia, Professor Moore said: 'It has been a great pleasure for me to help clarify statements in the *Quran* about human development. It is clear to me that these statements must have come to Muhammad from God, because almost all of this knowledge was not discovered until many centuries later. This proves to me that Muhammad must have been a messenger of God.' Consequently, Professor Moore was asked the following question: 'Does this mean that you believe that the *Quran* is the word of God?' He replied: 'I find no difficulty in accepting that'.[3]

The contents of the second verse point to the big bang theory concerning the origin of the universe and most of the geologists and nuclear physicists of the world now accept that theory:

> Dr Alfred Kroner is one of the world's renowned geologists. He is a Professor of Geology and the Chairman of the Department of Geology at the Institute of Geosciences, Johannes Gutenburgh University, Mainz, Germany. He said: 'Thinking where Muhammad came from. . . I think it is almost impossible that he could have known about things like the common origin of the universe, because scientists have only found out within the last few years, with very complicated and advanced technological methods, that this is the case.[4]

There are many more facts embedded in the Quran that have been, and are being, recognised or proven true by modern scientific knowledge. For example: the revolution of the sun, moon and planets in fixed orbits (36: 38-39), the fertilisation of plants by the

---

[3] Peachy, Dr. William (Daoud) et.al. eds *A Brief Illustrated Guide to Understanding Islam* p.10

[4] *ibid* p.14

wind (15: 22), sexual pairing of the plants and every other creation (36 35), the casting of heavy mountains into the earth so that it does not quiver or quake during its motion, (16: 15) etc. In the seventh century, when the *Quran* was being revealed to the Prophet Muhammad, very little was known about the science of astronomy, anatomy, agronomy, embryology, biology, geology or nuclear physiology. In any case, the Prophet was an illiterate person and living in a secluded part of the vast Arabian desert he could not have known anything about science. The only explanation possible therefore, would be that God Almighty revealed these facts to the Prophet Muhammad and that the *Quran* is the Word of God. About Muhammad and the *Quran* the Rev. Prof. William Montgomery Watt has this to say:

> I do, however, believe that Muhammad, like the earlier prophets, had genuine religious experience. I believe that he really did receive something directly from God. As such, I believe that the *Quran* came from God, that it is Divinely inspired. Muhammad could not have caused the great upsurge in religion that he did without God's blessings.[5]

The *Sunnah*
– the words and deeds of the Prophet Muhammad

The second source of guidance for Muslims after the *Quran* is the *Sunnah*, the practice and the example of the Prophet, and the *Hadith*, the reliably transmitted reports of what the Prophet Muhammad did, said or approved. The *Sunnah* is the exegesis, clarification and interpretation of the Divine revelations because all the Prophet's actions, sayings and recommendations were in perfect accord with those revelations. Belief in the *Sunnah* therefore is a part of the Islamic faith.

The devoted companions of the Prophet attentively heard, meticulously collected, diligently memorised or recorded the sayings, the sermons, the actions, the manners, the dealings, in fact everything, every act and every aspect of his life in this world. Some of his sayings and sermons explain and elaborate on certain

---

[5] 'The Last Orientalist' Rev Prof William Montgomery Watt *The Coracle* Iona Community, Summer 2000 Issue 3:51 pp.8-11

verses of the *Quran* and the examples and aspects of his life point to the best way of benefiting from the guidance of the *Quran*. The Prophet received the revelations from God through Archangel Gabriel. He understood the meaning and the interpretation of the Divine Commandments and lived his life in complete adherence to Divine guidance. His life therefore, or his examples (the *Sunnah*) and his sayings (the *Hadith*), give Muslims a perfect template and a practical demonstration of how they can build their lives according to Divine guidance. Devout Muslims therefore try to use that template, which in essence is the Islamic way of life. The *Quran*, the *Sunnah* and the consensus of theologians only, on matters not dealt with by the *Quran* and the *Sunnah*, make up the *Sharia*, the Islamic Religious Law.

The Five Pillars of Islam

There is no hierarchy and no sacraments in Islam and nothing equating to priests or bishops. Islam believes in direct communication with an Omnipresent and Omniscient God, who listens and responds to the prayers and penitence of His every creature. Hence, there is no need and no place for any intercessor or intermediary during the worship and supplications of His Creation. Nevertheless, there are *Ulema* (the learned), who guide and advise the Muslims in religious matters and *Imams* (leaders), who lead them in congregational prayers. They are trained in religious schools to dispense guidance and to lead prayers in the mosques. However, it is not compulsory or even necessary in Islam to have a trained Imam in a mosque, in fact any practising Muslim whom other worshippers request, can lead the prayers.

In Islam, every action that is performed with sincerity according to the Divine guidance is considered an act of worship. Hence, looking after one's family and parents, being good and loving husbands or wives, being considerate and generous to other members of the society, especially neighbours and next of kin, forgiving enemies and overlooking people's faults etc., are all considered meritorious acts of worship in Islam. However, there are certain rituals, the specific acts of worship and of obedience to God, that a Muslim must perform. These are known as the Five Pillars of Islam and they are:

1. *Shahada*: This is the declaration of faith in the following words:

> I bear witness that there is none worthy of worship except
> Allah the God Almighty, and I bear witness that Muhammad
> is His servant and messenger.

Thus, Muhammad is not divine and has no share whatsoever in divinity. He was a human being who was chosen by God to be His messenger to humanity. However, God did direct Muslims to obey, respect and love His messenger Muhammad. Hence, the respect and reverence shown to their Prophet by Muslims is so profound that it is difficult for non-Muslims to comprehend. Muslims respect him and love him more than any person or anything in this world. Muslims also have deep respect for all other prophets or messengers of God and they would resent any of them being mocked, belittled or reviled.

Shahada is the confession of faith. Every person who wants to be or considers himself a Muslim must genuinely accept and sincerely believe in this statement, as this is a prerequisite for accepting Islam as one's religion. Any person who intentionally makes this declaration theoretically becomes a Muslim. In addition, he also must believe in the angels, in all prophets and their scriptures and revelations from God, in the Day of Judgment and life after death. Lastly to be a true and practising Muslim, one must comply with the other following four pillars or requirements of Islam.

2. *Salah* – the act of worship: In Islam the worship of God consists of five prescribed prayers performed daily at dawn, midday, late afternoon, after sunset and about two hours after sunset or before going to bed. A true Muslim must perform all five prayers under all conditions. Only women during menstruation and the postnatal phase, insane and unconscious persons, children under twelve years and very old senile persons are exempt from this obligation. When a Muslim is offering his prayers he is in direct communication with God his Creator. It is a unique exercise in which every part and every muscle of the body joins the soul and mind in the worship and glorification of God. The bowing down and prostrating to God during the prayers five times a day, uttering supplications and repeating *Allahu Akbar* (God is the greatest) instil humility and

enhance the recognition of God's Majesty, to whom the prayers are offered and addressed. The prayers, performed regularly with devotion, strengthen the belief in God, generate morality and piety, purify the heart, cultivate the conscience and comfort the soul. Further, the prayers dampen temptation, discourage acts of wrong-doing and trigger a state of harmony with the world and everything in it.

Cleanliness is an essential requirement for worship in Islam. A worshipper must perform the prescribed ablution before prayers and ensure that his body, clothes and the place of prayer are all clean. The heart, mind and intentions must also be pure and clean before and throughout prayers. Prayers are offered facing towards the *Kaabah* in *Makkah*. The daily prayers can be performed any-where, but going to a mosque and praying in a congregation is more rewarding. Males must perform, if possible, their Friday prayers in a mosque with the congregation. However, women are not obliged to go to the mosque for their daily or Friday prayers.

3. *Sawm* – fasting: Fasting is another act of worship in Islam. A fast is observed every day from dawn until dusk during the month of *Ramadhan* for 29 or 30 days depending on the number of days in this month of the lunar calendar. Every Muslim is obliged to fast, but there are some exceptions: children who have not reached the age of puberty, the insane, the aged, the sick, travellers, expectant women, nursing mothers and menstruating women are all exempt from fasting. Fasting requires abstention from food, drink, smoking, all undesirable and evil actions, words, intentions, and desires. Intimate marital acts are also forbidden during the fasting hours. The month of fasting changes the entire course of a Muslim's daily life.

Ramadhan is the ninth month of the Islamic lunar calendar. As the lunar year is ten days shorter than the solar year, the month of *Ramadhan* is always ten days earlier than the previous year and thus revolves through all seasons. Whereas fasting in the months of winter in Scotland is easy, as the fasting period between dawn and dusk is only about 8/9 hours, it becomes very difficult and demanding in the summer months of June to August as the time between dawn and dusk then is about 19/20 hours. Nonetheless, Muslims consider *Ramadhan* the month of blessings and every adult and often some young children also, persevere in fasting even during the height of summer. The fasting regimen teaches patience, self-discipline and the valuable lesson of fortitude. By experiencing hunger and thirst, one learns to appreciate the plight of the deprived and the poor who are always hungry. It is a month-long annual exercise that builds and strengthens the character, willpower and adaptability of the devout Muslim, and prepares him to conduct his life in a righteous, unselfish, patient, compassionate and considerate manner for the subsequent eleven months.

4. *Zakat* – the Poor Dues: *Zakat* is the prescribed annual amount of 2.5% of one's savings and of the value of one's liquid assets and 10% of the agricultural produce that must be given to the poor and the needy. Normally Muslims perform this duty in the month of *Ramadhan*. Poor people with no valuable assets and very little savings are exempt from giving *Zakat*. Those who are liable must distribute the due amount to the deserving immediately because under the Divine decree they no longer have any moral or legal right to that part of their wealth. According to the *Quran*, it is a claim of the poor upon the wealth of the rich. In Islamic countries, the state collects the *Zakat*, in addition to other scheduled taxes, and distributes it to the needy. In non-Islamic countries the Muslims themselves are obliged to asses their assets, calculate the right amount of *Zakat* and deliver the total amount to the destitute. It can be given to any deserving person without any regard to his/her race, colour or creed. It is a duty decreed by God Almighty to be undertaken by Muslims for their own good and the greater good of the society they live in. *Zakat* is a unique institution that according to Islam purifies the wealth and the property of a Muslim, but above all, it purifies his heart from greed for wealth and selfishness. It encourages him to be more generous and charitable and to share his God-given riches with the less fortunate. The *Quran* is replete with verses exhorting Muslims to share their wealth, over and above their obligatory *Zakat* dues, with their poor relations and other needy people, and promising great rewards to those who do.

5. *Hajj* – the pilgrimage to the *Kaabah* in *Makkah*: Every Muslim, male or female, is obliged to perform the pilgrimage to the *Kaabah*, at least once in his/her lifetime, providing he/she is physically,

mentally and financially capable of doing so. Before embarking on the journey the prospective pilgrim must have sufficient funds to pay off his/her debts if any, cover the expenses of the journey and stay in *Makkah*, and leave sufficient provision for dependents during his/her absence.

Hajj is another unique feature of Islam. It is to obey the command of God and to commemorate the sacred rituals of Abraham and Ishmael at *Kaabah* and in the environs of *Makkah*. It is the largest annual religious gathering in the world with millions in attendance. During its course, prayers and peace permeate the atmosphere – peace with oneself, peace with other pilgrims, peace with animals and all living creature (because Islam forbids disturbing the peace of any creature during the ceremonies of *Hajj*) and most importantly peace with God. It is a powerful demonstration of the universality of Islam and the brotherhood and equality of man.

Pilgrims, male and female, flock to *Makkah* from every country and corner of the world; they are black, brown, yellow and white. They may be rich or poor, aristocrats or commoners but during the course of *Hajj*, they are all equal. The males dress is the same simple two pieces of unsewn white cloth – one round their waist to cover the lower part of the body and one over their shoulders. The females dress in their usual modest clothes covering their whole body except face and hands. They are there to glorify God, nobody and no-one else. Their supplications, rituals, and prayers are the same, all performed together as Islam does not allow any discrimination or distinction on the grounds of status, race or colour. In the sacred precincts no one gets any preference over the other; they stand and sit wherever they find space; everyone is equal before God in the House of God. They return from *Hajj* spiritually enriched and morally rearmed.

In this way the Five Pillars of Islam lay down the warp and wool of the Muslim life. The *Shahada* is intended to be a constant presence; the day is punctuated by the five prayers, and week by the Friday congregational prayer, while the *Zakat* and the *Ramadhan* fast occur once a year, with the *Hajj* coming in a lifetime. Linking the believer to the movement of the earth, the sun and the moon, these ancient mono-theistic rites, practised without alteration since the time of the Prophet, are believed to work a spiritual alchemy on the soul of the Muslim by providing a constant reminder of the beauty and truth which underlie and give meaning to the visible world.[6]

The regular observance of the above duties (the five Pillars if Islam) is meant to lead a person to fear of God and to righteousness. It should make him a law-abiding, responsible, caring and sharing member of society. In Islam, a person's conduct, integrity, civility, care and concern for others, is more important than just observing the rituals. If someone observes all his/her religious rites regularly but does not follow a responsible, compassionate and charitable life, then his observance of those rites is superficial and a pointless formality that is of little use to him. This is made very clear in the *Quran*:

> It is not righteous that you turn your faces (in prayer) towards East or West; but it is righteous to believe in God and the Last Day, and the Angels and the Scriptures, and the Messengers; to spend of your wealth, in spite of your love for it, for your kinsfolk, for orphan, for the needy, for the wayfarer, for those who ask, and for the ransom of slaves; to be steadfast in prayer and practise regular charity; to fulfil the contracts you have made; and to be firm and patient, in pain and adversity, and throughout all periods of panic. Such are the true believers, such are the God fearing. (2: 177)

Hence, the Islamic system is based on faith as well as actions that give credence to professed beliefs. Islam is a practical code of living in which feelings and intentions count for little until they are transformed into real actions.

Islamic Way of Life

Islam is a religion and a complete way of life. It is a comprehensive Divine charter that covers and conducts every aspect and every field of life. It guides a Muslim to live a peaceful and pious life in this world and to prepare for a successful and happy eternal life in

---

[6] Sheikh, A. & Gatrad, A R. eds, Winter, Tim J. in *The Muslim grand narrative*, Caring for Muslim Patients p.22

the hereafter. It tells him what his religious obligations are and what his worldly duties are. It inspires him to achieve intellectual and spiritual heights and at the same time, it motivates him to seek honourable, fair and just means to provide for his family and others in need. It encourages a Muslim to live a full and happy life enjoying the bounties of his Lord God and discourages him from becoming a hermit, an ascetic and/or a celibate for life. It instructs him how to behave in public and in private. It informs him what his obligations are towards his family, his parents, his colleagues, his employees, his employer, his superiors, his juniors, his friends, his foes, his rulers and his subjects. It advises him about what to eat, what to drink and what to avoid, how to eat and how to drink, how to sit and how to sleep, how to talk and how to walk. Hence, for a believer there is nothing concerning the ambit of human life that is not covered by the Islamic code.

As far as the everyday life of a Muslim is concerned, he is obliged to obey the injunctions of the *Quran* as translated into practice by the Prophet Muhammad and to observe with conviction and devotion the above-discussed five fundamentals (pillars) of Islam. If he does that, he can achieve excellence in the spiritual field and at the same time a high standard in his worldly life.

There is no division or separation between the sacred and the secular in Islam. Spiritual and temporal are not only complementary but also interdependent in the life of a Muslim. If he is good in his temporal life, he is bound to be good in his spiritual life and vice versa. For example earning his living as a professional or a trader is a secular act in the general sense, but it would be an act of worship for a Muslim if he undertook it with integrity and according to the values set by Islam, i.e. if he were working for someone, he must do his job with total commitment and honesty. If he is in trade, commerce or a profession he must be honest and fair in all his dealings.

Nonetheless, according to Islamic belief, God has given man the freedom of choice. Man is the best of God's Creation in this universe and indeed His vice-regent on this earth. The Almighty has endowed man with great potentialities but has left him with free will. Man is free to accept the Divine guidance or reject it. He is endowed with the faculty of choice; he is free to follow the right or the wrong path. God through His Prophets has shown human beings the right path, but He or His Prophets do not force them to follow that path and no-one else has the right to force anyone to accept a certain way of life or a certain religion. The *Quran* makes this point very clear in the following Divine declarations:

> There shall be no compulsion in religion. (2: 256)

> Say (O Muhammad) it is the truth from the Lord of you all. Then whosoever will, let him believe, and whosoever will, let him disbelieve. (18: 30)

Ethics and Etiquette: Islam directs a Muslim to be a compassionate, responsible, benevolent, pious and peaceful member of society. He must be a law-abiding, good citizen and support charitable and social organisations. To encourage Muslims to achieve and practise these qualities it imposes certain restrictions upon their behaviour: drinking alcohol or taking drugs and gambling are forbidden in Islam and so is the free mixing of unrelated adult males and females. Pre-marital sex, sex outside marriage and homosexuality are not permitted and considered cardinal sins. The charging or paying of interest is also prohibited. Breaking oaths or promises, lying, cheating, stealing and every other moral delinquency is condemned. Disloyalty to one's country where one enjoys equal rights and freedom to practise one's religion is inadmissible. Islam lays great emphasis on charity, love and compassion. Even to an enemy a Muslim is commanded to 'return evil with good.' In addition to *Zakat*, the 2.5% fixed poor due, a Muslim is obliged to share his wealth with the less fortunate, the orphans, the widows with no resources, the sick, the destitute and all those in need whoever and of whatever faith or race they may be.

A Muslim is enjoined to respect others' rights, feelings, freedom and privacy. Good manners and politeness in speech and action is considered a kind of charity in Islam. He/she is forbidden to suspect, spy, backbite or mock anyone. A Muslim should be kind and considerate to his parents, his relatives, his colleagues, his neighbours and anyone he comes across during the course of his daily life. He is directed to overlook people's faults, forgive others' excesses, visit the sick, and help those in distress. The *Quran* forbids a Muslim to enter any house or property without the explicit permission of the owner. He must not cause any inconvenience or harm to anyone especially his neighbours. The Prophet Muhammad is reported to have said: 'He whose neighbour is not safe from his mischief is not from us' (i.e. he is not a Muslim). The *Quran* declares:

> Show kindness to your parents and your relatives, to the orphan and to the needy, and to the neighbour who is of kin (to you) and the neighbour who is not of kin, and the colleague/fellow traveller, and the wayfarer and (servants/ slaves) whom your right hands possess. Allah does not love boastful and arrogant people. (4: 36)

A Muslim is required to dress modestly. A male must not expose in public any part of his body from navel to the knee and a female must cover all her body from head to feet except her hands and face. As regards food, a Muslim is allowed to eat all wholesome and pure foods and is forbidden to eat pig's meat, carrion and blood. The meat Muslims consume must be of animals killed according to the Biblical rite of cutting the jugular vein and draining all blood from the body of the animal. This prevents any diseases, carried by the animal in his blood, passing on to humans.

Islam teaches that a Muslim looks upon all humanity as one family under the Sovereignty of God. There is no concept of superiority in Islam on account of class, wealth or birth. Discrimination because of colour, class, race or ethnicity etc. is abhorred and forbidden in Islam. In the last sermon of his life addressing hundreds of thousands of believers gathered at the time of *Hajj*, the Prophet Muhammad declared:

> O people! Your God is one and your ancestor (Adam) is one. An Arab is not better than a non-Arab and a non-Arab is not better than an Arab and a white person is not better than the black person and a black person is not better than a white person. Piety alone is the measure of a person.

And on human equality, God declares in the *Quran*:

> O mankind, We have created you from a male and a female and have made you into nations and tribes for you to know

one another (and not to despise one another). Truly, the noblest of you in the sight of God, is the best in conduct. Lo! God is All-Knowing, All Aware. (49: 13)

Thus, In Islam there is no concept of inferiority or superiority of one nation or one person over the other; everyone is equal. Humility and affability are religious virtues in Islam. Piety and benevolence are the only criteria for any honour or superiority. The *Quran* condemns attitudes of false pride and superiority:

Turn not thy cheek in scorn towards folk, nor walk with pertness in the land. Lo! God loves not each braggart boaster. Be modest in thy bearing and subdue thy voice, Lo! The harshest of all voices is the voice of the ass. (31: 18-19)

Family Life: Marriage in Islam, for those who are capable of meeting the responsibilities involved, is a religious duty for men and women, and celibacy is discouraged. The *Quran* decrees that single men and women marry as soon as possible and enter into this blessed legal union. Marriage in Islam is a legal as well as a sacred contract with very serious commitment to mutual care, concern, love and fidelity. It is a commitment to life, to society and to the dignified survival of the human race. It is a commitment that married couples make to one another in which they find mutual fulfilment and self realisation, love and peace, compassion and serenity, comfort and hope.

Under the *Sharia* – Islamic law – no force or coercion is allowed in the union of two people. Both parties must give their free and unfettered consent before the religious ceremony can proceed to marry the two people concerned. If the woman or man is coerced even slightly into marrying the other person then that marriage is invalid. Under Islamic law the husband must give a dowry – a marriage gift (an agreed sum of money), befitting his means, to his bride after the marriage ceremony. Whatever he gives her belongs to her and whatever she owned before the marriage is also hers alone. The husband has no share or right to his wife's possessions, property or income. He is responsible for the adequate maintenance of and provision for his wife according to her customary standards and in accordance with his means. He must discharge these obligations willingly and sincerely. The marriage does not change the name of a woman and she is not obliged to adopt her husband's name. A woman can make her marriage monogamous if she chooses by inserting a clause in her contract annulling her marriage in the event of her husband taking another wife. The wife is not obliged to do the housework. However in order to promote and pursue a successful and harmonious married life and for the well-being of her husband and children she usually assumes these tasks as part of her uxorial duties. In the case of marital problems the elders or friends of the two families are obliged to make every effort to reconcile the parties. In the case of an irrevocable breakdown, divorce by the husband as well as by the wife is permissible.

Islam builds the family on a solid foundation that is capable of providing continuity, security, happiness and love. The *Quran* and *Sunnah* enjoin love and kindness, compassion and consideration, patience and piety, goodwill and equity as a pattern of behaviour for wives and husbands. The Prophet said that the best among the Muslims is the one who is best to his wife and the greatest blessing and happiness of life is a good and godly wife. In his last sermon the Prophet declared:

> O people! You have rights over your wives and your wives have rights over you. Treat your wives with love and kindness.

The Islamic family is not a nuclear one, it is extended to include the grandparents, grandchildren, uncles and aunts and their children. It is a sacred duty of the parents that they look after their children with care and concern, bring them up with affection and kindness, attend to the spiritual welfare and education of both the sons and daughters and their general well-being. A daughter is a blessing of God for a Muslim family and she should be brought up with particular love and care.

Islam puts great emphasis on education. The *Quran* repeatedly exhorts reflecting and learning, indeed the word *ilm* (knowledge) is mentioned over eight hundred times in it. The Prophet Muhammad said, 'Seeking of knowledge is an obligation upon every Muslim male and female.'

Hence, the Muslim mother manages the household in order to care for the education and the general welfare of the children and the Muslim father works and provides for the family. Reciprocally the children have a religious duty to love, respect and be obedient to their parents.

The mother has a special status in the Muslim culture and enjoys highest respect in the family. There is a saying of the Prophet: 'Paradise lies under the feet of the mother', meaning that if a person is obedient to his/her mother and keeps her happy he/she deserves paradise in the hereafter. Hence, when the parents grow old Muslims are obliged to maintain them, look after them, and attend to their every need with utmost affection and consideration. The *Quran* is very specific about the obligation of a Muslim to be more concerned and compassionate towards his parents in their old age. In Islam there is no concept of leaving one's old age parents in Old People's Homes when in their last days they badly need the care and especially, love and affection of their dear and near ones.

Jihad: – the concept of war in Islam. The word *Jihad* does not mean 'holy war'. Its primary meaning is 'struggle' and it is in this sense that it is chiefly used in the *Quran*.[7] According to a saying of the Prophet Muhammad, a holy war is a lesser *Jihad* whereas the greater *Jihad* is to struggle against one's own egos and evil temptations. Hence, to instil integrity and humility into one's own heart, to strive to control one's emotions, desires, avarices, prejudices, etc. are all part of the greater and nobler *Jihad*. Also, to uphold and speak the truth against intimidation and oppression to help someone in need or trouble, to help the oppressed, to struggle to establish justice in one's society and to struggle to earn an honest living are all *Jihads*, indeed greater *jihads* in Islam.

Islam means peace and Islam promotes peace. However, it is also a sober, rational and practical religion and as that, it acknowledges special circumstances under which someone or some nation may have to enter into hostilities. It recognises that for defence and the maintenance of peace and order, justice and freedom, sometimes a legal and just war, or the lesser *Jihad*, as the Prophet called it, is unavoidable. Nevertheless, Islam stipulates that every effort must be made and every avenue exhausted to resolve a dispute peacefully. War or hostile action must be the last resort. Further, Muslims are commanded by God never to begin hostilities, never

---

[7] Armstrong, Karen *A History of Jerusalem* p.295

to be the aggressors, never to break any treaties or oaths, never to reject an offer of peace, never to be the oppressors and never to violate the human rights of any people in war or in peace. In the course of a just war, Islam forbids the killing or harming of non-combatants, civilians, priests, monks, prisoners, those who put down their arms and those who take refuge in churches, synagogues and other places of worship. Also, during a war Islam prohibits the destruction of places of worship, people's habitations and properties, cutting down the trees and burning or destroying crops. Some of the Quranic declarations concerning war or *Jihad* are as follows:

> Fight in the way of God against those who fight against you, but begin not hostilities. Lo! God loves not aggressors. (2: 190)

> If they seek peace then you also seek peace. (8: 61)

> Keep your promises; you are accountable for all that you promise. (17: 34)

> For had it not been for God's repelling one set of people by means of others, monasteries and churches and synagogues and mosques, wherein the name of God is oft mentioned, would assuredly have been pulled down. (22: 40)

Under the Islamic law, an individual or even a group of people have no authority to declare a war, only a properly constituted Muslim state, or government is authorised to declare a war. Hence, the terrorists who try to legitimise their evil actions of bombing and killing innocent citizens under the label of *Jihad* are totally misrepresenting and indeed distorting the concept of *Jihad* in Islam.

Islam condemns all terrorism and extremism and prescribes moderation and a middle course in all affairs. The essence of Islam is to avoid all extravagances on all sides. Thus, there is no room whatsoever and howsoever for acts of terrorism in Islam. The Prophet Muhammad said:

> God has no mercy for one who has no mercy for others.

Bombing and killing innocent men, women and children, causing terror and violence in society, destroying houses, properties or public utilities are all diabolical acts forbidden and detestable in Islam. Suicide itself is a cardinal sin and so is the suicide bombing of innocent people. Sanctity of life, irrespective of religion, race or colour, is one of the most important principles of Islam. No one has the right to take an innocent life except God, the giver of life. In Islam the killing of an innocent person is equal to killing all mankind:

> ... whosoever kills a human being for other than manslaugh-
> ter or corruption in the earth, it shall be as if he had killed
> all humankind, and whoso saves the life of one, it shall be as
> if he had saved the life of all human kind. (5: 32)

Extremism and terrorism are unfortunately problems that all religions had and have to face. There have always been and will be extremists and terrorists claiming to be doing their evil deeds in the name of their respective religions. No religion preaches intolerance and terrorism. A religion therefore should not be blamed for the outrageous and irreligious acts of those who claim to be its adherents. However if there were genuine grievances of a section of the society then it becomes very easy for the extremists to exploit that situation and win the sympathy of some members of the community in support of their ill intentions.

The past history of Islam, some aspects of which have been referred to in the previous chapters, shows the unparalleled tolerance, moderation, compassion and justice demonstrated by Muslims, sometimes under very trying circumstances, during the one thousand years of their ascendancy in Asia, Africa and Europe. Intolerance, terrorism and extremism entered Islam in response to Western powers' injustices inflicted upon Muslims during the colonial, postcolonial and post-communist periods.

The current plight of Muslims in Palestine, Chechnya, Iraq, Afghanistan and Kashmir has worsened the situation. Groups that preach and practise extremism and terrorism are exploiting the Muslim masses by focusing on these issues. The sixty-year-old Israeli Palestinian conflict and the ever-increasing misery and oppression being suffered by the Palestinian people provide extremists with a compelling argument to win the support of some Muslims. Western countries', especially the United States' and Britain's, unflinching support for Israel and their unwillingness to enforce any UN resolution concerning Palestine, while they never fail to impose the implementation of a resolution affecting a Muslim country, or illegally invading a Muslim country, are other fertile sources for extremists to promote their ideas of hate and violence. The flagrant abuse of human rights and the atrocities being committed by the Russians in Chechnya and the United States in Iraq and Afghanistan are further fanning the flames of extremism in the Muslim world.

In order to arrest this dangerous situation the wrongs being done to Muslims in the above-mentioned parts of the world have to be addressed and stopped. Otherwise, in order to combat these wrongs and injustices certain misled or ill-advised Muslim individuals and groups, in their desperation and frustration, would keep spreading their unIslamic agenda and adopting extreme measures.

Extremism and terrorism are a contradiction of the Muslim law – the *Sharia*. To practise and promote terrorism is a declaration of war against God and the Prophet of Islam. It would therefore be very unfair to consider Islam *per se* and all its adherents to be militants and extremists because of the evil deeds of some aggrieved and frustrated Muslims. To put a stop to the nefarious activities of the terrorists the West must end its illegal and immoral interference in the affairs of Muslims and its occupation of Muslim countries. When no more wrongs and oppression is inflicted upon defenceless Muslims, when the West abandons its double standards and hypocrisy, when Muslims are given some space and they find their proper place in the comity of nations, only then the extremists and terrorists will lose their credibility in Muslim society.

It should not be forgotten that until not long ago, during their days of power, justice, tolerance, religious freedom and co-existence have been the hallmark of Islam and Muslim society. It was Islam that introduced freedom of worship, tolerance of other faiths and justice for all to the world and especially the West.

> How easy it is today to think of the West as the home of freedom of thought and liberty of worship, and to forget how as recently as the seventeenth century, Huguenot exiles

escaping religious persecution in Europe would write admiringly of the policy of religious tolerance practised across the Ottoman Empire. The same broad tolerance that had given homes to hundreds of thousands of penniless Jews, expelled by bigoted Catholic kings from Spain and Portugal, protected the Eastern Christians in their ancient homelands, despite the Crusades and the continual hostility of the Christian West. Only in the twentieth century has that traditional tolerance been replaced by a new hardening in Islamic attitudes. . . [8]

---

[8] Dalrymple, W. *From the Holy Mountain* p.168

Epilogue

MOST of the bias and prejudice towards a person or a group of people usually stems from ignorance. Our present-day world has become a global village and we human beings have become one another's close neighbours in that village. To live in peace and harmony we all have to get to know our neighbours better. We have to get to understand their way of life, their culture and even their faith. Only if we do that we can banish fear and hate from our society and the world.

In this connection, I would like to relate a small story I read sometime ago. A man was sitting in his lonely house in a mountain valley and looking out of the window. He became apprehensive when he noticed something far on the mountain moving towards his house. A little later, when that object moved relatively near he thought it was an animal. But, when it moved nearer, it became apparent to him that it was a man, perhaps a stranger. When the stranger moved closer to him he realised that he was armed. At this he became alarmed and began to prepare in order to defend himself. However, when the stranger came very close it suddenly dawned at him that he was his long-lost brother who had returned home.

Hence, East and West or Islam and Christianity are not irreconcilable, and never have been. Only ignorance, bigotry, injustice and double standards on the West's part and genuine grievances and frustration on the East's part are driving them apart. It is politics, not religion that is the cause of present tension between them.

Islam and Christianity have so much in common. They have lived together in harmony and interacted amicably in the past. Once the causes of their differences are justly resolved they will do so again, and the irrational and myopic prophesies of the 'clash of civilisations' will come to nothing.

The time has come for the world to recognise that the Jews, Christians and Muslims are the children of Abraham – and according to the *Quran*, that our different religious communities are part of God's plan. The *Quran*: 'For every one of you [Jews, Christians and Muslims], We have appointed a path and a way. If God had willed, He would have made you but one community; but [He has not done that in order that] He may try you in what has come to you. So compete with one another in good works'. (5: 48)[9]

God calls on all believers to worship him alone, to be grateful to him and to lead upright lives, especially by being generous with their wealth. The *Quran* also presents Muhammad as the person chosen by God to bring this message to the people of Mecca, to the Arabs, and then to the wider public. In the light of the great positive values of the teachings of the *Quran* and the practical successes which resulted from it, the inadequate perceptions of Judaism and Christianity cannot be accounted a serious weakness, such as to negate all that is sound and true. It is a Christian principal that 'By their fruit you shall know them', and Islam has certainly brought to millions a better life than they would otherwise have had. [10]

---

[9] Carnegie Corporation of New York: Annual Report 2001 p.61

[10] Watt, Rev. Prof. William Montgomery, *Muslim and Christian Encounter* pp.28-29

THE attack on Glasgow airport, on 30 June 2007, was the first terror incident in Scotland. It came as a terrible shock to everyone. However, considering that such attacks were associated with the so-called 'Muslim' terrorists the Scottish Muslims held their breath expecting trouble. When it became clear that it was indeed an evil act perpetrated by two 'Muslims' the Muslim community became tense and afraid of the repercussions against them. They became concerned about the possible racist attacks and police actions against the Muslim community, as had been happening in England. Nonetheless, the Islamic Centre Glasgow called an emergency meeting of the Muslim leadership on Sunday 1st July, to condemn this terrorist attack and to stress that the Muslim community and their religion abhors such evil acts.

When Strathclyde Police and the Scottish Executive came to know of the meeting, they both intimated to the Islamic Centre that they desired to attend. We, at the Islamic Centre therefore were delighted to welcome next day Assistant Chief Constable John Neilson and Mr. Kenny McCaskill, Minister for Justice in the Scottish government. To our very pleasant surprise Mr Alex Salmond, the First Minister, who was visiting Glasgow Airport that morning, after finishing his business there, also came to be at the meeting.

ACC Neilson assured the gathering that the Police would do everything possible to protect the Muslim community from any attacks by racists or bigots. Mr Alex Salmond expressed his appreciation for the valuable contributions of the Muslim community to Scottish society. He emphasised that Scottish Muslims were law-abiding and responsible citizens and nobody should blame them for this evil act. Mr McCaskill said that the Scottish government would protect the interests of the Muslim community. The Muslim community appreciated these assurances and gestures of goodwill and felt somewhat relieved of their tensions and fears.

However, that was not the end of this difficult situation. On 2nd July Chief Superintendent John Pollock phoned me to say that according to their information a car used by one of the terrorists was parked in an as yet unknown mosque car park and that they may need my cooperation in dealing with the matter. I assured him of my assistance. The next day he told me that they had now found out where the car was parked and he would contact me when they are ready for action. In the evening Mr Pollock and Inspector Ian McKim came to my house and told me where the car was located and asked me to accompany them to go to that Mosque to inform the management of the mosque about the planned action and seek their cooperation. In addition, Chief Superintendent Pollok outlined the need for the community to be aware of the significant interest this incident would generate in not only the local media but also the world's press and identified his concerns as to how this could, if not carefully considered by us both have a very negative effect on community tensions and encourage targeting of minority communities by mindless thugs. At this point all three of us worked on a strategy to counter the 'Finsbury Park comes to Glasgow' assumption that was sure to be raised by those who were ignorant of the true message of Islam preached at the Mosque.

At the Mosque, we discussed the matter with available members of their Management Committee who assured us of their full cooperation. They asked the Chief Superintendent if it was possible to perform their night prayers prior to initiating the policing operation, a request he agreed to accede. Following completion of prayer at 11.15pm we asked the Committee members to vacate the mosque and the car park and inform their congregation not to come for the morning prayers as the operation might last for the whole of the night. Soon after all the police teams and the necessary equipment arrived and the operation began after midnight. A blast was affected to make the car safe at about 4.00 am. Fortunately, nothing was found in the car and the operation finished about 5.00 am without bursting any doors, violating the sanctity of the Mosque, bundling innocent people in the police vans or using violence against any individual as had been happening in England. I was able immediately thereafter to undertake live interviews with numerous media organisations debunking the suggestions of a militant Islam being preached in Glasgow while the police incident officer described how the Muslim community had given every cooperation to the police enquiry.

In the last paragraph of the penultimate chapter of this book I had expressed my hopes that the Scottish police, if need be, would use the new legislation concerning terrorism with consideration and proper prudence and the enforcement of the anti-terrorism laws would not contravene the norms of traditional British justice and fair play. I am delighted to say that my hopes came true and as related above, during this serious incident, Strathclyde Police did act in the most considerate, humane and prudent way.

The Glasgow airport attack happened after I had finished this manuscript. Hence, I am including this piece in the postscript with the hope that other police forces in Scotland as well as in England learn lessons from it and realise that sometimes the cooperation of individuals and communities in tackling a serious and difficult situation can bring about desired and even better results and save much unnecessary violence, ill-will and animosity.

Sources Chapter 1

Adler, M. N. *The Itinerary of Benjamin of Tudela* (London 1907)

Anderson, Joseph, *The Orkneyinga Saga* (Mercat Press 1973)

Aitchison, Nick, *Scotland's Stone of Destiny* (Tempus Publishing 2000)

Bain, Joseph, ed. *The Calendar of Documents Related to Scotland* (Vol. 1, 1108-1272)

Bower, Walter, *The Scotichronicon* Vol. I, Book I (Aberdeen University Press 1993)

Brondsted, Johanne, *The Vikings* (Pelican, London 1965)

Brownlow, Rev Canon, M.A., trans. *The Hodeoporican of Saint Willibald* (Palestine Pilgrims Text Society, London 1891)

Dalrymple, William, *The Guardian* July 12, 2003

Dalrymple, William, *From the Holy Mountain* (HarperCollins 1997)

Daniel, Norman, *Islam and the West* (Oxford 1993)

Daniel, Norman, *The Arabs and Medieval Europe* (London 1975)

Encyclopaedia Britannica Vol. 12 (London 1959)

Ferguson, William, *The Identity of the Scottish Nation* (Edinburgh University Press 1998)

Fletcher, Richard, *The Cross and the Crescent* (Penguin Books 2003)

Frye, Richard, trans. *Ibn Fadlan's Journey to Russia* (Markus Wiener Publishers, Princeton 2005)

Harpur, James, *Sacred Tracks* (Singapore 2002)

Hussain, Farhat, *The Birth of Muslim Coinage* (Heritage Resources, London 2002)

Jones, Gwyn, *A History of the Vikings* (Oxford University Press 1973)

Levine Lee.I. ed. *Jerusalem Its Sanctity And Centrality to Judaism, Christianity and Islam* (Continuum, New York 1999)

Laurent, J. C. M. ed. *Peregrinatores Medii Aevi Quatour* (Lipsiae, J. C.Hinrichs Bibliopola 1864)

McIntosh, Alistair, 'Saint Andrew: Non-violence and National Identity', published in *Theology in Scotland* St Mary's College, University of St Andrews, Vol. VII: No. 1, Spring 2000

McRoberts, David, 'Scottish Pilgrims to the Holy Land' *(Innes Review* xx 1969)

Meehan, Denis, ed. *De Locus Sanctus* (Dublin 1958)

O'Donovan, John, ed. *Three Fragments* (Dublin, 1860)

Ouseley, Sir William, trans. *Kitab Masalik wa-mamalik tasnif Ibn Hawqal, The Oriential Geography of Ebn Haukal, an Arabian Traveller of the tenth century* (Oriential Press, London 1800)

Runciman, S. *The History of Crusades,* Vols. I (Cambridge 1954)

Smyth, A. P. *Scandinavian Kings in the British Isles* (Oxford University Press 1977)

Stefansson, J. *The Vikings in Spain* (Saga Book Viking Society 1909)

Allan, W.E.D. *The Poet and the Spae Wife* (Saga Book Viking Society, New York 1980)

Stenton, Sir Frank, *The Oxford History of England: Anglo-Saxon England,* (Oxford University Press. 1971)

The Arabian Journey (Moesgard Museum 1996)

Wilkinson, John, *Jerusalem Pilgrims before the Crusades* (Aris & Phillips Ltd, Warminster 1977)

Yeoman, Peter, *Pilgrimage in Medieval Scotland* (B. T. Batsford Ltd/ Historic Scotland 1999)

Stevenson, R. B. K. *Sylloge of Coins of the British Isles 6, National Museum of Antiquities of Scotland Part I* (Oxford University Press 1966)

www.sacredconnections.ndo.co.uk/holyland/scotlkandegypt.htm

Sources: Chapter 2

Anderson A. O. & M. O. & Dickson, W. C. eds. *The Chronicle of Melrose* (1936)

Armstrong, Karen, *History of Jerusalem* (HarperCollins, London 1996)

Calendar of Documents relating to Scotland Vol. III (1307-1357)

Clancy, Thomas Owen, ed. *The Triumph Tree* (Canongate, Edinburgh 1998)

Daniel, Norman, *The Arabs and Medieval Europe* (London 1975)

Fletcher, Richard, *The Cross and the Crescent* (Penguin Books 2003)

Hillenbrand, Carole, *The Crusades: Islamic Perspectives* (Edinburgh University Press 1999)

Hitti, Phillip K. trans. *An Arab Syrian Gentleman and Warrior in the Period of the Crusades, Memoirs of Usamah Ibn-Munqidh* (I. B. Taurus & Co., London 1987)

Hume, John, S. & Moss, Michael, S. *A History of Scotch Whisky Distilling Industry* (Canongate 1981)

Lane-Poole, Stanley, *Saladin and the fall of Jerusalem* (Greenhill Books, London 2002)

Laurent, J. C. M. ed. *Peregrinatores Medii Aevi Quatour* (Lipsiae, J. C. Hinrichs Bibliopola 1864)

MacQuarrie, Allan D. The Impact of the Crusades Movement in Scotland, 1095–c.1560, Thesis, presented for the Degree of Doctor of Philosophy in the University of Edinburgh in 1982

MacQuarrie, Allan D. *Scotland and the Crusades 1095-1560* (Edinburgh 1985)

McRoberts, David, 'Scottish Pilgrims to the Holy Land' (*Innes Review* 1969)

Proceedings of the Society of Antiquaries of Scotland Vol. XLVII, Relics Preserved in Dunvegan Castle, Skye, (Edinburgh, 1912-1913)

Runciman, S. *The History of the Crusades* Vol. I (Cambridge 1951-54)

Runciman, S. *The History of the Crusades* Vols. II, III Penguin Books

Ryan, Frances Rita, trans. *A History of the Expedition to Jerusalem 1095-1127* pp.121-122 (University of Tennessee Press, Knoxville 1969)

Simpson, T,B. *The Scottish Historical Review* Vol. XXXVII, (Edinburgh 1953)

Taylor, A. B. *The Orkneyinga* (London 1938)

Watt, W. M. *Influence of Islam on Medieval Europe* (Edinburgh 1972)

Watt, W. M. *Muslim Christian Encounters* (London & New York 1991)

Wheatcroft, Andrew, *Infidels* (London 2003)

Yeoman, Peter, *Pilgrimage in Medieval Scotland* (B.T. Batsford Ltd/ Historic Scotland 1999)

Sources: Chapter 3

1000 Years of Islam in Britain (Islamic Society of Britain, London)

Accounts of the Lord High Treasurer of Scotland, The (1507-8, 1567-69, 16) (1589- 93, 10: 404)

Anderson, Sonia, P. *An English Consul in Turkey* (Clarendon Press 1989)

Another Letter from Dr. Serarias, to Dr. Homes, Mr. Bruce and others (Printed for George Freeman, Anno Dom. 1665)

Asad, Muhammad (Weiss, Leopold) *Is Religion a Thing of the Past?* (Educational Press, Karachi 1960)

Blank, David, *Images of the Other – Europe and the Muslim World before 1700* (Cairo 1997)

Blount, Henry, *A Voyage into the Levant* (Theatrum Orbis Tararum Ltd., Amsterdam 1977)

Burnett, Charles, *The Introduction of Arabic Learning into England* (The British Library 1997)

Bruce, Duncan A, *The Scottish 100* (Carroll Craf 2000)

Calendar of Documents of Scotland 941.05 CAL (1509-1589) Vol., V., Vol. XXX. & (1589- 93, 10: 404)

Carnegie Corporation of New York, Annual Report 2001

Chew, Samuel, C., *The Crescent and the Rose* (Oxford University Press 1937)

Dalrymple, William, *White Mughals – Love and Betrayal in Eighteenth-Century India* (HarperCollins 2002)

Daniel, Norman, *The Arabs and Medieval Europe* (London 1975)

Donnachie, Ian & Hewitt, George, *Dictionary of Scottish History* (HarperCollins 2001)

Ellis, Markman, *The Coffee House* (Weidenfeld & Nicholson, London 2004)

Encyclopaedia Britannica Vol. 15 (London 1959)

Encyclopaedia Britannica Vol. 20 (London 1959)

Fletcher, Richard, *The Cross and the Crescent* (Penguin Books 2003)

Gibbon, Edward, *The Decline and Fall of the Roman Empire* (London 1937)

The Jewes Message to their Brethren in Holland; and a New Letter touching their further proceedings sent from the Kingdom of Scotland (Printed for George Freeman, Anno Dom. 1665)

Matar, Nabil, *Islam in Britain 1558-1685* (Cambridge University Press 1998)

Matar, Nabil, *Turks Moors and Englishmen in the Age of Discovery* (Columbia University Press New York 1999)

MacQuarrie, Allan, 'Ansalem Adornes of Bruges: Traveller in the East and Friend of James III' *(The Innes Review* XXXIII 1982)

MacQuarrie, Allan, The Impact of the Crusades Movement in Scotland 1095-c.1560, Thesis presented for the Degree of Doctor of Philosophy in the University of Edinburgh, 1982

McRoberts, David, 'Scottish Pilgrims to the Holy Land' *(Innes Review* xx 1969)

Paris, Mathew, *Chronica Majora* ed. Luard, Henry Richards, (1872-1884)

Phelps, Gilbert, ed. *The Rare Adventures and Painful Peregrination of William Lithgow* (London, The Folio Society 1974)

Quick, Dr. Abdullah Hakim, *Deeper Roots* (Ta-Ha Publishers Ltd., London 1998)

Rahman, H. U. *A Chronology of Islamic History, 570-1000 CE,* (Ta-Ha Publishers Ltd., London 1995)

Register of the Privy Council of Scotland 941 REG Vol. 12, (1619-1622) and Vol. 13, (1622-1625)

Schimmel, Annemarie, *The Empire of the Great Mughals* trans. Attwood, Corinne (Sang-e-Meel Publications, Lahore, Pakistan 2005)

Stern, S. M. ed. 'Three Letters from the Ottoman Sultana Safiye to Queen Elizabeth' in *Documents from Islamic Chanceries* (Cambridge University Press 1965)

Thorndike, Lynn, *Michael Scot* (London 1965)

Vesrtegan, Richard, *Restitution of Decayed Intelligence* (Antwerp 1605)

Sources Chapter 4

Bayly, C. A., *Empire and Information* (Cambridge University Press 1996)

Bryant, G. J., *Scottish Historical Review* April 1985

Buddle, Ann, *The Tiger and the Thistle* (National Gallery of Scotland, Edinburgh 1999)

Cain, Alex. A. M., *The Corn Chest for Scotland* (Edinburgh 1986)

Dalrymple, William, *City of Djinns* (HarperCollins)

Dalrymple, William, *White Mughals, Love and Betrayal in Eighteenth-Century India* (HarperCollins 2002)

Devine, T. M., *Scotland's Empire 1600-1815* (Allen Lane)

Devine, T. M., *The Scottish Nation 1700-2000* (Penguin 1999)

Dunlop, D. M., 'Scotland According to Al-Idrisi, c.A.D. 1154' *Scottish Historical Review* Vol. XXVI (Edinburgh 1947)

Faderman, Lillian, *Scotch Verdict* (London: Quartet 1985)

Fletcher, Richard, *The Cross and the Crescent* (Penguin 2003)

Fry, Michael, *The Scottish Empire* (Tuckwell Press & Birlinn 2002)

Grey, C., *European Adventurers in Northern India* (New Delhi 1993)

Hawes, Christopher, *Poor Relations* (Curzon Press 1996)

Hutchinson, Lester, *European Freebooters in Moghul India* (Asia Publishing House, London 1964)

Maan, Bashir, *The New Scots* (John Donald Publishers 1992)

Moesgard Museum (Denmark) The Arabian Journey 1996

Sources: Chapter 5

1000 Years of Islam in Britain (Islamic Society of Britain, London)

Accounts of the Lord High Treasurer of Scotland, The 1505-1508 and 1567, 1569

Bawcut, Priscilla, ed. *The Poems of William Dunbar* (Edinburgh, 1998)

Chew, Samuel, C. *The Crescent and the Rose* (Oxford University Press 1937)

Dunlop, D. M., 'Scotland according to Al-Idrisi' *Scottish Historical Review* Vol. XXVI

Encyclopaedia Britannica 1959 edition

Fryer. P., *Black People in the British Empire* (Pluto, London 1988)

Hechet, J., *Continental and Colonial Servants in the Eighteenth Century* (Northampton Mass., 1954)

Maan, B., *The New Scots* (John Donald Publishers 1992)

Mandville, Sir John, *The Travels of Sir John Mandville, The Version of the Cotton Manuscript in Modern Spelling* (London, Macmillan & Co. Ltd 1900)

Matar, Nabil, *Turks Moors and Englishmen in the Age of Discovery* (Columbia University Press, New York 1999)

Moesgard Museum (Denmark) The Arabian Journey, (1996)

Salter, Joseph, *The Asiatics in England* (London 1873)

Spears, Percival, *The Nabobs* (Oxford University Press 1932)

Visram, Rosina, *Ayahs, Lascars and Princes* (Pluto, London 1986)

Watt, W.M., *Influence of Islam on Medieval Europe* (Edinburgh 1972)

Woking Muslim Mission *The Islamic Review*

Ali, Kose, *Conversion to Islam, A Study of Native British Converts* (Kegan Paul International, London and New York, 1996)

(http://en.wikipedia.org/wiki/Abdalqadar as-Sufi al Murabit)

Sources: Chapter 6

Pickthall, Muhammed Mamaduke, *The Meanings of the Glorious Quran, An explanatory Translation* (A Mentor Book, New American Library)

Abdalati, Hammudah, *Islam in Focus* (American Trust Publications 1975)

B. Maan & Alastair McIntosh, an Interview with 'The Last Orientalist' the Rev Prof William Montgomery Watt, *The Coracle*, the Iona Community, (Summer 2000)

Carnegie Corporation of New York: Annual Report 2001

Dalrymple, W., *From the Holy Mountain* (HarperCollins 1997)

Dalrymple, William, *White Mughals* (HarperCollins 2002)

Fletcher, Richard, *The Cross and the Crescent* (Penguin 2003)

Peachy, Dr. William, et. al., General Editors *A Brief Illustrated Guide to Understanding Islam* (Darussalam, Houston, Texas1997)

Watt, Rev. Prof. William Montgomery, *Muslim and Christian Encounters* (London and New York 1991)

Winter, Tim J, *The Muslim grand narrative, Caring for Muslim Patients* edited by: A. Sheikh & A.R. Gatrad, (Radcliffe Medical Press 2000)